D1453646

Our Shadowed World

To David

With thanks
for your support—
that helped this
book on its way

Dominic

Aug. 2019

Westar Studies

Our Shadowed World

Reflections on Civilization, Conflict, and Belief

Dominic Kirkham

CASCADE *Books* • Eugene, Oregon

OUR SHADOWED WORLD
Reflections on Civilization, Conflict, and Belief

Westar Studies

Copyright © 2019 Dominic Kirkham. All rights reserved. Except for brief quotations in critical publications or reviews, no part of this book may be reproduced in any manner without prior written permission from the publisher. Write: Permissions, Wipf and Stock Publishers, 199 W. 8th Ave., Suite 3, Eugene, OR 97401.

Cascade Books
An Imprint of Wipf and Stock Publishers
199 W. 8th Ave., Suite 3
Eugene, OR 97401

www.wipfandstock.com

PAPERBACK ISBN: 978-1-5326-6173-0
HARDCOVER ISBN: 978-1-5326-6174-7
EBOOK ISBN: 978-1-5326-6175-4

Cataloging-in-Publication data:

Names: Kirkham, Dominic, author.

Title: Our shadowed world : reflections on civilization, conflict, and belief / Dominic Kirkham.

Description: Eugene, OR: Cascade Books, 2018. | Westar Studies. | Includes bibliographical references.

Identifiers: ISBN: 978-1-5326-6173-0 (paperback). | ISBN: 978-1-5326-6174-7 (hardcover). | ISBN: 978-1-5326-6175-4 (ebook).

Subjects: LCSH: Civilization—Western. | World politics. | Religion—Philosophy.

Classification: BL51 K53 2019 (paperback). | BL51 (ebook).

Manufactured in the U.S.A.

Biblical quotations marked (JB) are taken from the Jerusalem Bible © 1966 by Darton Longman & Todd Ltd and Doubleday and Company Ltd.

07/17/19

For the companions of my shadowed past

Rob & Jan

and Teresa

"The end of the human race will be that it will eventually die of civilization."

—Ralph Waldo Emerson

Contents

Preface

*"We as a people have to understand that this veneer of civilization
under which we live is thin, fragile and not universal."*

Michael V. Hayden, 2017
(Head of NSA and CIA 2006–2009)

Civilizations are formidable and frightening creations. Civilization is often seen as the opposite of savagery—the living city rising above the threatening wilderness, a progressive idea leaving in its wake a more primitive state. It is part of the narrative of this book that this understanding is quite mistaken. Rather, I contend, civilization brings its own form of savagery; and the greater the cities and the more "advanced" the civilization, the greater the scale of savagery. It is a story that culminates in our own times with one of the most incomparable acts of savagery imaginable—the Shoah, or Jewish Holocaust of the Second World War.

It is a story that can be perhaps best represented by the monumental concrete face, rising some fifteen meters high, which stands on a hill alongside the Road of Bones (human bones!) overlooking Magadan in the Kolyma region of Eastern Russia. Here in what has been called the capital of the Soviet Gulag this overpowering memorial—the Mask of Sorrow—was built in memory of all those countless millions of people who perished under the flimsiest of pretexts in the forced labor camps of Stalin's regime over a period of three decades. This modern pietà has an Aztec quality to it, with its grim visage and weeping tears of skulls, which bears witness to the industrial scale of slaughter that took place among civilized people. It would need all the capabilities of a modern state to exterminate twenty or forty million (the actual numbers will never be known) of its own people as occurred in Stalin's Russia and Mao's China.

The rise of civilization with the city-state some five thousand years ago in Mesopotamia, the "land between the rivers" also called "the cradle of civilization," saw the appearance of new forms of institutionalized savagery: organized violence or war, slavery, and the oppression of women, to name but three. And to support and defend the city-state there arose the organized expansion of savagery we call empire. Empire was invented by Sargon the Akkadian, one of the first identifiable figures of history, who also created the first legal code and thereby laid the foundations for legalized male domination, for civilizations have generally been patriarchal affairs. One of the earliest marks of civilization is the humble brick, and among other irrevocable precepts of Sargon was that a woman who dared to speak out of turn should have her teeth smashed, with a brick.

Civilization grew and proliferated largely through empire. It would be pedantic to rehearse the benefits that civilization has provided to humanity, but it is sobering to reflect on the human cost by which they were acquired. A typical boast of a victorious king and aspiring emperor, like that of the Assyrian Shalmaneser III, was that "I covered the wide plain with the corpses of their fighting men. I dyed the mountains red with their blood." Another king, Ashurbanipal, recorded, "I tore out the tongues of those whose slanderous mouths had uttered blasphemies against my God Ashur . . . I fed their corpses, cut into small pieces, to dogs."[1] The invention of writing—one of the key achievements and marks of civilizations—has, ironically, enabled us to chronicle the record of such savagery. Indeed, it is the grim determination of its victims not to be forgotten that provided the motivation for writers of many eras such as Varlam Shalamov, a victim of Stalin's Great Terror, whose *Kolyma Tales* bears witness to the truth of human savagery that must never be forgotten.[2]

Nor must its cause be forgotten. Let us be clear: it is human belief, both secular and religious, that provides the motivation and legitimation of savagery. As one of Stalin's activists, Lev Kopelev, would write of the goal of the universal triumph of Communism, "In the terrible spring of 1933 I saw people dying from hunger. Women and children with distended bellies, turning blue . . . corpses in ragged sheepskin coats . . . I saw all this and did not go out of my mind . . . Nor did I lose my faith. I believed because I

1 Quoted in Robertson, *Iraq: A History*, 79.

2 See Shalamov, *Kolyma Tales* (trans. Glad).

wanted to believe."[3] Belief provides the numinous justification for civilization as much as bricks facilitate its construction. The terrifying judgment of the papal legate Arnaud Amaury on the inhabitants of Béziers in 1209—"Kill them all. God will know his own."[4]—reverberates across the centuries from that "Age of Faith" to the modern faith-based caliphate of Abu Bakr al-Baghdadi in Syria/Iraq, which also now aspires to rule the world. As I write these words contemporary jihadists are perpetrating similar atrocities in that same part of the world where civilization began in the name of their beliefs. *Inshallah.* "God's will." *Plus ca change?*

In the meantime, empires have continued to rise and fall, and civilizations have woven people's noble ideals and religious beliefs into an ever-expanding remorseless spiral of savagery. One need only consider the Holy Roman Empire of Christendom, baptized with blood of thousands of butchered Saxons by its founder Charlemagne, and expanded by the swords of those merciless holy warriors of God, the Crusaders. Such were the Teutonic Knights, whose mission was to create a Christian civilization among the heathen Slavonic savages of the East. Whatever noble truths they sought to establish in the name of Christian belief, the Inquisition, which was also the instrument of their implementation, was perhaps the most cruel and savage institution ever devised. Its savagery shaped the minds of millions, and its legacy poisons the present in often unnoticed ways. It is a story I will endeavor to explore as one wonders to what extent the vast ambition of Caesaropapism and the Christian civilization or Christendom it created reflected the teaching of the humble Nazarene carpenter.

Civilization is paradoxical, even contradictory. Nowhere is this more evident than in the history of our most advanced and sophisticated contemporary world leader, the United States. Its iconic monument of the Statue of Liberty faces eastwards, welcoming the oppressed and impoverished of the Old World with the promise of prosperity and freedom in the New World. But this great civilization advanced westward on lands stolen from an indigenous population deemed savage, and was fueled by wealth created from slavery. The Indian Wars became a story of shame and savagery, an American holocaust. In the land of freedom, as Chief Little

---

3. Quoted in Merridale, *Night of Stone*, 219.
4. Quoted in Baigent and Leigh, *Inquisition*, 12.

Wolf mournfully reflected, "We only wanted a little ground where we could live"—in freedom. The same can be said for Palestinians who simply want to return to the homes for which they still hold the keys.

To many these are uncomfortable and indeed unwelcome thoughts, for the notions of civilization and savagery, "special providence" and spectacular destruction do not sit easily together. They are like ill-matched conjoined twins or the mythical brothers Cain and Abel, whose fratricidal enmity precedes the rise of civilization. So has it ever been. Rome, which sprang from the blood of Remus spilled by his brother Romulus, would become a mighty empire whose distinguishing features were patriarchy, slavery, hierarchy, and violent conquest of its enemies—aptly epitomized in the greatest popular spectacles of all, the gladiatorial games that took place in its most imposing and appropriately named monumental structure (given its colossal size), the Colosseum. The orgies of blood-soaked savagery that this masterpiece of civil engineering made possible—as in many other such structures across the empire—are without historical parallel.

Since those ancient times an exponential growth of the possibilities for violence and savagery has occurred as the flint-tipped arrow has given way to the nuclear missile. The twentieth century became characterized not only by the scope of genocidal savagery but also by the destructive violence of its warfare and weaponry. Now humanity had the power to destroy the whole of civilization in an atomic holocaust. And in the twenty-first century this shadow over the earth has been further darkened by an even more perilous threat: ecocide. As Al Gore wrote in his ecological manifesto, *An Inconvenient Truth*, civilization is destroying the planet.

The apocalyptic proportions of this new shadow arise from everything that humanity does—all its activities, all its ambitions, all its ideals and dreams. We are now compelled to confront the enormity of all we do and are, and to view ourselves in the context of this new reality. This book is an attempt to examine the nature of the civilization we have created. If any hope remains for us as a species, it must be that we can do better, that we will choose life—a life that will be good for all, just as in the aspiration of the biblical creation myth.

Though this book is the product of solitary reflection over many years, its publication has relied on the interest and skill of others who have been surprisingly generous with their time and talent. I am particularly grateful to the Westar Institute and commissioning editor David Galston in this respect but also to Tom Hall, who diligently scrutinized the text, and David

Lambourn, who so kindly provided the bibliography and index. My thanks are boundless even if my defects are many.

Introduction

A Personal Encounter with the Savagery of Civilization

*"It is with civilization that human 'savagery' becomes
an agonizing part of the human condition."*

A. B. Schmookler

Many people can recall an event that changed them forever—a completely unexpected incident that altered the whole course of their lives. It need not have been dramatic or traumatic in itself, perhaps it was no more than a chance encounter or an unexpected visitor, but it was an event whose powerful effects they only later began to recognize.

My chance visit to Poland in 1982 was such an event. At that time Europe was entering into a critical period of change with a sclerotic Soviet Union hovering on the point of collapse and increasingly restive satellite nations struggling to survive under its oppressive yoke. None was more disgruntled than Poland, where a fractious electrician from Gdańsk named Lech Walesa had taken the lead of the protest movement *Solidarnosc*. Solidarity threatened to topple the Communist hierarchy and was determined to settle for nothing less. In the face of an imminent Soviet invasion, Prime Minister Jaruzelski choose the least disreputable option, declared martial law, and put Walesa under house arrest.

It was in this volatile context that a Polish friend then living in Warsaw asked if I would like to visit for the Easter holidays. I readily accepted, and my life was never the same again. Though I had previously visited Poland

and Russia, and was quite familiar with their history and cultures from college studies under a tutor who was an East European refugee, nothing prepared me for a whole nation on the edge of a precipice. The atmosphere was not simply electric but volcanic, charged with what can be described only as an apocalyptic expectancy.

This sense was heightened by the Easter season itself, with its many dramatic church displays highlighting the theme of the conflict of good and evil with the possibility of a triumphal resurrection. But this was not just a theological or religious message, with which as a priest I was quite familiar, but a none-too-subtle theopolitical statement of resolution and revolution in the face of an overbearing atheistic tyranny (Soviet communism). It was all very much in tune with the traditional Polish messianic self-identity stretching back to Michiewicz and the early Romantics. The vibrancy of this tradition was something quite new to me and was made more intense by the fact that beyond anyone's wildest dreams a Polish pope had just been elected in Rome. Surely not only Poland's but all of Europe's destiny was about to be transformed—and they were definitely up for the fight.

I returned to England almost in a daze. The experience had quite disorientated me, and curiously the thing that seemed most difficult to come to terms with was the sheer ordinariness of life here in England: people strolled down the street without a care in the world, perhaps into a shop to buy something or for a game in the park—just doing as they pleased. It seemed impossible to imagine this was part of the same world as the one I had just left—a place of riots, revolution, and religious intoxication. When I spoke about this sense of disorientation to a Polish acquaintance, he fully understood; he told of a relative who had recently been for a visit to England and had to be carried out of a supermarket in a state of collapse, so overwhelmed was he not only by the abundance of goods, but by being free to buy whatever he wanted. Poland was a land of empty store shelves, rationed goods, and endemic scarcity—a place where one had to wait in line for everything, and even a delivery of toilet paper to a store could become a major event.

An even more immediate and powerful experience, indeed among the most significant of my life, was a visit to Auschwitz. Nothing could prepare one for the visual impact of that horrific place as an indelible testimonial to human cruelty. Even more difficult to accept was that what happened there was the product of an advanced, modern society of which I was a part. For Jews it was a *churban*, an event of utter destructiveness that defies comprehension; for those who survived the death camps it meant that life could never be the same. As is the consequence for torture victims in general, they experienced a loss of faith in humanity, felt radically detached from society, and lived with a question mark hanging over the very meaning and purpose of life. One of the first and most famous reflections on life in Auschwitz was Viktor Frankl's tellingly titled *Man's Search for Meaning.* The title of Primo Levi's *If This Is a Man,* was equally indicative and perhaps ominous, for in the end the memory proved unbearable, and he committed suicide.

For me, even more significant than the horrific historical facts of Auschwitz was their wider context—the question of how such events could have happened. What tragic flaw in the society and perhaps even the broader civilization had made it possible? In many ways Auschwitz seemed to symbolize the death of the civilization that made it possible. The consequences were seismic, and the implications have preoccupied me ever since.

One consequence was to question the very nature of evil. Both as a Catholic and a priest I was familiar with the notion of evil and its hypostatization (from the Greek hypostasis: foundation) in the figure of the devil— he whose satanic presence figured largely in those Easter posters in Polish churches, inferring implying that his current incarnation was the Soviet Union, famously described by Ronald Regan as "the evil empire." Surely in the case of Auschwitz the immediate agency of Hitler as a monster of satanic force could be blamed for all that had happened. Such an explanation left the rest of us as much in the clear as it did the many ordinary Germans who at the time denied any knowledge of what had happened in the death camps.

But I found this whole narrative—along with its assumption of an underlying evil as an external influence on humanity—not only unconvincing but so delusional as to amount to a state of denial. I began to see that the cause lay in the nature of humanity itself and the sort of society that we humans create. Events like the Holocaust were neither exceptional nor inexplicable, but the result of an aspect of humanity about which many were unwilling to inquire too deeply or too willing to dismiss as the work of evil monsters. As Holocaust theologian Richard Rubenstein commented, by our neglecting to recognize the nature of the human desire for destructiveness, an outpouring of evil had been unleashed upon millions of innocent victims.

Far more disturbing, and even threatening, is the recognition that people like Hitler and Himmler, the chief executive of the Holocaust, were not exceptional people, but ordinary human beings like you and me. Himmler was a loving father and family man who frequently wrote home regretting that his "duties" kept him away for so long. The same was true of the Auschwitz camp commandant, Rudolf Hoess, who was dedicated to his work and liked nothing better than listening to Mozart in the company of his family after a tiring day's work. It just so happened that his "work" was mass murder. Among recent historical studies, Thomas Weber's *Hitler's First War* documents Hitler's transformation from an unexceptional, conscientious soldier to a madman—a change driven by personal frustration and enabled by the society in which he lived: a society that provided many eager collaborators. Equally notorious purveyors of evil were Stalin, Mao, and Franco, who remain national icons. And one of the most shocking things about the social psychologist Stanley Milgram's research experiments was the ease with which ordinary people could be turned into killers, especially if they were conscientious. At the Nuremberg trials a Rorschach psychological test was given to all the accused Nazis, and all registered as normal!

Granted the individual flaws of the actors in this drama, it seems clear to me that contemporary history and society had created a matrix that made such events possible. Deeply implicated in this worldwide tragedy are the nature of European culture and the role of the church in the long and shameful history of anti-Semitism (though some dissemble even at this description, preferring to call it anti-Judaism, as if this were somehow more acceptable!). In fact, it was through the explicit and deliberate policies of the Catholic Church that twelfth-century Europe became what the medievalist Robert I. Moore termed in the title of a book a *Persecuting Society*, and has remained so down to the present day. As a Catholic priest, I found this increasingly difficult for me to cope with. Not only was the hierarchical church complicit, but the very nature of Christian religious belief and practice is tainted with anti-Semitism that is firmly rooted in the gospels and in other documents foundational to the faith.

And thus it was that just as I had come to reject the traditional understanding of evil, so I now began to reject traditional theism and much of the religious tradition in which I had grown up. For the death camp survivor Elie Wiesel there could be no belief in God after Auschwitz. For writers like Richard Rubenstein, in *After Auschwitz*, God cannot be exempted from what happened in history, and neo-Orthodox attempts at explaining this unspeakable evil as some sort of punishment or retribution must be rejected as utterly contemptible. Having arrived at these conclusions, after nearly thirty years as a religious and a priest I left the church and ministry.

This book, then is the outcome of a long personal journey and years of reflection. Though it may lack a compelling narrative, it does have the overall coherence of theme and purpose adumbrated above: the historical evaluation of our human predicament and what we call civilization. Many of the individual chapters have resulted from years of reflection and have grown old with me! They may have begun as reflections on particular topics—the nature of tyranny and ideology, of civilization and society, of ways of thinking and the nature of belief, of militarism and misogyny—but have widened out into meditations on humanity and where civilization has led us in its present predicament as it faces not only the threat of genocide but that of ecocide—the destruction of the planet. In a way the story of this book is how we created a civilization but devastated the earth.

I have been led to put these reflections in written form not primarily to see them published, nor to persuade others of a particular view. Rather, they have arisen as a consequence of my own search for understanding; I see them as explorations rather than conclusions. Others will have their own views, and mine are no more than pinpricks on a vast canvas; but perhaps they will serve as a prompt to the hopeful reflection that as a species we are able to do better, that humanity can become more humane.

Part 1

A Savage Civilization

I

A Threatened Ending
Religion, Politics, and Ecology
in a Conflicted Age

Humanity is forever teetering on the brink of an expectation that may appear as either salvation or catastrophe—or sometimes a combination of the two. This threatened end of the present state of things scholars variously call the eschaton (the end-times) or the apocalypse.

The latter word first came to be used in the Middle East of the fourth century BCE, during the tumultuous times that followed the conquests of Alexander the Great. It was a time when ancient empires and kingdoms were being replaced by a new Hellenic order, a time of cultural upheaval when older values and traditional identities were confronted by new philosophies and a new internationalism. That is to say, it was a time rather like our own! People wondered what on earth was happening and turned to the heavens for an answer. There, so seers proclaimed, books hidden from the beginning of time would be opened and the message of preordained destiny would be "uncovered"—in Greek *apokaluptein*, apocalypse.

The Hebrew Bible culminates at this point, with the prophet Daniel interpreting visions and uncovering—that is, revealing—the future. The New Testament finishes on the same note, with a newly inspired seer receiving the message from heaven: the scroll of the book must be eaten and its dire message of the end-times revealed. It is worth noting, however, that following the destruction of this evil world a "new heaven and a new earth" will follow, the holy city of Jerusalem will descend from heaven, and the servants of God and the Lamb will reign forever (Rev 21–22).

But though the word *apocalypse* was Hellenic and the context biblical, the concept of apocalypse was considerably older, several thousand years older. For its origin we must look to Zoroastrianism, the first of the great religions to understand the world in terms of a moral order and a teleological conclusion. Previously the world had been viewed through the medium of myth, of heroic conflicts that subdued chaos and ensured the natural cycles of fertility. Zarathustra proclaimed a moral order under the direction of one supreme being (*Ahura Mazda*—the God of Light), who directed all things to a final end, a day of judgment when books would be opened, the record of all past actions proclaimed, and our lives evaluated by a final decision that would stand forever.[1] Thereafter history would increasingly be viewed as periodic, progressive, even predestined, and having a final END.

This new vision from Persia slowly spread southward and mingled with the teachings of the Babylonian astrologers and their unparalleled renown for reading the signs in the heavens. It was here that the beliefs of seventh-century Jewish exiles would be transformed: divine intermediaries, angels, would announce the coming of the Messiah, the Righteous One, as the final days and Last Judgment approached. Subsequently, apocalyptic movements like the Essenes sought to put a date on the threatened ending and proclaimed the imminence of a final conflict that would precede the coming of the Righteous One. The gospels announced that this day was at hand, and Saint Paul promised that the long wait for the Anointed One— the *christos*—was over.

But there was an ambiguity in this message from the outset. John the Baptist had proclaimed the kingdom of God was at hand, as if God was to intervene in history, but then Herod intervened and beheaded John. So his message was taken up by Jesus, but with a difference. The shift in perspective was to the present but also to something else: to an intervening God was now added the need for human cooperation. As the Scripture scholar John Dominic Crossan put it, "The paradigm shift from *imminent* to *present* entailed a shift from unilateral divine *intervention* to bilateral divine intervention and human *cooperation*."[2] It is the latter critical element of the human response that became the more problematic. As Crossan goes on to note, God's kingdom arrives only insofar as people take it upon themselves

1. Cohn, *Cosmos*, 114.

2. Crossan, *Jesus*, 165 (italics original).

or enter into it; that is, "The lure of 'how soon' returned to haunt forever the new Christian-Jewish vision."[3]

But it did not happen. A thousand years later the feverish expectation returned when the monastic chronicler Rodulfus Glaber (Rudolph the Bald), in his *Five Books of History*, interpreted the events of the period from 1000 to 1033 as signs that the apocalyptic prophecy was about to be fulfilled, and that "Satan will be released when a thousand years of history have passed."[4] Another aspect of this popular view was that the Messiah would return when the Jerusalem temple and earth had been cleansed. The Crusades were launched to effect just such a fulfilment, Christendom having found a convenient enemy in Islam, which already had recast the biblical expectation with its own version of the final time and thus became the last of the great apocalyptic religions. The crusaders were confident that their success was preordained, none more so than Saint Bernard of Clairvaux, whose electrifying sermons were instrumental in launching the Second Crusade in 1145, but who died incredulous that it should have failed.

In place of the threatened apocalypse that did not arrive, millenarian movements periodically sprang to life, proclaiming that "now" was the time:[5] such was the prophecy of Joachim of Fiore (d. 1202), who proclaimed the Age of the Spirit. Another failed messiah was Sabbatai Zevi (d. 1676),[6] who was succeeded by the Hassidic movement of Jewish Orthodoxy, whose members still hope that "next year" will be the year. Yet another example is the Catholic Apostolic Church founded in 1832, which appointed the final twelve apostles to prepare for the coming of the end times. By this time the world was once again in turmoil in the wake of the French Revolution and in the thrall of the Industrial Revolution, which created a new sense of unprecedented change. This was reflected in the apocalyptic paintings of John Martin (1789–1854), which fascinated the early Victorians, for his awesome canvases of *Belshazzar's Feast* (1820) and *The Destruction of Sodom and Gomorrah* (1852) not only seemed to express a distant past but captured the contemporary mood of unpredictability, as did the tumultuous modern style of William (J. M. W.) Turner (1775–1851). Even popular depictions of the furnaces of Coalbrookdale took on an apocalyptic aura, with new overtones that befitted an increasingly secular industrial age.

3. Crossan, *Jesus*, 165.

4. See Lacey and Danziger, *Year 1000*, 179–84.

5. Cohn, *Pursuit*.

6. Scholem, *Sabbatai Sevi*.

Popular religious expectation reflected the unsettled and unsettling times. The prophetess Joanna Southcott—a widely influential *seer* of the early nineteenth century—received regular visits from the Holy Spirit promptly at five o'clock each evening, revealing to her that she would give birth to "Shiloh," who would gather the people together for the second coming. Her phantom pregnancy of 1814 was the talk of the time and something of a medical conundrum. Meanwhile John Wroe took advantage of the missing miracle to reveal that it was he who would fulfill this role and to make detailed plans for the Lancashire mill town of Ashton-under-Lyne to become the New Jerusalem described in the book of Revelation.[7]

But all these expectations, like those original hopes of John the Baptist for a unilateral divine intervention, came to nothing. Utopian dreams of an eschatological ending remained just that, dreams—or, as the perceptive and radical social commentator Karl Marx put it, an opiate of the people. Again Crossan's work helps in distinguishing between a rhapsodic and impossible *utopia* (Greek for "not-place"/nowhere) and a possible *eutopia* ("good-place"/ this place), which it is within our power to construct: "*Eutopia* imagines a social world of universal peace, a human world of nonviolent distributive justice where all get a fair and adequate share of God's world."[8] It is exactly this imminent or *realized eschatology,* of human willingness to act for the common good starting here and now, that is the crucial element of a transformed or transfigured world.

In the nineteenth century such an understanding of apocalyptic expectation was beginning to take shape under a new name, Communism, a new specter that now stalked the cities of Europe and proved a lightning rod for the growing resentment of the newly urbanized masses of impoverished workers. As Eric Hobsbawm has written, "Around 1840 European history acquired a new dimension: the 'social problem,' or (seen from another point of view) potential social revolution."[9] A new, purely secular millenarianism now haunted Europe, and theology gave way to ideology, transforming old utopian and apocalyptic dreams into revolutionary social demands. Marx provided the new millenarianism with a "scientific" basis grounded on an economic understanding of the inexorable march of history. Nothing could now alter mankind's final destiny.

7. Green, *Prophet.*

8. Crossan, *Jesus,* 137.

9. Hobsbawm, *How,* 41.

But once again it didn't happen. By the end of the twentieth century that dream was also in tatters, and its Soviet delivery system had collapsed. For all his brilliance Marx had overlooked one simple reality: nature. The environmental indifference and destructiveness of Soviet-style Communism was monumental and catastrophic. Vast industrial and agribusiness plans—like the cotton plantations of central Asia that desiccated the Aral Sea—proved apocalyptic in a manner and degree quite contrary to expectation. It was an environmental recklessness that was finally epitomized by the nuclear disaster at Chernobyl—a name ironically meaning "wormwood"—that inevitably drew attention to the passage in Rev 8:10, in which a star called Wormwood fell from heaven and poisoned rivers and springs so that the people died.

But Soviet communism was not alone in its environmental destructiveness. Western capitalism proved equally rapacious. In complete disregard of its optimistic ideology, its exploitation of the finite and fragile resources of the natural world turned out to be unsustainable. It took the new prophetic voice of Rachel Carson—a woman's voice at last!—in the face of abusive skepticism to alert the world to an impending ecological apocalypse. Ecologists such as Thomas Berry challenged thunderous disbelief to emphasize that "the basic disruption of all the basic life systems of earth has come about within a culture that emerged from a biblical-Christian matrix."[10] This was not accidental in a culture and belief system that viewed the earth as having been created for the benefit and delight of humanity.

Just as theology once gave way to ideology, now ideology had to make way for ecology. The coming of the Green Revolution seemed to confirm what two German academics, Rotteck and Welcker, had written in 1842 of the "proletarian revolution'" that replaced the conflicts of the feudal world: "No major historical antagonism disappears or dies out unless there emerges a new antagonism."[11] Ecocide, the shadow side of economic growth, had now become the apocalyptic specter stalking the modern secular milieu.

The two specters that now in particular overshadow the world are population growth and climate change—two seemingly insoluble crises that in turn reflect a disconnect of people and governments from the natural world. Ironically, it is in the Middle East, where civilization and apocalyptic sensibility first arose, where all the elements of an impending modern apocalypse have now coalesced. Satellite images show the area

10. Berry, *Selected Writings*, 106.

11. Hobsbawm, *How*, 42.

once called the Fertile Crescent and cradle of civilization reduced to an arc of increasing aridity and vegetation scarcity. Since 1900 the region has warmed by 1.2 degrees centigrade, and rainfall has declined by 10 percent, forcing an exploding population into overcrowded cities already straining under poverty, political oppression, and religious tensions.[12] The resulting frustration finds its expression—though not necessarily its cause—in such religious extremism as the so-called death cult of the Islamic State of Iraq and Syria (ISIS).

In Syria we now have the first modern conflict to be explicitly linked to climate change.[13] For a decade reports have linked rising temperature and the likelihood of civil strife to areas throughout sub-Saharan Africa. In 2015 a report to the U.S. Defense Department warned of climate change as a "threat multiplier"' and of water wars.[14] As Frank Femia of one Washington think tank says, ""You can't say climate change is causing ISIS to do what it's doing, but it [climate change] certainly has a role to play in the region.""[15] It creates the context of stress and chaos in which extremism and apocalypticism flourish. And while ISIS destroys all vestiges of history in pursuit of heaven, it overlooks the more potent portent of the present, for ecology defers to neither religion nor politics.

ISIS is itself a product of apocalypticism. From the outset Islam, following the monotheistic tradition of the so-called Abrahamic family of faiths from which it springs, had an apocalyptic expectation of a threatened or promised ending. The contemporary clash of this tradition with modern Western civilization has created a new context for its manifestation. Ever since the dismemberment of the Ottoman state and caliphate, the Muslim world has suffered a deep sense of grievance, particularly over the arbitrary creation of the mosaic of modern Middle Eastern states (created to suit Western interests), which provides the context of contemporary conflict. As one radical preacher urged, "Your father's Islam is what the colonizers left behind, the Islam of those who bow down and obey. Our Islam is the Islam of combatants, of blood, of resistance."[16]

ISIS adherents believe in an imminent apocalypse that only the most devout will survive. Their attempt to restore a caliphate aims to create a

---

12. Bawden, "Climate"; see also Kelly et al., "Climate."

13. Bawden, "Climate Change"; see also Kelly et al., "Climate Change."

14. United States Department of Defense, "National Security."

15. Quoted in Holthaus, "Hot."

16. Quoted in Roy, *Jihad*, 25.

space where believers—as well as nonbelievers—can kill and be killed and so earn martyrdom. Its values invert those of normal civilization: "You love life, we love death," its adherents taunt. As Roy says, this narrative "has the power to fascinate fragile individuals suffering from genuine psychiatric problems."[17] Its certainties have great appeal to those adrift in the ambiguities of modernity or torn by the cognitive dissonance of conflicting values. Not only does it open up an opportunity for an increasing number of "lone wolves" to make a lasting affirmation of identity—like some character out of a novel by Dostoyevsky or Conrad—but it gives a rallying point for those newly converted to Islam to express their commitment. These converts to Islam in France, Belgium, and Britain as well as born-again Muslims who after living highly secular lives suddenly renew their allegiance, constitute the core of jihadists who operate beyond the traditional frameworks of religious organization in the pursuit of radicalism and death. Their bloodlust sets them apart as did the mark of Cain in the mythical past.

Where civilization began, an apocalypse of planetary proportions now looms; the four horsemen of destruction, war, famine, and death are once again in the saddle. Many tremble at this descent into chaos, but the contemporary Middle East merely reprises the inexorable pattern of civilization; for as Lewis Mumford observed in his monumental study *The City in History*, the essence of civilization has always been the exertion of power in every form.[18] The city became the paramount expression of this truth as an instrument of aggression, domination, and conquest. As Plato declared in *The Laws,* "In reality every city is in a natural state of war with every other."[19] The consequence of this thirst for power became expressed in empire, as with Sargon, King of Akkad, who was the first to create an empire, seeking to dominate all he beheld.

Again, nothing expresses this state more clearly than ISIS in Syria. Though the rest of the world looks on aghast as ancient cities like Nineveh and Nimrud are utterly destroyed, they forget that these cities themselves represent and recapitulate centuries of destruction. The palaces built by Sennacherib bear witness to his power and his total annihilation of Babylon and other rivals: "The city and houses from its foundation to its top, I destroyed, I devastated, I burned with fire. The wall and the outer wall, temples and gods, temple tower of brick and earth, as many as there were,

---

17. Roy, *Jihad*, 23.

18. Mumford, *City*, 66.

19. Mumford, *City*, 65.

I razed . . . I made its destruction more complete than that by a flood."[20] Civilization has always stood on the neck of the vanquished, and now ISIS apes this attitude and behavior, and, though perhaps unwittingly, continues the story of civilization.

Here, then, we see a pattern of events closer to home than we might like to think. As Patrick Geddes[21] has pointed out, each historic civilization begins with a living urban core, the polis, and ends in a shattered ruin— a necropolis, a city of the dead, of fire-scorched ruins, empty workshops, heaps of meaningless refuse, the population massacred or driven into slavery. Mumford cites mighty Rome as the perfect example of how one civilization after another, having achieved power and centralized control, fails to reach "an organic solution of the problem of quantity."[22] In fact, on reading his description of Rome's breaking point—the suffocating numbers, rising rents, and deteriorating housing conditions; the overexploitation of resources—one could almost mistake it for the London news, or for news from many great contemporary cities. As he concludes, "When these signs multiply, Necropolis is near, though not a stone has yet crumbled."[23]

After five millennia of brinkmanship are we facing the impending end of civilization? Some think so; consider Naomi Oreskes and Erik Conway's unequivocal title *The Collapse of Western Civilization*, or Jared Diamond's all-inclusive *Collapse*. The looming possibility brings with it a poignant awareness of the fates of the Harappan, Roman, and Khmer civilizations, to name but three—and a sharp reminder that the Maya and a number of other civilizations from central and southern America collapsed under environmental stress and subsequent violence. Of these spectacles, which were alarmingly similar to what we see in Syria, perhaps the most graphic examples are those of the Moche and the great metropolis of Teotihuacan— the place "where time began" . . . and then ended!

After each collapse, apocalyptic as it may have been to those involved, new beginnings were always made somewhere else. So what if anything is different now? The answer is devastatingly simple: all preceding collapses were regional events initiated by localized factors—there was always "somewhere else." But today's global society has many features of a single global civilization and is threatened by such global phenomena as climate

20. Quoted in Mumford, *City*, 68.

21. Geddes, *Cities*.

22. Mumford, *City*, 277.

23. Mumford, *City*, 281.

change, ocean acidification, collapsing ecosystems, and exponentially expanding overpopulation. There is no longer a "somewhere else."

Archaeologist Ronald Wright warns that we have become victims of a "progress trap" of our own making.[24] Our belief in progress has, he argues, hardened into an ideology, "a secular religion, which like the religions that progress has challenged, is blind to certain flaws in its credentials."[25] This was always evident, but little noticed, even at the outset when the drainage of land and cultivation of crops made the first towns of Sumer possible. But these very technological developments in time created salt pans that ruined the land, destroyed the crops, and starved the cities—a process that was among the first installments of the "progress trap."

Since then the human species has become infinitely more inventive, expansive, and powerful. Wielders of flint knives could be overpowered by those with bronze or iron swords, who in turn would fall to those with muskets and canons; now the whole of humanity can be exterminated with atomic weapons. This may be a logical progression and material progress of sorts, but the final step is one too far; when the progress trap is sprung one last time it brings apocalypse.

We now have entered what has been called the Anthropocene (and perhaps the final) stage of our history.[26] Politics, Religion, and Ecology (PRE) have combined to form a new matrix of modernity; a *prelude*, but to what? Previously, each impending threat of doom came and went: the apocalypse didn't happen. Will the same be true again? Today Christian Zionists still proclaim the end, and in the United States 60 percent of the population are said to believe that the prophecies of the book of Revelation are accurate and that the End will come in their lifetime. Jesus will return and take those confirmed in the Christian faith up to heaven in 'the rapture.' In Israel, Amos Oz noted how religious students were "crude, smug and arrogant . . . bursting with messianic rhetoric, ethnocentric, 'redemptionist,' apocalyptic—quite simply inhuman"—students for whom Arab human beings under "our dominion" might never have been.[27] Zealots increasingly agitate for possession of the Temple Mount, the destruction of the Dome of the Rock, and the rebuilding of the third temple to prepare the way for the return of the Messiah. Such actions would almost certainly trigger an

24. Wright, *Short History.*
25. Wright, *Short History,* 4.
26. Schwagerl, *Anthropocene.*
27. Oz, *In the Land,* 132.

Armageddon—the battle to end all battles—and confirm the expectation of Zarathustra all those millennia ago and not far from the Megiddo of biblical prophecy!

Perhaps a change of worldview and lifestyles and thinking will result in hope for the future. Perhaps a new awareness and mindfulness will enable us to change our ways. Perhaps the survivors of an impending catastrophe will be sufficiently chastened to create a better world. But will it happen? We stand on the brink of the unknown.

So what should our response be? What should we do in what may be the last days of humanity? Fortunately, the Cambridge theologian Don Cupitt has given us a very good answer in his recent book, *Ethics in the Last Days of Humanity.*[28] He argues that our response should be unstinting generosity of spirit in the present moment—what he calls *solar living,* that is, simply following the example of the sun and pouring ourselves out for the good of all life. "If we can pause a while in our rush to expend all available natural resources, and instead learn how to live by expending *ourselves,* we may feel ourselves becoming fit to inhabit this earth for a while longer yet."[29]

Like Nietzsche, Cupitt argues that we need to free ourselves from all forms of *ressentiment*—a term more all-embracing than its English equivalent of "resentment" and denoting all forms of reactionary, negative feelings. It is the complete openness to humanity that marks humanitarianism as the culmination of human moral understanding and an expression of our final completion (the *eschaton* in biblical terminology). In fact, Cupitt goes further than this. For him *humanitarianism is eschatological.* Humanitarianism is the ultimate and final expression of our understanding of the meaning of life.

It may come as a surprise to many how recent this understanding is. A study of the usage of the word *humanitarian* reveals that it emerged in the nineteenth century as an effect of the rationalism of the Enlightenment on Christian thinking that in turn gave rise to *philanthropy* and a concern for general human well-being.[30] It arose out of a specifically Christian matrix and, as Cupitt points out, its origins are rooted in the teaching of "the Jesus of history" (as opposed to "the Christ of faith") that proclaimed the immanence of the kingdom of God and demanded a total generosity of spirit,

28. Cupitt, *Ethics.*

29. Cupitt, *Ethics,* 72.

30. Williams, *Keywords,* "Ideology."

NOW. His message was very much in keeping with the apocalyptic spirit of his age, though it demanded an eschatological state of living that was soon to be occluded by the rise of the church and "the Christ of developed ecclesiastical Christianity" with its increasingly exclusivist doctrines and pretentious hierarchy of privilege.

Interestingly, this has become clearer in the light of modern biblical scholarship and textual studies such as those by the distinguished Scripture scholar John Dominic Crossan. In a number of works, particularly *The Power of Parable*, he explores how even the evangelists (mis)interpreted the original teaching of Jesus in ways which were both inadequate and contradictory of the original intention.[31] What is particularly disturbing is the way in which the terminology for Caesar Augustus in Roman imperial theology became normative for describing Jesus in later Christian theology: *Quibus imperavit Augustus, imperavit Christus* (Christ is the only legitimate successor to Augustus-Caesar). Thus, the humble messiah who preached unconditional love and who rode peaceably on a donkey was transformed into the vengeful king riding on a warhorse crushing all his adversaries and wading through blood "as high as a horse's bridle, for two hundred miles." (Rev 14:20).[32]

As confidence in church-based Christianity now languishes, Cupitt argues, the historical Jesus, the posttheistic Son of Man, has rightly grown in stature and is "now manifest as a cosmic figure" for our times. A historical example of this change may be seen in the story of nurse Edith Cavell, whose current centenary deserves remembrance. It is noteworthy that her memorial in Trafalgar Square bears only one word in large capitals: HUMANITY. Though a devout Christian who would have rejected the term, she can be seen as a martyr to the ideal of humanitarianism—not to mention as a feminist icon in the midst of a male, militaristic world. It was her simple actions of caring for wounded soldiers regardless of nationality in the interests of humanity—her last words were, "Patriotism is not enough"—that now sets this bar of judgment above all other standards, whether nationalistic, ideological, political, or religious. Regardless of our beliefs, our ultimate criterion of individual and collective worth must now and hereafter be our humanity, our humaneness.

It is on this count that theocratic governments such as those in Iran and Saudi Arabia, and groups such as ISIS and other despotisms so notably

31. Crossan, *Power*.
32. Crossan, *Jesus*.

fail. As countless migrants flee such states they cry, "We are humans!" Instinctively they turn to the West, hoping to find, if not some existential salvation, at least a better way of life. More generally, victims of natural disasters the world over have come to expect and even demand generosity: "What took you so long?" they ask rescuers and aid workers. Curiously, the standard of generosity implicit in the new humanitarian ideal is widely accepted as a right, *sans frontiers*. A broad humanitarian generosity is now expected of the West and continues to make it exceptional. Surely this must be the basis of all future ethical systems.

This ethic challenges the pervasive cult of greed and personal ambition that has become so destructive of our world. We must stop asking, What do I want? What can I afford for myself? The questions must be, What can I give? What can I afford for others? The quest for ever greater consumption and acquisition of goods has led to increasing inequality and social instability, while members a neofeudal, privileged elite retire into ever more securely gated estates and fortified mansions. A life-affirming alternative was defined by those great Victorian do-gooders, in whose view a society that benefits everyone is better for everyone; it brings happiness and satisfaction, peace and contentment. That is the kind of apocalyptic consummation the book of Revelation promised. We need it now!

2

A Mirror to European Civilization
The Meeting of "Otherness" and Savagery

Although anniversaries and centenaries come and go, the issues they raise and the controversies they generate tend to linger on. A case in point is the five hundredth anniversary of the discovery of America in 1992. Or at least that was the way innumerable articles and studies put it. But apart from the details of what took place in that fateful year of 1492, far more important and equally elusive is the perspective from which we must now view and evaluate them. Exactly what was "discovered"? For the Latin American writer Ignacio Ellacuría it was clear that what was "discovered"— in the sense of revealed or uncovered—was Europe itself and the nature of its civilization.

Ellacuría did not mince words: "Thus, five centuries ago, with the 'discovery' of the so-called 'new world' what was really discovered was the true Spain herself, the reality of Western culture and the church as they were then."[1] In this perspective it was above all the conquistador, the dominator, who laid himself open to discovery. In reality it was what we now condescendingly call the Third World that discovered the First World in its most negative and truest aspects; the plunder and destruction of a continent was the harbinger of what Europeans had to offer the rest of the world in

---

1. See Ellacuría, "Fifth Centenary." I am quoting here from the lecture notes of Jon Sobrino, which he handed to me after a lecture I attended.

an epoch of discovery, colonization, and conquest—all the while passing themselves off as benefactors of the world.

This theme was taken up by another distinguished voice, a survivor of a U.S.-backed *contra* massacre, the Jesuit liberation theologian Jon Sobrino. In a powerful address delivered in Salford Cathedral titled "500 Years: Reflections for Europe from Latin America" he stated unequivocally that "in the reality of the South (or Third World), with all its poverty, injustice and death, the North (First World) can recognize itself, as in a reverse mirror-image, through what it has produced."[2] This metaphor of a mirror—recalling those polished obsidian mirrors found in burial caches throughout the Americas—was also used by the Mexican writer Carlos Fuentes. In his quincentennial study, *The Buried Mirror: Reflections on Spain and the New World*, he challenges us to think about how our understanding of the world has been shaped and evolved in the face of the radically "other."[3] We look into a mirror and see disconcerting and disturbing reflections.

For Sobrino, recalling the events of 1492 and analyzing the reality of 1992 was the means of understanding the state of humankind on our planet, and the crucial question is whether unity is a product of unification and growth of the human family achieved by truly accepting "otherness," or whether "it is to be considered as a means of shaping the world into antagonists, a unity of superiors and inferiors, of executioners and victims." For him, "the Western, democratic and Christian civilization of the humanism and renaissance in vogue in 1492, just as with the enlightenment and modernity of the past five centuries, has been incapable of humanizing the Third World, just as it has been incapable of humanizing Europe itself."[4] If these challenging sentiments, however irksome, are difficult to deny, then we need to ask why.

The European expansion, in this case led by the Spaniards, was driven by the insatiable quest for ever greater wealth and power at any cost, and always underpinned by a sense of divine legitimation. The ambiguity of this motivation was well expressed by the distinguished Austrian historian Friedrich Heer when he wrote, "The enthusiasm of the early Spaniards who first voyaged to the Americas was stirred and sustained by mythological and eschatological expectation, by hopes of finding Paradise, by fantasies

2. The lecture notes were privately distributed after the event.

3. Fuentes, *Buried Mirror*.

4. I am quoting here from the lecture notes of Jon Sobrino, which he handed to me after a lecture I attended.

of mounting a global crusade against Islam."[5] The discovery of a new world was even placed on a par with the original act of creation and the incarnation, and the conquest of America was presented as an extension of the *Reconquista*—the crusade against Islam and paganism to create one catholic world order. But regardless of such ideological motives as Christianizing the natives, the existence of indigenous people was seen as a means to an end; the primary goal was, as Sobrino noted, "to make the Spaniards rich, and later when that supply became exhausted, black Africans were enslaved so that they could in turn become instruments, just like modern sources of energy."

The justification for all this took place in many and varied ways: ecclesiastically (the bull of Pope Alexander VI divided the new domains between Spain and Portugal), theologically (this was the providential reward for the reconquest of Spain from the Moors), politically (there were no legitimate owners of the lands), anthropologically (Indians were inferior and not even fully human), ethically (the evil and perverse customs of the Indians demanded suppression), and so on. But many and varied though these justifications may have been, the premise was always the same; namely, that the Europeans were going to stay in those lands and defend what was already held in possession in order to get rich. The few solitary voices raised in opposition, such as that of Bartolomé de las Casas and Francisco de Vitoria, were drowned out by the chorus of conquest.

The situation had changed little for many of the poorest inhabitants of South America when modern liberation theologians began to articulate the needs and rights of the poor. Their theology was denounced by the Vatican for being politically motivated, just as the initial voice of protest had been denounced as heretical and seditious. Material interests of international conglomerates and appropriately named "vulture hedge funders" proved virtually unassailable, and political demands for security and stability ensured the survival of right-wing cabals. The wealth of nations overwhelmingly benefited an elite who often had strong Western ties and who, like General Pinochet, saw themselves as virtuous defenders of catholic order.

Just as it did five hundred years ago, an underlying eurocentricism still measures everything according to how well it benefits the First World. This egotism is compounded by an underlying indifference and ignorance which, in the words of the theologian J. B. Metz, "removes the so-called Third World to a faceless distance." The result is "a kind of cultural strategy

5. Heer, *Holy*, 168.

for the immunization of Europe . . . an attempt to set themselves apart in their minds from the global challenges facing humanity . . . a new variety of tactical provincialism."[6] Metz's observation is currently reflected in the desire to isolate Europe from the "'swarms" of migrants who threaten her insularity yet are often the consequences of her actions.

This current mind-set of disinterest and indifference disguises a deeper mentality of arrogance and contempt that was already embedded in the minds of the conquistadores, five hundred years ago. When Columbus stepped ashore on the Bahamas in 1492, he was welcomed by the Taino people, a hospitable multiethnic people who had inhabited many of the Caribbean islands for over a thousand years and had a well-ordered and peaceful society. These he summarily denounced as heretics and while women were raped he began mass burnings: at one *auto-da-fe* eighty *caciques* (chieftains) were burned alive. After twelve years of genocidal butchery and disease brought by the Spanish, the islands had been depopulated. In such a case we may well ponder just who exactly were the savages.

We may also ask why this should have happened: what was the origin of this behavior and mentality? Columbus seems to have had an apocalyptic view of the world and to have seen himself as chosen for a divinely inspired mission—the fulfilment of the single-minded dream of the Christian monarchs Ferdinand and Isabella for Christian uniformity and the reconquest of Muslim lands. The genocide (for this is what we would now call it) of the Taino people was the same treatment accorded to deviant or defiant groups across medieval Europe, from the so-called Cathars of Languedoc to the Prussians and Slavic peoples targeted by the great northern Teutonic crusades. This became the pattern for future European expansion.[7] Ethnic or racial difference was not initially significant; the fact that people seemed to believe different things was sufficient indictment. The infamous instruction attributed to the papal legate Arnaud Amaury authorizing the massacre of the entire population of Béziers in 1209 sums it up: "Kill them all. God will know his own."[8] This is how a confessional civilization dealt with "'otherness."

It is highly ironic that the point at which the church reached the zenith of its power and influence—the so called Age of Faith during the twelfth and thirteenth centuries—should also be the time when it was most alienated from the spirit of its humble, pacifist founder as recorded in the

---

6. Metz, quoted in Sobrino, *Principle*, 77.

7. Christiansen, *Northern*.

8. Quoted in Baigent and Leigh, *Inquisition*, 12.

gospels. A vast monasticized power structure, run by an elite clerical caste and operating from palatial residences and grand cathedrals with elaborate liturgies, epitomized the very opposite of numerous dominical teachings on wealth and power, privilege, and elitism. Indeed it violated the central gospel message of beatitude, peace, and reconciliation. It is perhaps not surprising, then, that numerous dissenting apostolic movements of *poverelli* or poor men (and women)—groups of Christians seeking to recapture the original gospel spirit of simplicity and apostolic fraternity—sprang up across western Europe, exposing this difference and dissenting from the hierarchical objectives of ecclesiastical reform and centralization.[9] These movements were generally condemned as heretical. Thus arose the increasingly bitter paradox that centralization of ecclesiastical authority resulted in an ever-growing diversity of opposition at the peripheries that was deemed subversive or heretical.

Again, one asks how this had come about. The historian Friedrich Heer was in no doubt: he attributed it to the reforming policies of Pope Gregory VII (1073–1085).[10] In the titanic power struggle that took place between the Holy Roman Empire and papacy in the eleventh and twelfth centuries, Gregory's solution to the corrupting influence of worldly kings was "to turn both secular clergy and laity into monks." By this means he would wrest the church out of secular control. Himself a monk, Gregory now imposed celibacy on the clergy as an unequivocal good but with significant consequences, as Heer indicates: "Celibacy also activates drives which impel men to overweening ambition, greed, vanity, envy and contentiousness. The unbridled clerical passion for contention . . . has from the eleventh century kept the Christian world in a state of constant turmoil."[11] But he goes further in asserting that the energies Gregory unleashed in his reforms came to define European Christendom and set up "tremendous disorders"; as a result, Pope Gregory "kindled more hatred in Europe than any other ruling figure since the days of the Neronian emperors."[12]

Strong words! But like all revolutionaries—and his pontificate is among the most decisive events in shaping the succeeding millennium— Gregory had the purest of motives. Among these was to prepare or cleanse the world of evil for the millennial return of Christ. The instrument to

9. Sheldrake, *Spirituality*.

10. Heer, *Holy*, 51–65.

11. Heer, *Holy*, 56.

12. Heer, *Holy*, 57.

attain this submission to the cross of Christ was the crusade, and it was Gregory who gave the first concrete expression of this idea. His plan was twofold: outwards beyond Christendom to unify all Christian people under papal authority, and inwards within Europe towards the suppression of heretics and deviants through a violent purgation. Though we tend to think of the Crusades in terms of the attempted reconquest of the Holy Land this extra dimension was only provided by Gregory's successor, Urban II, and was a manifestation of the intrinsic savagery already tearing Europe apart. The more immediate target of the papal plans to renew Christendom was the Holy Roman emperor, Henry IV, whose nemesis Gregory became as he sought to destroy the emperor's claim to the leadership of Christendom.

One element of this new reality was the creation of what is perhaps the most inhumane and iniquitous institution of terror ever devised by humankind—the Inquisition.[13]

This comprehensive apparatus of persecution was codified by the Fourth Lateran Council of 1215—itself a high-water mark of medieval ecclesiastical power—and laid the foundations of what has justly been called a "'persecuting society."[14] Characterized by confessional, racial, and ideological intolerance, the inquisitional mentality was to become a distinguishing feature of European society until modern times. Initially an attempt to unify Christendom through the extermination of "deviance" or "dissent" represented by so-called heretics—of which the fabricated medieval Manichee is perhaps most famous—the program of persecution soon grew to embrace Jews, Moors, lepers, homosexuals, prostitutes, and with the later witch hunts, women in general.[15]

The original motivation and enduring mentality behind this somber history has been brilliantly analyzed by the medieval historian R. I. Moore, among others. As he writes, "Heresy was varied in its origin, incoherent in its convictions, inarticulate in its forms; the myth which the bishops made of it was clear, simple and universal."[16] Disparate individuals were "welded together" to form coherent stereotypes that would then define and identify the objects of persecution; "the construction of the stereotype on a basis of reality gave it a real and potent existence of its own." Like the crusade, the inquisition would become an essential instrument for the papal purgation

13. Green, *Inquisition*.
14. Moore, *Formation*.
15. Levack, *Witch-Hunt*.
16. Moore, *Formation*, 85

of Christendom and creation of a theocracy. As Heer has noted, in the end and regardless of the doctrinal content, heresy would simply be high treason against the pope.[17]

By the sixteenth century, the mentality of suspicion and the methodology of persecution had become so embedded in the fabric of European society that it would continue to morph into further expressions of contempt for such differences as those characterizing colonial peoples. Shakespeare's *Tempest*, set on the shores of the new world, presents Caliban as a stereotype of the primal savage, while later settlers would view the natives as monkeys. As with the North American Indians, so later with the Australian Aborigines, who were originally classified (and hunted) as "'vermin" and only in 1949 recognized as citizens!

The unfortunate practice of caricaturing the medieval period as one of superstition, stagnation, and obscurantism to provide a foil for the dynamic quality of modernity and Enlightenment has itself obscured many of the deeper, enduring continuities that arose in that period. As Moore succinctly summarizes the medieval matrix, "The creation in this way of a single account of the victim as an enemy of God and society, which might be transferred at will to any object, either a class of persons already existing, such as Jews, whom it might be desirable or convenient to persecute, or a new one, such as sodomites or witches, which by an act of classification might be invented for the purpose, was a crucial stage in the development of the model of persecution."[18] And this prescription came to be a defining characteristic of European society. Europe's totalitarian regimes of the twentieth century would become adept at its application. The mentality of suspicion and denunciation was as clearly operative in socialist states and the McCarthyism of the twentieth century as it was in the Albigensian Crusade of the twelfth.

Modern states, such as that created by Ferdinand and Isabella in Spain in the fifteenth century, came to be characterized by centralized power, ideological uniformity (in this case Catholicism), and mechanisms of violent coercion that provided the template for both the mentality and methodology of persecuting societies for centuries to come. On this trajectory one can also include the Soviet Union, notable for its paranoid labelling of "wreckers," "saboteurs," and dissidents, as well as for its secret police, its

17. Heer, *Holy*, 57.
18. Moore, *Formation*, 160.

systematic surveillance, and its show trials. And, lest we forget, Franco's fascist Phalangists and the culminating inferno of the Nazi Holocaust.

Some writers, such as the distinguished sociologist Zygmunt Bauman, have presented the Holocaust and racism as the logical product of the eighteenth-century Enlightenment and the inevitable consequence of modernity.[19] Bauman, like Michel Foucault, believed that a central feature of modernity was the urge to dominate, divide, and classify, and that binary oppositions such as between "the self" and "other" were expressed, for the Nazis, in the presence of the alien Jew within the border of the state/self. True as this may be, it unduly restricts one's perspective by ignoring the religious foundations of the Enlightenment and those essential elements rooted in medieval Christianity.[20] All the features that Bauman attributes to modernity are clearly present in embryonic form by at least the fifteenth century, when the word *state* took on its modern meaning,[21] and particularly so when it comes to persecuting and exterminating the "other." It is from these roots that both the Enlightenment and modern genocidal mentality emerged, though without the two necessarily being concomitant. After all, the Nazis loathed the Enlightenment *philosophes* and derived their key inspiration from writers like Herder and Fichte, who were Romantic reactionaries with an equal loathing of the Enlightenment. As Herder said, "I am not here to think, but to be, feel, live."[22] In this sense the Holocaust was a reaction against Enlightenment modernity rather than its product.

As Max Weber described it, the rise of the modern bureaucratic state was predicated on the practice of control and would have been impossible without these deeply rooted precedents. The recent trial of Oskar Gröning, the "Accountant of Auschwitz," reminded us that such a program of mass extermination would, like the earlier heresy trials and witch hunts, have been impossible without the massive administrative resources of the state with its myriad of "'professional" practitioners.[23] Inquisition and Holocaust alike testify to the awesome capabilities of clerical administration and bureaucratic detail. In a somewhat more felicitous context, the continuities between past and present were well expressed by Sir Charles Peers in 1931, when as Chief Inspector of Ancient Monuments he said of his staff at the

19. Bauman, *Modernity and the Holocaust.*

20. Siedentop, *Inventing.*

21. Siedentop, *Inventing,* 347.

22. Berlin, *Crooked,* 40.

23 See Cowell, "Oskar Gröning."

Office of Works, "Mute, modest and meritorious they are, in these present times, the authentic successors of those monastic orders whose relics they study to preserve. Their deserts are known only to their heads of departments: they live in obscurity and die in poverty."[24]

A small detail, yet a key element, of this ubiquitous and enduring reality remains in the use of the word "clerk"—from the Latin *clericus,* priest, and interchangeable with the word "cleric." It is a reminder of the time when the administration and entire legal apparatus of states was wholly in the hands of clerics/churchmen, without whom the state would have been unable to function. Such bureaucracies, Moore and Levack remind us, were solely responsible for constructing and administering the apparatus of persecution and terror. As Levack writes, "Beginning in the thirteenth century, however, the ecclesiastical and secular courts of western Europe abandoned the early medieval system of criminal procedure and adopted new techniques that assigned a much greater role to human judgment in the criminal process."[25] This "inquisitorial" process would subsequently reshape the legal landscape of Europe. One of the new techniques introduced was the process of judicial torture, predicated on the assumption that interrogation would lead to a confession of the truth. Even now we are assured that waterboarding is not torture but "legitimate interrogation." But the distinction remains hazy—or is it just a matter of the appropriate classification? This was exactly the sort of detail that so preoccupied the inquisitors of old.

Surprising as it may seem, a restructured and renamed Inquisition still survives in the Catholic Church. It is now called the Congregation for the Doctrine of the Faith, but no thought has ever been given to any expression of remorse or regret for the past, for the incalculable ocean of anguish, or for the innumerable judicial murders. In fact, as was the case under the direction of its previous prefect, Cardinal Ratzinger, later Pope Benedict XVI, it continues to function in very much the same inscrutable way as ever, quietly trying to frustrate, change, and ruin careers.[26] In the secular world the recent War on Terror has revealed the extent to which the past, in both its mentality and methodologies, remains embedded in the present. And of course the same must be said of underlying racist attitudes that continue to simmer below the surface of respectability.

24. Quoted in Thurley, *Men*, 147.
25. Levack, *Witch-Hunt*, 71.
26. Baigent and Leigh, *Inquisition*, 233–62.

All this is redolent of how the Old World of Europe with its model of the closed Catholic state was formed and then shaped the formation of modern Europe and then was revealed, or uncovered, as the real discovery for a New World. But the discovery of 1492 has contributed to our understanding of our own civilization an even longer-term perspective that is only now becoming apparent. Only during the last century have archaeologists come to realize that Central and South America were the home to a whole host of civilizations, many of considerable sophistication, stretching back over five thousand years.[27] Apart from the well-known Maya, Aztec, and Inca civilizations, numerous smaller civilizations have been uncovered along the Pacific Rim: the Moche, Nazca, Chimu, Tiwanaku, and many more. Many of these, like the fabulous city of Teotihuacan, arose and disappeared without trace before being replaced by others long before the conquistadores arrived. Why a city that was greater in size than its contemporary Rome disappeared is still unclear; but when the Aztecs rediscovered its remains some six centuries later, they were overawed by its size, and thinking it must have been built by a race of giants, gave it the name we now know: "the place where men became gods" or "the place where time began."[28]

No doubt it was the repeated experience of disaster that caused the cosmologies of New World societies to be modeled on a cyclical catastrophism in which civilizations arose and then collapsed and disappeared completely, with a new phase of growth to begin only later. When the Spanish friar Fray Bernardino de Sahagún tried to discern what had happened in this strange new world, he learned from the natives of the divine creation of new suns that rose phoenix-like from the ashes of collapsed worlds. In the allegory of the Fifth Sun it was claimed a new world had been created by the intervention of Tecuciztecatl and Nanauatzin, and in this world the Aztec Empire arose and reached its zenith in the century that preceded the Spanish invasion of 1519. One of the decisive reasons for the puzzling collapses of the Aztec and the equally mighty Inca Empires to a handful of Spanish adventurers was the seemingly fatalistic acceptance that this is how it must be.[29]

27. Davies, *Ancient*.

28. See Cooper, *Lost Kingdoms*—that is, Jago Cooper's BBC miniseries *The Lost Kingdoms of Central America*, which aired in 2014 on BBC Four; see especially the fourth episode, called "The Place Where Time Began."

29. D'Altroy, *Incas*, 139.

This overall pattern of civilizations that appear and disappear is very different from our experience in the Old World of the West. The succession of civilizations from Mesopotamia and Egypt through Greece and Rome and down to the present has mostly been seen as a continuous narrative; as one civilization ended another took its place and the baton was handed on. The only threat of a total break came during postclassical times, between 400 and 1200, but even then sufficient strands of learning remained to maintain the link. The overall effect of this surging but cumulative narrative of achievement—like the tide rising ever higher—is that we tend to view the world through a paradigm of continuity and progress. We presuppose that life will go on and survival will be ensured. The lesson from the New World is that this paradigm might be wrong; our confidence might be misplaced.

Indeed, we might do well to take the New World pattern of events as a warning. Recent archaeological research shows that invariably the end came as a result of environmental and ecological stress.[30] As the rains failed and agricultural land ceased to be productive, the rituals of the Moche and Nazca became increasingly desperate, but to no avail; at Lambayeque their gruesome futility is all too apparent in the record of its blood curdling rituals. At Teotihuacan, the ceremonial center seems to have been systematically dismantled and ransacked. As was the case with the first civilization of the Olmecs, so with many of the later Mayan sites: great cities became unsustainable in the face of a growing population and the degradation of agricultural land through overproduction; and the result was a forced abandonment, after which they were swallowed up by the jungle. All these factors mirror the threat that now faces our global civilization. Our cities may be vaster and more sophisticated, but the basic determinants reflected back to us in the mirror of these ancient civilizations remain as remorseless as ever.

The "discovery" of 1492 was indeed dramatic, not least for those ancient slate-black pyrite mirrors into one of which the god Quetzalcoatl is said to have peered and screamed out in anguish as he saw reflected in its dusky surface the pale visage of a human face whose wan features seemed the harbinger of a reign of death and destruction.[31] Subsequently, such wraiths would indeed appear from across the eastern seas just as the ancient legends had foretold. The gruesome nature of their savagery would be the true discovery of 1492; it is a dark truth that still shadows our world.

30. Diamond, *Collapse*, 136–77.
31. Fuentes, *Buried Mirror*, 11.

3

Europe's Heart of Darkness

How Auschwitz Challenges Our
Understanding of Civilization

Most people in the United Kingdom are familiar with *A–Z* maps. This brilliant innovation allows us to find our way around unfamiliar places with ease, for just a glance gets us to where we want to be.[1] Auschwitz is an intriguing name in that its first and last letters are the first and last letters of the alphabet, and what it denotes provides an A-to-Z guide to some of the deepest and darkest labyrinths of the European mind and history. At a glance it takes us to the very heart of the experience of Europe—a heart of darkness many would still prefer not to recognize.

In the ancient world certain places were credited with the dubious distinction of being entrances to the underworld. No one who walks under the infamous arch of Auschwitz—with its iron and ironic motto, *Arbeit macht frei* (Work makes you free)—can doubt that for the modern world

---

1. The innovation is that the maps began, rather bizarrely with Phyllis Pearsall (1906–1996) getting lost on the way home from a London opera in the 1930s while using a standard street map, so she decided to check all the streets for accuracy by walking them and finished up walking every street in London! The unprecedented level of accuracy was what distinguished the subsequent A–Z from all other street maps simply by the fact of Pearsall physically checking them out rather than just referring to other maps as other publishers had done. A second innovation came from the fact that the maps were produced in easily accessible book form. As a result the A–Z dominates the market for street maps of the UK.

this really was the gate of hell. For here one is not simply engulfed by a meandering sprawl of buildings (it was originally an old military barracks) but swallowed up in the labyrinth of the European culture that created it. Joseph Conrad famously attempted to enter this dark world by using the imagery of a journey up the primordial river of a dark continent. The result—*Heart of Darkness*—has been called, with a certain grim foreboding, the first novel of the twentieth century. Yet hindsight lets us see that his protagonist, Józef Korzeniowski, could just as well have stayed in his native land and journeyed to the upper reaches of the Vistula for the location of his novel. For there, indeed, is to be found the true heart of darkness.

Auschwitz lies at the heart of Europe. This statement is first of all, and in its simplest form, a statement of geography. Open any map of Europe and trace an arc from the Urals across northern Scandinavia to the Iberian Peninsula: the center point of this arc lies precisely at Auschwitz.

This is not an accident. Nothing about Auschwitz is an accident. Like everything else about it, the planning was meticulous, carried out with a cool dispassionate rationality that in view of the intent makes this place all the more disturbing. A glance at the railway map that hangs in one of the cell blocks (now a museum) epitomizes this intent. From this focal point the rail network reaches out across Europe like a giant spider's web, the furthest points all equidistant from the center. As the accompanying precise and detailed timetables make clear, their traffic was to converge on this point in constant and uninterrupted flow. So important was this flow that nothing else was allowed to take priority over it. As the Polish poet Czeslaw Milosz remarks in his autobiography *Native Realm*, "The colossal energies that were mobilized to implement this system—that is, wasted on purely arbitrary goals—ought to fill one with awe at a century in which technology prevails over material advantage."[2]

The "arbitrary goal" of this system was the transportation of humans; its purpose their extermination. Of course, it takes more than a system to provide a goal or purpose. It requires an idea. Auschwitz is the final expression of an idea. Curiously enough, Conrad anticipated and described this requirement exactly: "The conquest of the earth, which mostly means the taking away from those who have a different complexion or slightly flatter noses than ourselves, is not a pretty thing when you look into it too much. What redeems it is the idea only; not a sentimental pretense but an idea; and an unselfish belief in the idea—something you can set up, and bow

---

2. Milosz, *Native*, 4.

down before, and offer a sacrifice to."[3] That idea is racial superiority, and it is a quintessentially European idea.

When Europe was beginning to emerge as a world power in the sixteenth century, the foundation of this idea was already implicit in the narrative of conquest and enslavement. The motive, of course, was economic, but the raison d'etre lay in the belief that those who are not like us are inferior to us and therefore can be (ab)used by us. Amer-Indians, Africans, Aborigines—it hardly mattered since the slave trade and destruction of native kingdoms would fill the coffers of European states, lubricating the wheels of commerce, industry, and technological growth. And each country seemed to be able to contribute something to the extraordinary ideological and economic nexus that arose. The British, practical as always, showed the way in perfecting the technicalities of the slave trade; when things went awry, the Spanish came up with concentration camps as a way of curtailing insurrections among the slaves; the pseudoscientific musings of the French count Joseph Arthur de Gobineau provided the myth of a master Aryan race; the German philosopher Friedrich Nietzsche provided the new moral code of the superman, and the German composer Richard Wagner offered the benediction. Thus it went on. As Milosz remarked of the new racial thinking, "that idea acquired a life of its own and was found not only among advocates of naked force but also, in a veiled form, among many democrats."[4] In short, it was generally thought to be a good idea.

If the idea of racial superiority was immensely seductive, its converse—the implied inferiority of others—proved immensely destructive. It resulted in the intentional degradation and demonization of other races, which became a key feature of European colonialism. One missionary map of Asia that was produced in the 1840s simply labeled India as the abode of devil worshipers in need of civilizing. In Tasmania the native Aboriginal population was hunted to extinction as vermin after the manner of fox hunting in the Home Counties, with heads kept as trophies and the skin of the last victim made into a tobacco pouch for the governor.[5] This grotesque example of human commodification is a striking portent of the lampshades made of human flesh at Auschwitz.

3. Conrad, *Heart*, 20.

4. Milosz, *Native*, 5.

5. The missionary map was one I saw on a TV documentary on the subject but don't have any reference, as this was not a published copy. See Wikipedia, "Aboriginal Tasmanians," which deals with the genocide.

The pathway from European colonialism to concentration camp is nowhere more clearly marked than in the story of Germany's colony in present-day Namibia. Though Germany came late to the great African land grab, it did so with a sense of absolute right to what the kaiser called "a place in the sun" and *Lebensraum* (living space). The fact that the land was already occupied by native Herero people was irrelevant; for since they were regarded as a lower form of primate, the men were massacred and the rest rounded up into death camps. And as was noted earlier, this first genocide of the twentieth century was overseen by *Reichskommissar* Heinrich Göring, whose son, Hermann, would become *Reichsmarschall* of the Third Reich.[6] This was not a coincidence. A good many Nazi functionaries who had learned their trade in the German colonies were, in the words of Viktor Böttcher (governor of Posen in 1939 and former civil servant in the Cameroons), fully prepared "to perform in the East of the Reich the constructive work they had once carried out in Africa."[7]

It is important to recognize that in the second quarter of the twentieth century Western civilization was about to encounter its most dangerous foe—not Nazism, but itself. The novelty of Nazism lay in its colonial attitude toward other European nations, which were now to experience the treatment previously reserved for more distant peoples and nations. It was this that the historian Mark Mazower noted as what "primarily differentiated Hitler's empire from Stalin's,"[8] and what made the Second World War different from all previous conflicts.

In Eastern Europe the Germans found a "non-Aryan" Slavonic people who stood in the way of *Lebensraum*. To the likes of the SS chief Heinrich Himmler, the destiny of these "Mongol types" was to be slaves to their Aryan masters. In his influential work of 1926 *People without Space*, Hans Grimm—who had formerly lived in German South West Africa before it was ceded at the Treaty of Versailles—argued that the German people needed to resume the eastward colonial and civilizing expansion that they had begun in the Middle Ages. For the first time the attitudes of modern European colonizers toward people outside Europe were to be applied to continental neighbors. As historian Niall Ferguson writes, "Auschwitz

---

6. Ferguson, *Civilization*, 189.

7. Ferguson, *Civilization*, 190.

8. Mazower, *Dark*. 163

marked the culmination of state violence against racially defined alien populations."[9]

Underpinning the warped notion of racial superiority lay another distinctive feature of European culture: science. Not only did an unrivaled superiority of technology enable world dominance and the sense of superiority that went with it, but behind it was an overwhelming confidence in scientific theory that amounted to a deadly hubris. This provided a basis for the dynamism and commitment that fueled the idea of racial superiority. When Francis Galton returned from his fact-finding mission to Africa in 1851, he declared that he had seen enough of savage races to convince him of the need for a rigorously scientific application to the improvement of the human gene pool by selective breeding—a science he called eugenics. Soon his racial theory and programs to improve "racial hygiene" were being promoted by authorities in Germany—and by none more actively than Dr. Eugen Fischer.[10] Drawing on experience from Africa and studies of Herero skulls, his influential study *Principles of Human Heredity and Race Hygiene* became a standard work on eugenics that was eagerly read by one impressionable young agitator then in prison and busily engaged in writing his autobiography, *Mein Kampf*. Fischer would go on to become director of the newly established Institute for Anthropology, Human Heredity, and Eugenics, and was also made a Gestapo Special Commissioner. Among his students was Josef Mengele. When Holocaust survivor Dr. Viktor Frankl reflected on the genesis of Auschwitz in his book *Man's Search for Meaning*, he pointed to scientists and academics as the main culprits.[11] The laboratory had become the antechamber of the crematorium.

The assumed verities of that science—we would now call it pseudoscience—gave theories of racial stereotyping a position of almost unquestionable authority in the European mind.[12] In the Aryan view of things, improving the quality of the race was second only to maintaining its purity. The science of "racial hygiene" demanded not only the elimination of "degenerates" but compulsory programs of eugenics for whole populations. Race laws could be wide-ranging and involved segregation, forced internment, sterilization, euthanasia, marriage control, and breeding programs— all enthusiastically promoted in the 1930s in countries as far apart as the

9. Ferguson, *Civilization*, 190.

10. Bauman, *Modernity and Ambivalence,* 32–33; Ferguson, *Civilization*, 190.

11. Frankl, *Man's Search*; see Bauman, *Modernity and Ambivalence*, ch. 1 (pp. 18–74).

12. Bauman, *Modernity and the Holocaust.*

United States and Australia as well as in Germany. As George Bernard Shaw fervently proclaimed, "Nothing but a eugenic revolution can save our civilization." And the archbishop of Freiburg, Conrad Gröber, defended the new laws so vigorously that a local Gestapo official felt it necessary to ask him to tone down his statements.[13]

The mind-set resulting from such views made modern racism much more potent than earlier prescientific forms of prejudice and gave a degree of legitimacy to the daily routine of camps like Auschwitz. A scientific determinism seemed both to demand and justify it, and overrode every other consideration typified by the sadistic experiments of Dr. Joseph Mengele and others. This category includes, for example, tests of the limits of human endurance—the results of which, it might be noted, provided invaluable data to NASA, the United States space program. And exterminating people was apparently hard work. Testifying to the arduous demands of his daily routine, Commandant Rudolf Höss recorded, "Often, at night, I would walk through the stables and seek relief among my beloved animals." Himmler spoke to the guards of an "unseen duty . . . to be always consistent, always uncompromising" that was hard to achieve; and at the Nuremberg trials Wilhelm Frick declared, "I had to do [my job] as well as I could," while Franz Stangl of Treblinka spoke of "my profession; I enjoyed it. It fulfilled me."[14] Compassion or regret were so entirely out of place as to be beyond consideration by people with such a mentality.

But the existence of Auschwitz cannot be explained merely in personal, local, or even national terms. It was made possible only by the modern industrialized society that emerged in Europe during the nineteenth century. Lacking this context it could not have functioned, for the murder of people on an industrial scale of millions presupposes industrialization. It required not only a sophisticated communication network and organizing bureaucracy, but it also needed the industrial production of synthetic chemical poisons, the invention and manufacture of efficient furnaces and ovens to dispose of the bodies, and mills for the recycling of human hair and clothes. Above all it demanded the work ethic of capitalism and the accompanying disciplined workforce. It was no accident that the motto over the gates to Auschwitz lauded, however cynically, the merits of work. And this is how the camps were justified to the general public: work experience—but with a difference!

13. Koonz, *Mothers*, 286.
14. Koonz, *Mothers*, 413.

The original camp at Auschwitz soon mushroomed into the vast labor complex of Auschwitz-Birkenau, which provided slave labor to nearby chemical plants, themselves the sophisticated icons of modern industrialization. The treatment of the workforce was not much different from that typical of the early stages of industrialization and recorded, for example, in Engels's *Condition of the Working Class*, a book based on his personal experience of Manchester cotton mills. Indeed, the motto "Work makes you free" is not far removed from the sort of aspiration that emblazoned the crests of newly incorporated northern mill towns, exalting the virtues of labor. The appalling conditions under which people were then expected to live and work were justified in the sight of many by the economic theories that underpinned capitalism. It was not abnormal for children to be routinely collected from orphanages and Work Houses to be worked to an early death in mills and mines, just as it was not abnormal for the slaves who produced the cotton to be worked to death on plantations. Capitalism regarded people as the instruments of production and little more. At its worst—or most typical—it showed the same cruel and indeed criminal indifference to human well-being that is still alive and well in the sweatshops of today's world.

Furthermore, the movement of vast numbers of people to work in concentration camps signaled one more step in a great process of industrialized alienation and dehumanization that typified modern Europe. The number of people consumed by the industrial complex of the concentration camps is staggering—possibly as many as twenty million, of whom six million were Jews. These numbers are largely symbolic, for the true numbers will never be known. In a sense, neither are they of primary importance, for as Josef Stalin once opined, one death is a tragedy, a million is merely a statistic. The statistics themselves do not matter as much as the searing personal tragedies that underlie them; the latter are almost too unbearable to recount and certainly beyond ordinary comprehension. And more than any other place it is Auschwitz that has come to symbolize this ocean of suffering.

None shared more horribly in this than the Jews. After Auschwitz the two-millennial presence of Jewish society in much of Europe ceased to exist. This reflects a peculiarly European antipathy, what Robert Wistrich in his devastating chronicle of European anti-Semitism has called "the longest hatred."[15] An essential element in mass murder and genocide is the de-

---

15. Wistrich, *Anti-Semitism*.

monization of a whole people. Over time a complete disconnection arises between what the perpetrators believe to be true of their victims and what is really the case. This disconnection and the complete lack of empathy that it produces has been identified by the neurologist Simon Baron-Cohen as the essential constituent of evil.[16] This sense of separation and alienation is tellingly reflected by an incident recounted by Vishniac, the famous photographer of the last days of the Jewish ghettos of central Europe. One day he invited a Nazi to look down his microscope at two blood samples, one Jewish and one Aryan, and see that there was no difference. The Nazi refused on the basis that he was not going to be tricked by a Jew![17]

This alienation had become deeply embedded in European society over a period of two millennia, for it arose from religious intolerance and was fostered by the Christian host community. As Erasmus once acerbically commented, "If it is the part of a good Christian to hate Jews, then we are all good Christians!" His contemporary Martin Luther was more specific in regarding Jews as the devil's spawn. In his tract of 1543, *Concerning the Jews and Their Lies,* Luther advocated a comprehensive program of eradication starting with the burning of synagogues and homes. What we now describe as institutionalized racism became embedded in the Lutheran state church of Germany and many other churches; indeed the vitriolic anti-Semitism of Austrian Catholicism had a formative influence on the mind of the young Adolf Schicklgruber (a.k.a. Hitler).[18] In the public mind Jews were an alien and potentially subversive presence; what Auschwitz represented was the culmination of this tradition of suspicion and hatred, for it brought together a genocidal intent with a modern industrialized capacity. The consequence was catastrophic.

Clearly there were many factors in the etiology of the Holocaust, streams that grew and coalesced to become an overwhelming torrent of destruction. Some of these have been mentioned above: the nature of European colonialism with its implicit sense of racial and cultural superiority, the emergence of a scientific culture, the development of a modern industrial society that dehumanized its workforce, and the long history of anti-Semitism embedded in the foundational culture of Christianity. No doubt other more immediate factors such as nationalism, economic and political instability, and the fear of Communism are also involved. But even

---

16. See Baron-Cohen, *Science of Evil.*

17. This comes from an incident recorded in a TV documentary.

18. Heer, *God's.*

then the story is not complete. Nor does it really penetrate into the heart of darkness that lies within a whole civilization and so address what is perhaps the most sinister aspect of all: how Europe came to be in its very structure a persecuting society.

It is only recently that this topic has been addressed by the seminal work of the medieval historian R. I. Moore.[19] His thesis is simple: that with the emergence in the eleventh century of a clearly defined European Christian culture, Christendom, the church had gained a position of unrivaled power over both the minds of its believers and the states that ruled them; yet despite this it felt threatened by heresy. Whereas by the year one thousand CE religious heresy was something of a distant memory associated with christological disputes, suddenly it became a preoccupation of church authorities for whom the emergence of popular religious movements threatened the church's legitimacy.[20] Within a few generations institutions were being established to track down dissent, and victims were being subjected to the previously unheard of cruelty of being burned alive. The result was what is perhaps the most inhumane and iniquitous institution of terror ever devised by man—the Inquisition.[21] This comprehensive apparatus of persecution was codified by the Fourth Lateran Council of 1215—itself a highwater mark of medieval ecclesiastical power—and laid the foundations of what Moore calls a "persecuting society." Characterized by confessional, racial, and ideological intolerance, the inquisitional mentality driving this state of affairs was to become a distinguishing feature of European society until modern times.

From an initial attack on heretics a program of persecution grew to embrace whole sections of society.[22] As Moore observes, disparate individuals were "welded together" to form coherent stereotypes that would then define and identify them as objects of persecution: "the construction of the stereotype on a basis of reality gave it a real and potent existence of its own." Clearly, the creation of "a single account of the victim as an enemy of God and society, which might be transferred at will to any object, either a class of persons already existing, such as Jews, whom it might be desirable or convenient to persecute, or a new one, such as sodomites or witches,

---

19. Moore, *Formation*.
20. Moore, *War on Heresy*.
21. Green, *Inquisition*.
22. Levack, *Witch-Hunt*, 166–77.

which by an act of classification might be invented for the purpose, was a crucial stage in the development of the model of persecution."[23]

By the sixteenth century, the mentality of suspicion and the methodology of persecution had become so embedded in the fabric of European society that it would continue to morph into further expressions of contempt for such differences as those characterizing colonial peoples. Curiously, the unfortunate practice of caricaturing the medieval period as one of superstition, stagnation, and obscurantism has served to provide a foil for the dynamic quality of modernity and Enlightenment; and unfortunately this has obscured many of the deep and enduring evils that arose in postmedieval Europe and came to be defining characteristics of European society.[24] This error has caused many to see the Holocaust as a consequence of the Enlightenment, with its formative influence being attributed to the nature of modernity.[25] In fact its roots, like those of modernity, are much deeper.[26]

When all of this is recognized we can see the error in viewing the Holocaust as primarily an outcome of modernity. It is not so much that the Holocaust revealed the hidden possibilities of modern society in turning ordinary people into murderers (as Zygmunt Bauman argued) as that it was the ultimate expression of a persecuting society whose mentality, institutions, and judicial processes had been consciously shaped by early medieval Christendom. And it is not hard to detect the continuities, not only in the subjects of persecution (particularly Jews) but in such methods as the detailed clerical administration needed to organize states of terror: *cleric*, *clerk*, and *clergy* share a single root. In fact all the features that Bauman attributes to modernity are clearly present in embryonic form by at least the fifteenth century,[27] and in particular the template of persecuting and exterminating the "other." It is from these roots that the modern genocidal mentality emerged, and with it came the possibility, indeed the probability, of Auschwitz.

What then is the moral of this story? It is the simple fact that savagery and civilization are not so far apart as we might wish to think. Reflecting on his experiences in war-torn Poland, Czeslaw Milosz observed that "the fate of twentieth-century man as identical with that of a cave man living in

23. Moore, *Formation*, 160.

24. Siedentop, *Inventing*, 350–51.

25. Bauman, *Modernity and the Holocaust*.

26. Spencer, *Evolution*, 94–109.

27. Siedentop, *Inventing*, 347.

the midst of powerful monsters."[28] The liberal optimism of the nineteenth century with its belief in progress is now gone forever. Commenting on the events that took place at Auschwitz, the *Macmillan Encyclopedia* tersely remarks that they have "raised serious doubts as to the validity of Western civilization."[29] But just as many seemed oblivious to the Holocaust's beginnings, incredulous at its existence, and overwhelmed by its revelations, so now many seem to have comfortably forgotten it—or, *pace* Jean-Marie Le Pen, dismissed it as a "'detail of history," a peculiar feature of the German past that "they" must come to terms with. But nothing could be further from the truth; the tomb of the millions who died at Auschwitz is in a very real sense the tomb of the civilization that made it possible.

28. Milosz, *Captive Mind* (preface), ix–xvi.

29. Isaacs, ed., *Macmillan Encyclopedia*, s.v. "Holocaust" (p. 581).

4

The Rebirth of Tyranny
How Politics Became a Form of Savagery

One thing that has characterized the coming of modernity is tyranny. We are prone to talk of material progress, social reform, and cultural enlightenment, but this primitive form of political organization flourishes as never before. The strongman—often an ex-general with attitude—continues to overpower other forms of government—sometimes with popular appeal, sometimes with brute force. It is an unsettling fact that tyranny seems to have metastasized in the twentieth century, and this in spite of John Stuart Mill's optimistic prognosis two centuries ago that one of the marks of civilization was "the progressive limitation of the tyranny of the strong over the weak."[1] What went wrong?

At the mere mention of the word a number of names spring to mind: Pol Pot, Mao, Mobutu, Franco, Stroessner, Stalin, Robespierre . . . As we roll back the historical record we find no shortage of candidates. Across wide swaths of Asia, the Middle East, Africa, and South America they reappear with depressing regularity. In fact the minute one is deposed, another is in the wings ready to take over: get rid of a monarch and you get a megalomaniac; end a colonial regime and a kleptocrat appears; overthrow a Shah and an ayatollah rises from the sands. History may not repeat itself, but the various forms of authoritarianism are depressingly familiar.

---

1. Mill, "Coleridge," 31.

And the would-be tyrant need not be famous—or infamous. That something of the tyrant lurks in all of us may help to explain the abundance of ambitious actors waiting for an entrance cue. Just as every priest is said to become a pope in his own parish, so we may say that every government official and even every parent tends to become—or at least is sometimes tempted to become—a petty tyrant, imposing his or her will beyond the limits of reasonable restraint, dominating others by power of position or personality. It seems that the inclination to tyranny, like paranoia, is a latent human trait that needs only the appropriate circumstances in which to flourish. One need look no further than the incidence of office bullying or appeals to industrial tribunals to see how common the phenomenon is.

In a recent book *The Psychopath Test*, Jon Ronson looks at traits that characterize the tyrant, and how such characteristics help people rise to positions of dominance in the world of business.[2] Indeed, the cut and thrust of business and commerce seems ideal territory for the tyrant; one major investment bank actually used psychometric testing to recruit covetous and self-serving people because their characteristics exactly fitted them for senior corporate financial roles. Dick Fuld, the fearsome head of Lehman Brothers, was not called "the Gorilla" as a term of endearment; for one who snarled at his staff that he wanted to rip out his competitors' hearts "and eat them before they died," this soubriquet was not entirely metaphorical.[3]

Such Aztec inclinations in the boardroom have prompted further speculation about the way societies function. In an unregulated world it is often the least principled people who rise to the top. The very fluidity of group dynamics seems to invite the emergence of the strongman to restore some kind of order with a stamp of authority that cannot be challenged. The Kray brothers tried it in the East End of London just as Genghis Khan carried it off on the plains of Mongolia and Stalin in the Soviet Union. Turmoil begets tyranny, though the tyrant would never recognize himself to be such a person; in modern parlance he would always be "responding to crises" or "taking the necessary steps." Both Robespierre and Stalin—equal contenders for the Golden Globe in tyranny—were thrust into worlds that had imploded on themselves and strove to create order. But they did not regard themselves as tyrants—indeed, quite the contrary. Looking back at the great famine that caused millions of deaths in the Ukraine, Stalin expressed annoyance at how much trouble he had been caused by peasants refusing to

2. Ronson, *Psychopath*.
3. See Ward-Proud, "Charismatic."

38

follow his progressive collectivization program and thus bringing so much devastation on themselves. No sense of any responsibility there! Nor did Robespierre for a moment doubt that all his policies were aimed at preventing the return of the tyranny that had preceded him.

The fact that Robespierre could refer to Louis the XVI as a tyrant, just as American revolutionaries referred to George III, shows a reversal in the original understanding of the term. This contradictory view of the tyrant is curious. Originally, kings and nobles may have been regarded as despots, but they represented established order; it was the usurpers and revolutionaries who provided the tyrants of the new order, or at least so it was in the ancient world. But in medieval times the understanding of tyranny underwent a radical change of meaning, thanks largely to scholars who reflected on the fate of kings in the Old Testament—especially those who, like Saul, "rejected the word of God" and in doing so became tyrants and thus led to their own inevitable overthrow.

The twelfth-century jurist Gratian provided the theological and legal framework for this new understanding of the role of a ruler. The *Decretum*, his wide-ranging compendium of canon law, emphasized the overriding restraints of the law. Not long afterwards, John of Salisbury's political reflections, *Policraticus*, devoted many pages to considering what to do about tyrants who refused to acknowledge the rule of law. Drawing on the stories of bad kings in the Old Testament, who incurred divine judgment, he came to the radical conclusion that "It is not only permitted, but it is equitable and just to slay tyrants."[4] It was such thinking that provided the essential intellectual context for the formulation of the Magna Carta, with which the bishops and barons confronted King John in 1215.

The growth of Protestantism in the sixteenth century prompted significant debate over the nature of tyranny and how easily rightful kings might become oppressors of their people. Emperor Charles V was particularly sensitive to this issue, seeing himself as the defender of all his people—even the newly discovered Indians of America; and in an address to the *Consejo Real* delivered in Madrid in 1528 he described princes who sought foreign conquests as tyrants. Though he struggled to keep his European territories together he was always aware of becoming a tyrant himself and "that monstrous thing, a universal monarchy." In his abdication address he begged forgiveness for any injustices he had unwittingly committed.[5]

4. *Policraticus* bk. 3, ch. 15.
5. Heer, *Holy*, 167.

In the influential Geneva Bible of 1560, the word *tyrant* appeared more than four hundred times to describe an ungodly ruler who subjected a nation to his cruel whims. Aware of the seditious implications of such a word, another monarch with distinctly tyrannical tendencies adopted an alternative strategy to that of Charles: James VI of Scotland and I of England had as one of his main concerns that the term should be removed from his Authorized Version of the Bible. But it was too late, for the new understanding of tyranny had already taken root among Puritans who, despite the widely accepted notion of the divine right of kings, would use the biblical condemnation of "tyrants" as a primary weapon with which to challenge the monarchy. To the dismay of crowned heads across Europe, hostility to tyranny created the republican English Commonwealth. Alas, no sooner had one tyrant been removed than another, in the person of Cromwell, took his place.

A crucial factor in understanding Robespierre and such contemporaries as Danton and Saint-Just was the knowledge of classical history and precedents that they brought to bear as an interpretive cipher of their own circumstances.[6] Of the situation in which they found themselves, Camille Desmoulins, a friend of Robespierre, wrote, "We were brought up in the schools of Rome and Athens, and in the pride of the [Roman] Republic, only to live in the abjection of the monarchy."[7] For the French revolutionaries it was foolishness to imagine that the past, with its disdain of tyranny, could be admired without condemning the present. Yet their attribution of tyranny was modern: in the past it had been the tyrant who overthrew the ancien régime and acted beyond the law.

For the Greeks the title of tyrant was not necessarily the reproach it has since become, nor was *tyranny* a pejorative term. As Charles Freeman notes in *The Greek Achievement*, tyranny "provided a model for an alternative distribution of resources" in a time of social instability; but it was essentially a transitional phenomenon that reflected "a lack of maturity in city government."[8] It provided a valuable way of addressing perceived injustices, and for this the tyrant could expect the gratitude of the people. For example, Pisistratids of Athens presided over the emergence of the city as a major trading center and enhanced the Acropolis, while Polycrates of Samos oversaw a golden age, the vestiges of which (such as the water

6. Scurr, *Fatal.*

7. Quoted in Scurr, *Fatal,* 28.

8. Freeman, *Greek.* 99.

supply system) still impress tourists. It was only later that tyranny acquired its negative connotations from historians who were now dismissive of this predemocratic form of government that they deprecated because of its precarious and unrestrained nature.

Nor for all their fabled brutality are tyrants necessarily unprincipled. One thing that stands out about Robespierre, apart from engineering the blood-drenched Reign of Terror, is the nobility of his principles: not for nothing was he known as the Incorruptible. His friends regarded him as a simple, even puritanical man, just as Svetlana Stalina said of her father, "He was a very simple man. . . . There was nothing in him that was complicated."[9] Goebbels similarly found that the great appeal of Nazism lay in the purity and simplicity of its principles! Perhaps it is typical of tyrants that they have a single vision, simple final solutions, even a dream of uncorrupted innocence; it's just a shame that people's imperfections get in the way of achieving the ideal polity. So it was in Huxley's fictional *Brave New World*.

Despite this, the contexts in which tyrannies arose in the past have some remarkable similarities to those of the present. In seventh-century Greece—as in eighteenth-century France, nineteenth-century Russia, and twentieth-century China—new industrial growth and commercial developments were providing opportunities for the emergence of a prosperous middle class between the peasants and nobility, who wanted political representation. Social change and dissatisfaction with the status quo crystallized around a strongman who, with some populist support and charismatic appeal, could seize control of the state by violence and redistribute wealth. Such was the *turannos*—the usurper of power who acted outside the law.

But the very act of usurpation created a crucial weakness: political instability. The tyrant could not expect the reverence or loyalty formerly granted the ancient regime that had preceded him; what had been gained by one campaign of violence could be lost to another. The usurper always lived in fear of being usurped; in his mind the shadows of conspirators were never far away. Thus, a culture of suspicion—the surveillance state—would become a defining trait of tyranny. Robespierre's Committee on Public Safety took to issuing took to issuing certificates of civic virtue (*civisme*); checks doubled as identity cards, in order to reassure good citizens: a CCV to go with your CV!

---

9. Quoted in Usborne, "Life and Death."

If the fate of the tyrant was to remain insecure, his defense was paranoia. In this he merely revealed a deeply human trait. Despite its pejorative connotations, paranoia is in fact an essential part of the human tool kit of survival, as indeed it is for all primates who live in complex social groupings. Even as I write, the news announces a new piece of research indicating that people with a more dominant prefrontal cortex have more friends. This, of course, is the most recently evolved part of the front brain that enables us to "mentalize" and guess what other people are thinking.[10] And working out what others are thinking—even if we have no wish to eliminate them—is a key survival strategy for us all. The alpha male, or successful tyrant, is just better at it than most! Those who can intuit what others are thinking and therefore anticipate their behavior, particularly that of rivals, have the advantage of being able to spot and eliminate potential rivals. Thus, paranoia begets terror.

There is no better example of this state of paranoia and terror than the reign of Henry VII. Himself a tyrant who had overthrown the rightful king, Richard III, and having but tenuous claims to legitimacy, Henry was obsessed with the possibility of conspiracy and morbidly suspicious of even his closest advisors, a disposition that only increased with time. Contemporaries noted that his sharp gaze and distant visage concealed a calculating viciousness, a calm demeanor masking a savage intensity, *suaviter ac saeviter*, as the Milanese ambassador Soncino observed. Thomas Penn tellingly describes the highly charged situation in his biography *Winter King*, quoting a contemporary drama by the poet laureate John Skelton, who pictures a court stalked by Dread, "confronted by doubleness and inconstancy at every turn, people creeping just out of his eyeline, whispering in corners as they looked him up and down, unable to be sure of anything or anybody. A kind of terror had settled on the royal household. And it stemmed from the king himself."[11] This was a world of which Machiavelli was the quintessential observer, and his advice was that the prince keep his subjects "in danger at his pleasure."

Whether ancient or modern, the dynamics of tyranny are nowhere more clearly observable than in the lives of Robespierre and Stalin. They were products of Europe's two great revolutions. From the outset both had a subliminal fear of the unseen reactionary enemy, and both possessed the necessary cunning and ruthlessness to deal with the situation. Since the

10 Pappas, "Social."

11. Penn, *Winter King*, 105.

challenge to authority most likely comes from those closest to the center of power or those with the greatest capabilities, it was such people who were in most danger of being eliminated. As the tyranny matures, therefore, the tyrant becomes an increasingly lonely figure and like Macbeth essentially friendless. In place of companions the tyrant chooses to be surrounded by pliant minions who secure their own survival by zealous compliance. The paradigm example was the diminutive private secretary of Stalin, Alexander Poshrebyshev, whose wife was imprisoned and executed in the Great Purge of the 1930s. Stalin refused his request for clemency reassuring him with an affected gesture of concern, "Don't worry, we'll find you another."[12]

As for the wider society, tyranny requires that potential fomenters of opposition be identified and eliminated. Robespierre's Law of Suspects, like article 58 of the Soviet Penal Code, served precisely to effect the immediate liquidation of suspects who proved guilty "either by their conduct, their contacts, their words, or their writings."[13] In fact, just about any action could be deemed suspect. As the Reign of Terror reached its climax, the infamous Law of 22 Prairial went even further: one's demeanor and speech, what one thought, even *that one thought*, became suspect. Thus tyrannies are wont to make enemies arbitrarily. People who read books, who wear glasses, who write, who speak certain words or phrases, who think differently—all such were prime suspects in the eyes of Pol Pot and Chairman Mao, people in dire need of "reeducation." Paradoxically, the purportedly progressive force of modern civilization, and even modernity itself, has been characterized by the increasingly regressive savagery of its tyrannies.

General Franco's coup against the Spanish Republic in 1936 is a case in point. Like those of Hitler, Mao, and Gaddhafi, the tyranny of Franco emerged in the context of a weakened state that emerged after the collapse of the established order of the preceding ancien regime. The difference in Franco's coup against the reforming government of the Second Republic was that it sought to reestablish the "real Spain" of traditional religious and monarchical values in the face a putative international conspiracy of Jews, Freemasons, and Bolsheviks.[14] In a manner replicated in the contemporary Weimar Republic, it fed on widespread anger that a great country had been reduced to shambles by deep social divisions that politicians seemed

---

12. This anecdote was related by the Cambridge historian David Reynolds on the BBC documentary *World War Two: 1941 and the Man of Steel.*

13. Quoted in Scurr, *Fatal*, 258.

14. Preston, *Spanish.*

unable to bridge. During the preceding century every form of government had seemed to fail; neither monarchy (both absolute and constitutional), nor democracy nor socialism nor anarchism nor coalitions could hold the nation together. Proffered solutions led only to greater chaos. Interminable political wrangling fomented an increasingly hate-filled violence that left even seasoned politicians frustrated and in despair. Franco decided to sort out the mess once and for all.

This determination led to another distinctive feature of Franco's tyranny. Under those of Robespierre and Stalin it took time for the bloodletting of a reign of terror to gather momentum, but for Franco it was from the outset an integral part of his coup, as Paul Preston's new study The Spanish Holocaust makes clear. In Franco's march on Madrid the infamous "Column of Death" was given explicit orders "to smash the cruel rabble with a great hammer blow that would paralyse them" forever.[15] On numerous occasions Franco showed complete indifference to reasonable pleas for clemency—he was interested only in a body count, and the higher the better. This total intolerance was partly a product of Franco's colonial experience in the Spanish Foreign Legion in Morocco, where parades of an entire battalion could take the form of troops presenting arms with the severed heads of "terrorists" on their bayonets. Franco's nationalists often referred to their republican opponents as "rif"—a term of contempt for the Moroccan insurgents—and he even used Moroccan mercenaries, no doubt knowing that the return of "Moorish" troops to the mainland shocked even many of his supporters. In transferring colonial attitudes and methods to his fellow countrymen, Franco anticipated the tyranny of Hitler, a distinctive feature of which was the German treatment of fellow Europeans in much the same way that Germans had treated Africans. As the Nazi governor of Posen, a former civil servant in the Cameroons, made clear in 1939, his task was "to perform in the East of the Reich the constructive work they had once carried out in Africa"—that is, exterminating the natives.[16]

To excuse their brutal measures modern tyrannies have found it necessary to acquire the further distinctive attribute of a guiding ideology. It is perhaps no accident, and indeed rather indicative, that this word was first used at the height of the Reign of Terror in Paris. It was in this context that the rationalist philosopher Destutt de Tracy coined *ideology* to denote "the

15. Preston, *Spanish*.
16. Ferguson, *Civilization*, 190.

science of ideas."[17] What he had in mind was the new kind of thinking that characterized the work of French Enlightenment thinkers, the *philosophes*, whose rationalism challenged so much of what had gone before. The new word was needed "in order to distinguish [rationalism] from ancient metaphysics." It is no coincidence that from this late eighteenth-century period the *isms* begin to appear in our language, for those great conglomerates of nebulous ideas such as rationalism, romanticism, nationalism, and secularism are hard to pin down but generally persuasive. Such was the birth of *ideology* and its recognition of the power of the ideas that was soon to become the tyranny of ideas.

For the philosopher Hegel, one of the great exponents of this new worldview, history was the record of a great tide of inevitability upon which humans were swept to their collective destiny whether they realized it or not. The grand unitary vision could sometimes be attained by the prophet himself, as in his *Philosophy of History*, which revealed that "the history of the world is none other than the progress of the consciousness of freedom."[18] It was up to the great leader who guided the bark of state—one like the "Great Helmsman," as Mao liked to be called—to recognize and realize a people's historic destiny. An overwhelming, cohesive, and persuasive idea with popular appeal had the power to sweep all before it; to be the guardian and exponent of such an "ideology" was to acquire near invincibility.

For Robespierre that idea was "the General Will." In his speeches he was forever calling for governing authority to "give the people that which already belonged to them" and expressing his love of "the People" and their intrinsic goodness.[19] All of this, of course, was derived from the most persuasive "ideologue" of all, Jean-Jacques Rousseau. From his youth Robespierre had idolized Rousseau, and like many since was captivated by the persuasive eloquence of his radical thoughts. Yet their emotive potency and toxicity bore little relation to their veracity, and perhaps that is why de Tracy sought to distinguish ideology from metaphysics. Despite Rousseau's manifest nonsense, his famous claim that "Man is born free but everywhere is found enslaved and in chains" has a mesmeric power over certain minds. As the critic Emile Faguet remarked, "It would be equally correct to say

---

17. Williams, *Keywords*, "Ideology."
18. Singer, *Hegel*, 15.
19. Quoted in Scurr, *Fatal*, 153.

that sheep are born carnivorous but everywhere eat grass";[20] Sartre simply parodied the idea, quipping, "Man is condemned to be free."

One who acutely observed and participated in the consequences of the new ideology that was reducing Parisian life to chaos was Napoleon—that archetypal Man of Destiny, whom large parts of Europe would soon have reason to regard as a tyrant. But he was dismissive of ideology: "It is to the doctrine of the ideologues . . . [that] one must attribute all the misfortunes which have befallen our beautiful France."[21] And thus *ideology* soon acquired a pejorative sense. This was subsequently reinforced by the revolutionary thinking of Marx and Engels, who in their *German Ideology* dismissed ideology as "upside-down" thinking, fanciful speculation detached from "the material life-conditions of the persons inside whose heads this thought process goes on."[22] In its place they wanted something more scientific. Instead of the General Will they proposed a "scientific socialism" based on what they saw as the irresistible absolute of history, dialectical materialism.

In fact, their belief in a value-free "scientism" that could lead to a clear understanding of reality and of the material laws that governed it was simply naïve; positivism is no more credible in its assumptions than the disparaged ancient metaphysics. As Rupert Sheldrake recently pointed out in *The Science of Delusion,* all science is underpinned by powerful dogmas and a metaphysical baggage that many are happy to assume without questioning.[23] Rather than eliminating ideology, all that Marx had done was to replace one with another that was even more potent and would give millions cause to tremble. Under the illusion of "scientific certainty" Marxism was presented as an unequivocal reading of history, the "iron laws" of which, like the rails of a steam train, bore an ideological juggernaut against which there could be no resistance. The tyranny of ideology had become the ultimate legitimator of tyranny, the indispensable accessory of any would-be tyrant, and the inspiration for the total intolerance of Franco, Pol Pot, and their like for "those who do not think as we do." As Margaret Thatcher used to ask, "Is he one of us?"

The tyranny of ideas in turn begets further tyrants. The fact that the ideas of Marx had no more veracity than those of Rousseau but were, as

---

20. Quoted in O'Brien, "Jean-Jacques Rousseau," 62.
21. Williams, *Keywords,* "Ideology."
22. Williams, *Keywords,* "Ideology."
23. Sheldrake, *Science.*

Napoleon noted, merely "diffuse" and "contrived" ideologies, did nothing to limit their appeal. The reason is not hard to find: people need an idea to live by, some overarching, cohesive understanding that gives purpose to life. At one time this function was provided by religious faith, but the growth of secularism undermined that option. Since the Enlightenment humankind has increasingly come to accept the presence of an external world that is mechanical and indifferent to human presence. This has, of course, reinforced the need to re-create a dream of innocence, a single vision that will give hope, an ideology to serve as a pseudo or replacement religion. The very fragility of such a construct seems to engender a doubt-destroying fanaticism. An exasperated Austrian officer who was interrogating the young revolutionary terrorist Felice Orsini perceptively exclaimed, Orsini's nationalism had become "a religious monomania."[24]

Though modern tyrants are often deemed to be irreligious, this is far from the truth. Understanding the need for religion, both Robespierre and Hitler denounced atheism. Robespierre proclaimed the need of the French people to place their trust in "the conception of an incomprehensible power, which is at once a source of confidence to the virtuous and of terror to the criminal."[25] In return the *Chronique de Paris* reported, "There are some who ask why there are always so many women around Robespierre at his house. . .It is because this Revolution of ours is a religion and Robespierre. . .is the a priest at the head of his worshippers."[26] And as Adam Zamoyski recounts in his study *Holy Madness*, nineteenth-century nationalism acquired all the trappings of a replacement religion, with such secular messiahs as Garibaldi in Italy and Kossuth in Hungary. Ideology inexorably became a monomania!

Ultimately, those in thrall to the tyranny of an absolutist doctrine do not imagine that human beings matter. Despite all the promises of better things to come, individuals are of no concern in the immediate present. The growth of human dispensability under modern tyrannies is staggering. When the Bastille fell, there were seven inmates; five years later over seven thousand filled the prisons of Paris to the bursting point, awaiting the guillotine. Czarist Russia had incarcerated several thousand political prisoners, but the Soviet Union held millions behind bars. During Mao's Great Leap Forward some forty million or more disappeared, but we will

24. Zamoyski, *Holy*, 101.

25. Scurr, *Fatal*, 215.

26. Scurr, *Fatal*, 215.

never know the true number because individuals simply did not matter, and nobody could be bothered to count. At a single site, the pits at Butovo near Moscow, over one hundred thousand bodies were disposed of. During Stalin's purges the overwhelming message of tyranny was clear: human life is worthless. The familiar phrase "You are dust" perfectly conveys tyranny's casual indifference to life. As the poet Osip Mandelstam wrote in one of his last letters, "I am treated like a dog. I am a shadow. I do not exist. I only have the right to die."[27]

Tyranny originated in the popular desire for a more just society, but in the service of ideology it became a powerful force for the oppression of people. It is deeply disturbing that tyranny should have become such a dominant feature of political life in the twentieth century, and even more tragic is the escalating scale and frequency of tyranny in modern times. It is as if a virus had found the ideal host and caused the social breakdown, violent transformations, and global wars that have characterized our world. Now a resurgent religious extremism that is born of a disillusionment with modernity has been added to the mix. Not without reason did the anthropologist Claude Levi-Strauss suggest that his discipline, the study of human behavior and society, would be better named "entropology," since it was in fact the record of the breaking down and destruction of cultures.

Yet as in ancient times, tyranny remains essentially a transitional stage of political organization on the way to greater individual freedom in a settled democracy. In our own time we have seen this spirit asserting itself—even if not always successfully—in the old Soviet empire and in the Middle East. The struggle to end tyranny and establish democracy is often precarious, just as was the struggle of the Greek city-states against the Persian Empire. Yet there is still hope of respite. Today powerful multinational institutions like the International Criminal Court and the European Court of Human Rights have arisen in the wake of immeasurable human suffering. These deserve our support, if only in recognition of the innumerable lives that have already been destroyed and continue to be destroyed by tyrannies. The tyrant who trades in fear has now something more to fear than the unseen assassin.

But something else is needed. Modern tyranny has thrived on the elixir of exhilarating ideas—ideologies characterized by "religious monomanias" of absolute conviction and closed minds. The challenge is to dispel the illusory nature of all ideologies and confront the state of mind that

27. Quoted in Merridale, *Night*, 256.

supports them. Let us have the courage to deny the acceptability of any repressive ideology or absolutist fundamentalism. Brought to trial himself by reactionary groups, the crusading Spanish judge Baltasar Garzón Real, who had confronted both General Pinochet and the legacy of General Franco, recently observed, "There is no ideology involved, just hundreds of thousands of victims."[28] In the end, tyranny falls not to the assassin's blade but to the accusing testimony of myriad victims whose memory will not be forgotten and whose pleas for justice now echo in the very courts of law that the tyrant would usurp. It is to the shades of those once deemed no more than dust that tyrants must now be made to answer.

28. Fotheringham, "Judge."

5

Of Mothers and Men
How an Ancient Antagonism
Defines Civilization

In the beginning was the war of the sexes—or so it seems! The world's oldest known piece of literature, the epic Babylonian creation story *Enuma Elish*[1] tells us that the male gods formed a plot to eliminate the "Great Mother," Tiamat, who ruled the universe, and chose Marduk to be their leader and do the dirty deed. After a bitter conflict, Tiamat was slain, and from her dismembered body was made heaven and earth. Now Marduk reigns supreme.

Only a story . . . or is it? In the nineteenth century a German academic, J. J. Bachofen, came up with a rather clever theory: through the analysis of ancient myths and rituals, he surmised, one could gain an insight into forms of social organization for which no material evidence now remains.

Ingenious! But many didn't find it so, especially when they began to read some of the conclusions he had come to. His great work, *Das Mutterecht* (*The Mother's Right*),[2] now sounds strangely prescient even in the choice of title; but in the late nineteenth century the notion of women's rights was almost incomprehensible. For he postulated a Neolithic matri-centric society that preceded the patriarchal, urban societies; over many millennia, he argued, an agriculturally based society in which women

1. See Fromm, *Anatomy*, 124–25.

2. Bachofen, *Myth*.

made up the dominant force of innovation and organization had laid the foundations of what we now call civilization—until their leadership was forcibly usurped by a new patriarchal order.

Bachofen contrasted the two kinds of society and their underlying characteristics thus: "Whereas the patriarchal principle is inherently restrictive, the maternal principle is universal; the patriarchal principle implies limitation to definite groups, but the maternal principle, like the life of nature, knows no barriers. The idea of motherhood produces a sense of universal fraternity among all men, which dies with the development of paternity."[3] And he proposed much more along similar lines as he expounded his theme of how patriarchy and the subsequent form of civilization it fostered came to be characterized by destructiveness and cruelty as it sought to gain control of nature, control of slaves, and control of women.

Provocative? So it seemed to contemporary Germany, with its overwhelmingly patriarchal society and decidedly classical tastes. Such ideas were greeted with derision, a bit like those of that other contemporary German scientist Alfred Wegener, who made the bizarre suggestion that continents move and wander about! The surprising thing is that a century later the empirical evidence has vindicated Wegener's theory, and the brutality of recent history has shown Bachofen right. Ironically, when plate tectonics was being established as the foundation of earth sciences in the 1960s, the first edition of Bachofen was being published in English. Changing gender concepts has proved more difficult than moving continents!

But movement there has been. We may be at first inclined to dismiss Bachofen's writing as typical nineteenth-century romanticizing of the past, much like Arter Gobineau's fantasizing of Aryan origins; but ancient sites like Catal Huyuk in Anatolia, now a focal point of pilgrimage for feminists, have provided overwhelming evidence of the matriarchal structure of Neolithic society, focused on the figure of the Mother Goddess. Noteworthy are the words of archaeologist James Mellaart, who was in charge of the excavations: "a continuity in religion can now be demonstrated from Catal Huyuk to the great 'Mother Goddesses' of archaic and classical times, the shadowy figures known as Cybele, Artemis and Aphrodite."[4] Shadowy now but once overpowering. And he could have added the Virgin Mary/

---

3. Bachofen, *Myth*, 80.

4. From Mellaart, *Catal Huyuk*, quoted in Fromm, *Anatomy*, 214.

Theotokos, whose cult drew its inspiration from such figures, as we see reflected in the "borrowed" liturgical texts for the Feast of the Assumption.[5]

This ancient matriarchal culture has now been eclipsed by the exclusively male perspective of the great monotheistic religions focused on Our Father. The key figure was now "the big man" (*lugal* in the lexicon of the first city-states of Mesopotamia): patriarchy had become established as the natural and divine order of things, and soon it was difficult to imagine that things could ever have been otherwise. In this new order women were seen not only as a threat but as a corrupting influence. The earliest law codes of Sargon and Hammurabi insist that they must be kept veiled and out of sight, and that if they spoke in public their teeth should be broken. The seminal myth of creation has Adam in pole position with Eve not only an afterthought but also the first lawbreaker, thus beginning a long line of thought, which stretches from Aristotle to Freud, that sees women as either defective males (Aristotle) or as castrated men (Freud)! Despite the obvious incongruity of such an arrangement—with Man giving birth to the Mother—it has now been accepted as staple diet for millennia and the basis for viewing the "natural" order.

For example, Hesiod, one of the first and most influential Greek writers, recorded in his *Theogony* the primal myth of Pandora, the first woman and Greek equivalent of Eve.[6] Her opening of a "box" of plagues that have afflicted mankind ever since is well known—except that it isn't and never was a box. In the original text the word used, *pithos,* denotes a vase with the particular shape of a womb. In the mythic imagination of the Greeks, in other words, all the evils of the world originated in the first woman's womb and thus bespeak her very nature—though we might not wish to be too specific in polite society! Before that, when only men were present, everything was just wonderful. And that is why they so consistently denigrated and marginalized women. Of course, though we tend not to think of Greek civilization in this way because it has so long been revered as something of an ideal and certainly the foundation of ours, it was probably the most misogynistic society that has ever existed.

How did such a fundamental change come about? Lewis Mumford in his classic *The City in History*[7] gives us the background detail of changes in material culture that would lead to such a dramatic transformation. He has

---

5. See Shoemaker, *Ancient.*

6. Hall, *Introducing,* 71.

7. Mumford, *City,* 11–39.

portrayed how small villages of the Near East were gradually transformed into the great cities of Babylonia, and how what we now call civilization was a consequence of the development of agriculture that came to define the Neolithic period. This urban revolution created an entirely new kind of culture, one "dedicated not just to the enhancement of life, but to the expansion of power."[8] New technologies—such as pottery, which was initially associated with agriculture—led to a new mentality. Instead of attending to a purely natural order in which one waited for things to happen, one could employ will and intention to *make* things happen. As the celebrated archaeologist Gordon Childe, who coined the term "Neolithic Revolution," put the case, "building a pot was a supreme instance of creation by man."[9] (So in the biblical myth God shapes Adam from red clay—*'adamah* in Hebrew—very much as would a potter.) As a consequence of subsequent developments, by the dawn of the third millennium organized industrial and military power was on a scale never to be surpassed until modern times.

As important as were the subsequent material, social, and political changes in lifestyle, the psychological change was even greater. The social psychologist Erich Fromm reflected on this transformation, finding it apparent that no longer was the fertility of the soil seen as the source of all life and creativity, but rather the intellect, which produced new inventions, techniques, abstract thinking, and the state governed by laws: "No longer the womb, but the mind became the creative power, and simultaneously, not women, but men dominated society."[10]

Here was a society no longer based on customary usage and consent, a concentric society without hierarchy; it was now a polity centrally directed by a dominant male minority that was authoritarian, hierarchical, and inclined to violence. The benefits of civilization were bought at the price of elite (male) domination, constant warfare, escalating conflicts, and slavery.[11] The possibility of coercion, upon which the power of kings and priests now rested, led to a new concept: the individual as a slave, an economic instrument to be exploited and discarded. On such rested the wealth of such ancient empires as Babylonia, Assyria, Athens, and Rome; and this model came to characterize civilization in the new epoch of patriarchy.

8. Mumford, *Myth.*

9. Childe, *Man.*

10. Fromm, *Anatomy,* 224.

11. Leick. *Mesopotamia.*

Bachofen's proposal that a patriarchal society was neither the natural order of things nor even the original arrangement, but in fact a carefully contrived convention ruthlessly imposed on a formerly matriarchal society was taken up by feminist writers of the nineteenth century, who increasingly began to question its contemporary acceptance in the modern world. It is a curious historical chiasm that just as the Neolithic farming revolution and subsequent urban revolution had led to the transformation (and deterioration) of the status of women and matriarchal society, so the two great social upheavals of modernity—the French and Industrial Revolutions—would provide both the context and opportunity for a new evaluation of the role of women and the consequent challenge to patriarchy.

By now a whole new social world was emerging as a consequence of a burgeoning industrialization that consigned a large section of society, both male and female, to the role of instruments of production, reducing them to enslaved automatons within the factory system. This unnatural and inhumane way of living led utopian thinkers and radical reformers to question the whole nature and purpose of society. Among the foremost of these was Robert Owen, an enlightened and visionary mill-owner who claimed that the exploitation of workers was a reflection of a wider mentality of competitiveness and domination that expressed itself most completely in the subjugation of women. Though we remember Owen now in general terms as a social reformer, his paramount concern was the status of women, for their role was crucial to the proper restructuring of society. Indeed, he and his fellow radicals recognized the male monopoly of money and single-minded pursuit of power to be the root of the problem, and most apparent in the "enslavement" of women. As Barbara Taylor has noted in her study of the central role of women in radical nineteenth-century thought, "*Homo Economicus,* the atomized, competitive individual at the centre of bourgeois culture, was the product of a patriarchal system of psycho-sexual relations."[12]

For the first time, women began to denounce this patriarchal order in what was and by some still is regarded as, scandalous terms. "All women are slaves . . ." is the way Mary Wollstonecraft had her fictional heroine Maria decry the situation in a novel of 1798. Others compared black slavery and the condition of women in a supposedly civilized country, one in which a husband has complete and unassailable command over not only his wife's labor and property but body as well. Ninety years earlier, Mary Astell had

12. Taylor, *Eve,* 38.

asked the key question, which in 1700 infuriated her male antagonists: "If Absolute Sovereignty be not necessary in a State how comes it to be so in a Family?"[13]

The fact that it *was* so exposed the profound double standards not only in society but also in the mentality of the men whose duplicity and prejudice shaped it. Even enlightened reformers like William Wilberforce failed to draw the parallel between the enslavement of Negroes and the enslavement of women. And a century later Herbert Asquith—whose Liberal government introduced the unprecedented social reforms that laid the foundations of the modern welfare state—adamantly refused to consider the issue of women's suffrage. Victorians seemed to have progressed from regarding women as virtual domestic slaves to valuing them as domestic pets—"a good companion to a man," but still to be kept firmly on a leash!

Increasingly women refused to accept such a status. Vociferous campaigns began to challenge the duplicitous misogyny of a patriarchal society; Josephine Butler led an attack against the Contagious Diseases Act of 1864 that demeaned women as no more than seductive animals threatening the military prowess of the armed forces. Other protests, like that of the Bryant and May match girls who sought better working conditions, weakened the class divisions among women that mirrored the patriarchal hierarchy and led aristocratic ladies to join with working women in a common cause that bridged the class divide.

Such women, generally dismissed as subversive eccentrics, went on to challenge all the defining characteristics of society. Typical were the writers Catherine Ogden and Mary Florence, who attacked what they called the militarism of patriarchal societies (like Britain and Germany), in which everything else was in thralldom to this all-consuming Moloch. In their powerful essay "Militarism versus Feminism," written in 1915, they argued that militarism and the war that was its insane apogee subverted every social pursuit to a destructive end. The foundations of this were to be found, they wrote, in the patriarchal nature of Judaism and later Christianity, an ethos that provided the necessary religious legitimation for both war and the suppression of women: "The Hebrew idea of women is the idea of that primitive militarist, the patriarchal nomad," whose religion was "in its original essence a militarist religion, the religion which conquered Canaan for its God of Battles."[14]

---

13. Taylor, *Eve,* 32.
14. Kamester and Vellacott, eds., *Militarism,* 68.

The carnage of the Great War gradually began to unsettle previous convictions: perhaps there was something in what they said after all! But by no means did this exhaust the strange conjunctions that underlay the functioning of patriarchy. In his recent book *The Alphabet and the Goddess* Leonard Shlain has put forward the more subtle thesis that the coming of literacy and the invention of the alphabet (a product of Semitic society) have, by "reinforcing the brain's linear, abstract, predominantly masculine left hemisphere at the expense of the holistic, iconic, feminine right one in both sexes," upset a delicate balance that hitherto existed between men and women, undermining the status of the latter so that patriarchy and misogyny followed.[15] Here we find a very modern take on that seismic Neolithic transformation.

With its many echoes of Bachofen, much of Shlain's book is a catalogue of prejudice directed against women and feminine images, but for him the key text is the Old Testament, which he believes to have literally changed the sex of God. "The first book written in an alphabet was the Old Testament and its most important message is the Ten Commandments. The first [commandment] rejects any goddess influence and the second bans any form of representational art."[16] Modern biblical exegetes have had a field day prying open carefully concealed traces of such ancient references to the femininity of God as El Shaddai—formerly translated "God of the High Places," but increasingly rendered "the God of Breasts"![17]

If the "People of the Book" were among the original villains, according to Shlain things became decidedly worse during the Reformation, which saw the invention of printing and the resulting reassertion of the primacy of the Word of God in reformed theology. In another of those parallelisms with echoes from a distant past, the consequence was a conscious assault on traditional feminine imagery, this time reflected in the frenzied destruction of images of the great Mother, Our Lady, and the glorious medieval Lady Chapels. And not only images were at risk. No less savage in this renewed war on women were the great witch hunts that spiraled out of control at this time—and all of which took place in the most literate of societies![18]

All this sounds very disturbing, but in essence it is not really novel. In fact, on rereading the *Enuma Elish* one finds a surprising coincidence of

---

15. Shlain, *Alphabet*, 7.

16. Shlain, *Alphabet*, 64–71.

17. Lumpkin, *Sacred*.

18. Levack, *Witch-Hunt*

ancient myth and modern practice. Before Marduk is chosen to be supreme king he has to pass a test: he has "to destroy and create," and only when the gods "beheld the efficiency of *his word* they rejoiced and did homage."[19] This is the key to the myth, the significance of which the psychoanalyst Erich Fromm pointed out as being "that man has overcome his inability for natural creation—a quality which only the soil and female had—by a new form of creation, that by the word (thought)."[20] Marduk has overcome the natural superiority of the mother and can now replace her; the male god creates the world by the word. Thus the biblical story begins where the Babylonian myth ends and culminates in the Christian myth that begins, "In the beginning was the Word . . .(and) the word was made flesh."[21] Of course women retain their uses as functionaries and facilitators of patriarchy, for their useful instrumentality (under the condition of strict anonymity) culminates in the Christian myth of the Word made flesh. This is how patriarchal man reconfigures the world.

But no longer! As the biblical story of the fall intimates, with the coming of knowledge innocence is lost, for the possession of the word exposes power—and the jealously guarded arcane traditions of ancient hierarchies: for once we know how patriarchy came to be fabricated, it no longer looks so natural and daunting, so secure or inevitable. By launching the eighteenth-century feminist challenge to this foundational myth of patriarchy, women made it clear that this view of their innate deficiency was no more than a social construct reinforced by religious belief—and worse yet, a canard that portrayed them as the cause of "the first transgression," the so-called "fall of man," and the subsequent woes of humanity. Women would henceforth variously be viewed as "the weaker sex," "temptresses," and a corrupting influence on their nobler counterparts. They needed to be restrained or closeted away. So pervasive and pernicious was this view that Mary Wollstonecraft—usually seen as the founder of modern feminism—wrote (in 1794): "We must get entirely clear of all notions . . . of original sin . . . to leave room for the expansion of the human heart."[22]

And such is still the position today. Some feminists see that misogyny and monotheism are simply two sides of the same coin, for patriarchy continues to fight a rear guard action against its critics, a battle that becomes

19. Quoted in Fromm, *Anatomy*, 225 (italics added).
20. Fromm, *Anatomy*, 225.
21. John 1:1 & 1:14.
22. Quoted in Taylor, *Eve*, 25.

increasingly bitter as it becomes more desperate. One wonders why in the late twentieth century the Vatican would still condemn works such as those of a nun, Lavinia Byrne, to be destroyed for merely raising the issue of the place of women at the altar![23] And the unstated reason is fairly obvious: once the roles of women are reappraised and the myth of the primacy of Adam with his subsequent fall is challenged, the whole soteriological edifice, together with its requirement for clerical mediation, comes tumbling down. No longer is there any real need for any of it—or for "them."

Whether it be the curia in Rome or ayatollahs and imams elsewhere, the story is always the same whenever these repositories of ancient patriarchal tradition fight to maintain it. The power of domination is never relinquished willingly; the law of the jungle (and of civilization) is that power is not given but has to be seized. The only consolation is that it will be! As societies become more open, inclusive, and democratic the priestess and goddess return, now in transfigured forms.

Over the last century an Iconic Revolution has been under way restoring equilibrium between male and female, word and image. Women can no longer be regarded as possessions to be locked away for private use. They are now equal partners on the public scene where girls consistently outperform boys and often leave the male ego badly bruised and disoriented. Yet for those early radicals like Mary Wollstonecraft it was always a central concern that the sexes be accorded equal regard and that men accept "rational fellowship instead of slavish obedience." For social reformers like the followers of Robert Owen the dream was "that women should be educated in order that whatever capacities they possess may be permitted to grow to their full height."[24] To many, especially in the Islamic world, this is anathema; but only in this way can humankind fully develop its inherent potential.

Indeed, the degree to which this end is achieved would be a useful criterion of social progress, and even of civilization itself. For utopian visionaries like Charles Fourier, "Social progress and changes of period are brought about by virtue of the progress of women towards liberty, and social retrogression occurs as a result of a diminution in the liberty of women."[25] In the whole evolutionary account of humankind's social development, the

23. Byrne, *Woman.*

24. Taylor, *Eve*, 234.

25. Taylor, *Eve*, 29.

position of women can be seen as a primary index of humanity's progress from savagery to civilization.

So, was civilization worth it? Or can we imagine a better way of living? Just as utopian socialists and feminists in the nineteenth century looked forward to a radically different society characterized by cooperation, equality, and fairness, so Bachofen had looked back to prehistoric times and wrote movingly of a "maternal principle" that underpinned society: "It is the basis of the universal freedom and equality so frequent among matriarchal peoples, of their hospitality, and of their aversion to restriction of all sorts."[26] Subsequently, modern anthropologists have written of the nature of hunter-gatherer societies in which "there is no peck-order based on physical dominance at all, nor is there any superior-inferior ordering based on other sources of power such as wealth, hereditary classes, military or political office."[27] Perhaps this still provides the blueprint for a better future.

In the many millennia of the Stone Age in which humans emerged from their primate ancestry, it was the subordination of primate instincts for dominance, selfishness, brute competition, and indiscriminate sexuality that enabled what the ethnographer Sahlins called "the greatest reform in history, the overthrow of human primate nature."[28] This is what secured the evolutionary future of the species because "it substituted kinship and cooperation for conflict, placed solidarity over sex, morality over might."[29] Yet these are the very signs of progress that the rise of civilization would reverse, and in their place we see the emergence of cities based on institutionalized violence and conflict. Mumford wrote of the destructive, death-oriented myth that empowered the new post-Neolithic urban order: each historic civilization begins with a living urban core but ends in a common graveyard—"fire-scorched ruins, shattered buildings, empty workshops, the population massacred or driven into slavery."[30] It could be the wars of the Babylonians or the Israelite conquest of Canaan . . . or Kosovo or Syria or the Ukraine; but in the end it results from man's passion for unlimited, god-like control over other people and things. In short, the record is not so much of progress as destruction.

26. Fromm, *Anatomy*, 219.

27. Fromm, *Anatomy*, 195.

28. Fromm, *Anatomy*, 190.

29. Quoted in Fromm, *Anatomy*, 190.

30. Mumford, *City*, 68.

But such aggression with its resulting destructiveness does not tell the whole story. Fromm identified it as only one element of a syndrome, observing "that we find aggression regularly together with other traits in the system, such as strict hierarchy, dominance, class division, etc." Based on his clinical experience as a psychoanalyst Fromm identified the passion for unlimited, god-like control over men and things—as we find in the ancient Sennacherib and the modern ISIS to be the root and essence of sadism. This finds its most complete expression in the mistreatment of women and sexual perversion; for Fromm "it ranges from the wish to cause physical pain to a woman . . . to humiliating her, putting her in chains, or forcing her complete obedience."[31] And of course these are exactly the things that feminists strove to eliminate from Western capitalist societies, and that now characterize the behavior of radical Muslim movements. The sadism of patriarchal societies gives full rein to the primitive instincts that matriarchal societies had sought to overcome.

As we look back over the panorama of history we cannot help but wonder whether it could have been different if women had been given more prominent roles! A case in point is the rise of the universities in western Europe. Progressive as it may seem, this pivotal but paradoxical development had the effect of excluding women from learned discourse, marginalizing them, and overshadowing such an esteemed role and stature as that enjoyed by Hildegard of Bingen, the learned abbess. The rise of an all-male Scholasticism had a yet more sinister effect in creating a way of thinking about women that lead inexorably to the obscene witch hunts that flourished in the sixteenth century. Marginalization led to demonization. Even in today's universities, Muslim fundamentalists seek to reverse the equalities that have been gained in modern times only after great effort. Patriarchy never gives up without a fight.

The distinguishing feature of patriarchal societies has always been that their Fathers, Fuhrers, and Fundamentalists lead them through endless cycles of catastrophe. It is therefore ironic to hear aged patriarchs railing against this very condition while at the same time refuting and refusing mothers and matriarchs their rightful place of equality in the ordering of the world. Secure in the founding myth of their social hierarchy and convinced of the creative power of the divine male, the acolytes of Marduk march blindly onward. Marduk's battle rages on!

---

31. Fromm, *Anatomy*, 373.

6

Another Face—Another Fate
The Stranger in Our Midst

Not many words in the English language begin with an *x* but you can hardly open a newspaper these days before one springs out at you. I refer in particular to *xenophobia*; it's all over the place and all around us in public discourse, with statesmen using it to defame one another and various foreign ministries accusing Britain of becoming increasingly chauvinistic. And what with the furore over Romanians and Bulgarians "flooding the country" it's not only our European neighbours who are trotting out such rhetoric either. Recently, the Toronto *Globe and Mail* carried a piece on our current sulky national sentiments with the comment, "These xenophobic attitudes are harming Britain's economy."[1]

It seems the "nasty party" is mutating into the "nasty country." But let's be fair—it's not only Britain. Immigration with its consequent tensions is high on the agenda of concerns in many European countries, notably France and Italy, who think they've had quite enough of it. Even that most welcoming of countries, the USA, has generated some very nasty politics over Mexican migrants and the deterioration of traditional WASP status caused by Hispanic influence. So corrosive is the issue that in March 2013 the Republican National Committee felt compelled to explain why it lost the 2012 presidential election and now needed to distance itself from extreme right-wing Tea Party influence by admitting, "We have become

1. Saunders, "Britain."

expert in how to provide ideological reinforcement to like-minded people, but we have lost the ability to be persuasive with, or welcoming to, those who do not agree with us on every issue."[2] In other words, closed minds and closed borders are not winning them any friends.

Even in the Jewish state of Israel African migrant workers have protested draconian new detention laws that allow migrants without visas to be detained indefinitely. This clear violation of basic human rights is all the more surprising in a country born of the need to escape such arbitrary oppression and presently home to a people who for centuries have themselves endured pariah status as persecuted aliens.

So what's going on and what's gone wrong? Of course all sorts of issues are involved: pressure on public services, overpopulation, economic uncertainty, quality of life, and so on and so forth—and all have some significance and truth. But underlying them is a dominant global feature of modern society: namely, the migration of people in vast numbers never before seen or imagined. Homogenous societies that have lived for centuries or even millennia in snug isolation now find themselves challenged by "outsiders," beset by strangers in what is now a radically different milieu. As Vince Cable recently opined, politicians are largely helpless in the face of this human flood, and it is futile to pretend otherwise.

One response to this reality is xenophobia. You may think this to be one of those old Greek words, dredged up from less enlightened times, but you'd be wrong. When I went to look up this word in the old *Chambers's Twentieth Century Dictionary* from the turn of last century, I was surprised to find it wasn't there. In fact, it wasn't coined until the early part of the last century, and before that its nearest cognate was *xenomorphia*: "irregular shape."[3] The appearance of a new word is indicative of a new reality, and the new reality of the late nineteenth century was the mass movement of peoples from the poorer areas of southern and eastern Europe to find better lives in the New World of the West. The shadow side of this movement was the growing fear of strangers like the Jewish refugees from the Russian pogroms, whose appearance in tens of thousands in London's East End prompted riots and the introduction of passport control.

But this is only part of the story. If we can learn anything from the history of the twentieth century it must surely be that even the most advanced and sophisticated civilization is neither as secure nor as enlightened as

2. Barbour et al., "Growth," 4.

3. See Davidson, ed., *Chambers's*, s.v. *xenomorphia* (p. 1140).

nineteenth-century liberalism imagined it to be. After all, just prior to the outbreak of the Great War a century ago, few would have thought possible such a ferocious conflict among the cosmopolitan nations of Europe . . . but it was. Or who would have imagined that the Weimar Republic could have given way to the neobarbarism of Nazism . . . but it did. Or who would have thought that in the late twentieth century Europe could again teeter on the brink of civil war as tourist resorts like Dubrovnik and Olympic sites like Sarajevo were being shelled to oblivion? . . .But it happened. Like grinding tectonic plates, times of stress reveal deep-seated forces at work in the churning social subconscious, forces that suddenly disrupt the seemingly calm surface of our constrained and constructed worlds with unexpected ferocity.

In fact the root of the problem lies deeper than the mercurial tides of history. It is an aspect of the sort of creatures we are and of the social worlds we construct. In his celebrated study of why men kill, the distinguished psychoanalyst Erich Fromm makes a penetrating and disturbing observation about how we humans are distinguished from other animal species. All animals, he notes, recognize other members of their species instinctively—by reflex reactions to smell, color, form, and so forth. But we are, as it were, flawed creatures: "Precisely because man has less instinctive equipment than any other animal, he does not recognize or identify co-species as easily as animals."[4] As a result, secondary features such as language, dress, and customs assume a greater place in determining who is cospecific. From this follows the paradox that because humans lack an instinctive sense of species identity, they are inclined to experience the stranger as belonging to another species. In other words, *"it is man's humanity that makes him so inhuman."*[5]

To explain this startling conclusion Fromm proposed that "only in the process of social and cultural evolution has the number of people who are accepted as human increased." A further insight, this time from the perspective of an anthropologist, comes from Mary Douglas, who focused on the way humans distinguish themselves and the importance of social world they create in sustaining their identity: "In each constructed world of nature the contrast between man and not-man provides an analogy for the contrast between the member of the human society and the outsider."[6] We

4. Fromm, *Anatomy*, 175.

5. Fromm, *Anatomy*, 176 (italics original).

6. Douglas, *Implicit*.

find solace in the homogeneity of the society in which we live and security in the social cohesion it offers by defining itself in contrast to outsider, the foreigner who is denigrated for being "non-us" or even less than human because his speech resembles animal-like sounds. The ancient Greeks coined the word *barbarian* by mocking what they took for the subhuman "ba-ba-ba" mumbling of foreigners. We don't seem to have made all that much progress in the more than two millennia since!

This polarity of thought is common to humans and the way they construct their worlds; it is evident in such common antitheses as inside and outside, home and abroad, good and evil, right and wrong, enemies and friends, male and female, light and dark, dead and alive. This symmetry is reassuring, for it is when under threat from enemies that we really know our friends, and it is no accident that a people's social cohesion and mental stability often improve in times of war, when under threat from outside. But such symmetry is a contrived artifice, an illusion that serves to disguise the reality of ambivalence, to dispel those indeterminate "twilight" states when things are neither one way nor the other, neither light nor dark, neither dead nor alive, when contrasting forces hang in uncertain balance. In ancient cultures, such as that of the Celts, these transient states and uncertain times raised the kind of fear and trepidation that could be restrained only by the strictest of taboos and most solemn of rituals. We may like to think we are different, but the evidence is otherwise.

In his study *Modernity and Ambivalence*, the sociologist Zygmunt Bauman makes clear why such deeply ingrained phobias survive when he observes, "There are friends and enemies. And there are *strangers*."[7] Foreigners are "out there," but strangers are in our midst. Boundaries are not only crossed but confused, and our ordered world is threatened. As Bauman explains, "The stranger is, indeed someone who refuses to remain confined to the 'far away' . . .The stranger comes into [our] life-world and settles here, and so—unlike the case of mere 'unfamiliars'—it becomes relevant whether he is a friend or a foe. He made his way into [our] life-world *uninvited*, thereby casting me on the receiving side of his initiative, making me on the receiving side of his initiative . . . all this is a notorious mark of the *enemy*."[8]

The enemy within! How often have we heard this denunciation in the twentieth century as ideologically driven states sought to consolidate their

---

7. Bauman, *Modernity and Ambivalence*, 53.

8. Bauman, *Modernity and Ambivalence*, 59 (italics original).

grip in the face of "spies," "wreckers," "aliens," "fifth columnists," "subversives"—all of which fearmongering condemns the very fluidity of peoples and porous borders that result from the trade, migration, interaction, and communication that are the hallmarks of modern global society? It requires the fanatical oddity of a hermit state like North Korea to show how crushingly impossible human life would be in a hermetically divided world—as was the situation in such fossilized states of the old Soviet bloc as Albania and Romania. Recently, a former British ambassador to Bulgaria wrote in a blog post about his experience at the time of the collapse, when new instructions called on him to become "a proselytiser for all things Western" (including freedom of movement!), "to help Bulgaria start rejoining the civilized world." How sharp and shameful a contrast he sees in the government's present attitude of hostility and its call "to demonize Bulgaria, as though it was some evil, hostile power intent on overwhelming our fragile state."[9] This is precisely the transition from awareness of *foreigners* "out there" to the fear of *strangers* "over here" of which Bauman wrote.

Bauman saw such intolerance as a natural consequence of the attempt to insure order in the modern state by establishing strict limits on incorporation and admission. This he saw as the outcome of "the dream of legislative reason" that had been the goal of Enlightenment philosophers, a dream he rather prosaically called a "gardening ambition": just as the gardener subdues the wilderness and brings order by rooting out unwanted growths and species, so the social purist or "monist," such as a Robespierre or Goebbels, would purify society. And since this was a scientific age, new sciences like eugenics would make such improvements possible; as the distinguished naturalist and evolutionist Ernest Hackel wrote, "by the indiscriminate destruction of all incorrigible criminals, not only would the struggle for life among the better portions of mankind be made easier, but also an advantageous artificial process of selection would be set in practice, since the possibility of transmitting the injurious qualities would be taken from those degenerate outcasts."[10]

The same philosophy could be applied to such other "degenerate outcasts" as Jews or Gypsies, who did not quite fit into the perfectly cultivated society. Other new "sciences" like phrenology or craniology would help define and identify just who these various people were. By the end of the eighteenth century such ideas were becoming well established. In 1799, for

9. Thomas, "Britain's."

10. Bauman, *Modernity and Ambivalence*, 31.

example, the Manchester surgeon Charles White drew on the work of the Dutch anatomist Peter Camper to create a helpful analysis of the "regular gradation from the white European down through the human species to the brute creation, from which it appears that in those particulars wherein mankind excel brutes, the European excels the African."[11] By the twentieth century Nazis were sending out scientific expeditions across the world in furtherance of this exercise in racial gradation.

Underlying such "scientific" exercises some anthropologists have seen a much older and more deeply ingrained authoritarian attitude that goes all the way back to the Neolithic domestication of animals. As historian Keith Thomas notes in his study *Man and the Natural World*, "human rule over the lower creatures provided the mental analogue on which many political and social arrangements were based." This was a view reinforced by many centuries of Christianity, during which learned clerics would harangue "inferior" humans such as "the poor silly naked Indians, just one degree (if they be so much) remov'd from a monkey" or the poor brutes who inhabited the Essex marshes in the 1700s—"people of so abject and sordid temper that they seem to have . . . by conversing continually with the beasts to have learned their manners."[12] It was a "learned" view that nomadic people, such as hunter-gathering Indians who did not colonize the land, were not only inferior, but less than human. This categorization could also be extended to include migrant and "feckless" people such as Gypsies and the Irish.

With the expansion of European colonization these attitudes became inseparable from the civilizing mission of imperialism. A noteworthy example was the Germany's colonization of South West Africa. Though Germans came late to the great African land grab, they did so with a sense of absolute right to what the kaiser called "a place in the sun" and *Lebensraum* (living space). It was irrelevant that the land was already occupied by the Herero people; and because they were regarded as a lower form of primate, the men were massacred and the rest rounded up into death camps. Overseeing this first genocide of the twentieth century was *Reichskommissar* Heinrich Göring, earlier noted as father of Hermann, future second-in-command of the Third Reich. And as also noted, many of the Nazi functionaries were simply reprising their earlier misdeeds in Africa[13] and inflicting on fellow Europeans practices formerly reserved for people outside Europe; indeed,

---

11. Thomas, *Man*, 136.

12 Thomas, *Man*, 42.

13. Mazower, *Dark*, 161–84

this "marked the culmination of state violence against racially defined alien populations."[14]

It is this unsavory truth that we are still trying to come to terms with. Resurgent xenophobia may be an indication that we are not doing very well. But there is hope, for in contrast to the pseudoscience that underpinned so much racial hatred in the past, new scientific understandings of human origins totally discredit the concept of race. In fact, the most remarkable thing about our human population, vast as it is, is that humans are among the most genetically uniform of mammal species. A random sample of about fifty chimpanzees from west Africa exhibits greater genetic diversity than all seven billion of us! No doubt this is due to humanity's near brush with extinction some seventy thousand years ago. The near catastrophe caused by the Toba volcanic eruption now ensures that we are all fundamentally the same.

This human unanimity was recently underlined by the work of Australian ecologist and explorer Tim Flannery. In the course of biological surveys carried out in remote parts of New Guinea he occasionally met people who not only had never met an "outsider" before but whose ancestors left Africa at least fifty thousand years ago. "Yet," he writes, "when we met, after fifty millennia of separation, I understood instantly the meaning of the shy smile on the face of a young boy looking at me . . . There was much natural magic to those unforgettable meetings."[15] Despite this commonality in expressions, emotions, and gestures—a phenomenon that fascinated Darwin over a century ago—Flannery goes on to say, "We've been very good at living as if our family, our clan or our nation is the only truly civilized and 'proper' group of people on Earth, and believing this has enabled us to kill and rob and main each other without seeing that we are damaging ourselves."[16] Nothing is so challenging to such a belief as meeting "the other," the stranger in our midst. One might add that perhaps nothing will do us more good.

And this leads to a final thought on that word *xenophobia*—that it's not really an English word at all, but a mongrel concoction. In fact, the whole of the English language is a glorious concoction of foreign words from around the world set in a grammatical matrix from northern Europe, a syntactical and grammatical amalgam that in the nineteenth century would no doubt

14. Ferguson, *Civilization*, 190

15. Flannery, *Here*, 123.

16. See Flannery, *Here*, 120–35.

have been construed Germanic. The very fact English has such a global reach is precisely because of its potential for inclusivity, and it continues to absorb and reconfigure strange words from just about anywhere. This is also true of England and the English—they keep on assimilating strangers from everywhere on the planet. This has become the very nature and distinguishing feature of the English; how fortunate that the mongrel word and the hybrid population affirm xenophobia to be but a small part of their story!

7

A Shadowed Past
The Search for Human Identity and Origins

We live in troubled times! Even well-established democracies such as the United Kingdom and the United States seem neither united nor stable. Old European states like Hungary and Poland have seen the resurgence of extreme forms of populism based on the affirmation of national identity. In Germany and Spain we have seen the reemergence of fascist parties—AfD (Alternative für Deutschland) and Vox are ghosts from a disturbed past. In Greece, the birthplace of democracy—as we are so often reminded—mass demonstrations have arisen over the adoption of a historic name, Macedonia: On January 20, 2019, more than two hundred thousand Greeks from all over the country took to the streets of Athens to protest a neighbouring state's use of the name with shouts of "Hands off our Macedonia" and "We will never give up our identity."

That last word, *identity*, seems to be the crux of the issue: who are we, as a people and as individuals? As one of the Greek protesters succinctly phrased it, "This issue isn't about nationalism, or far right populism. It's about who we are . . . That's all we have left."[17] And it's an increasingly widespread and significant sentiment. In August 2017 Charlottesville in Virginia witnessed serious rioting concerning the statue of the Confederate general of the Civil War, Robert E Lee. The intimidating equestrian statue and the argument over whether it should stay or go became the focus for a

17. Carassava, "200,000 Protest."

69

Unite the Right rally demanding that the statue be left alone. The opposing rally of civil rights activists led to the clash of two ideological groups seeking to express two distinct identities, black and white.

What was particularly disturbing about the Unite the Right rally were the flags and symbols being carried. Not only were there the old Confederate battle flags and the Gadsden flags (icons of the earlier revolutionary War of Independence), but there were also Nazi swastikas and the emblems of the Ku Klux Klan and all the paraphernalia of white supremacists. Here was a very particular and long-lived narrative of identity that was obviously far from moribund. It is a narrative that reaches back to the discovery of the New World itself, a place inhabited, or so it seemed to Europeans, by less than human peoples—caribs, calibans, cannibals. When Francisco de Vittoria (1483–1546), the celebrated Dominican theologian and putative founder of the concept of international law, argued for their natural rights and equal treatment in *De Indis*, he caused outrage: readers demanded that Vittoria face condemnation for heresy and imprisonment from the emperor, Charles V. Others preferred to see the natives as little more than monkeys, a sentiment that still echoes in the chanting football (soccer) crowds of today and bananas thrown onto the pitch.

Writing about ongoing racism on the football terraces (areas for soccer spectators to stand), chief sportswriter Matt Dickinson of the *Times* drew attention to the "unconscious bias" that resides not only on the terraces but in boardrooms and affects behavior "more perniciously than a single discriminatory comment." At issue here is societal prejudice and cultural assumptions that simply assume white privilege without stopping to think about the negative consequences of racism. As Dickinson perceptively observes, "It is challenging to think about what is absent. And so, white privilege becomes 'dull, grindingly complacent."[18] The sobering reality is that supremacist thinking is based on an underlying cultural image, the result of a very long-term process of hundreds of years of "indoctrination" that certain groups of people are more worthy than others.

The power of cultural prejudice and deeply embedded images in the psyche predetermine much unthinking behavior and can be found at work throughout history. When it comes to models of self-understanding there are two very different metanarratives of identity and of human engagement with the world which, even if not always articulated, may be characterised as collaborative and manipulative. On the one hand, the ancient

18. Dickinson, "John Barnes."

hunter-gatherers and primal people have a deep sense of being a part of the earth as a shared habitat with other creatures and plants all of which taken together make life possible and with which human origins and identity are intertwined. This is expressed, for example, in the totem poles made by the First Nations tribes on the Pacific Coast of Canada. Symbolically, these embody the tribal history and identity that draws its living spirit from the land and is rooted in a specific place and ecology, just as are the trees in the forest. On the other hand, farming communities that developed in the post-Neolithic world of agriculture and animal domestication did so through the appropriation of a specific area that was divided up, allotted, and manipulated. In time this made possible the growth of complex social units, cities—such as Ur and Sumer—and the origins of what we now call civilization. Controlled by powerful elites cities, came to provide people with a sense of identity. In time the empires they founded would dominate the world.

The clash between these two narratives of identity and origin can be clearly seen in the process of colonization. In America, for example, the land was seized and partitioned by "settlers," and the identity of the First Nations was all but destroyed. But the mutually defining hostility of the eponymous cowboy and the Indian is as old as civilization itself, echoed in the ancient myths such as that of the fratricidal bothers Cain and Abel, the nomad shepherd and hunter in dispute with the settled farmer and citizen. Until recently it was the manipulative narrative of civilization with its powerful technologies that always triumphed, as in the United States where railroads extended across the prairies in the nineteenth century, with their "iron horses" belching fire and smoke accompanied by the scarcely comprehensible destruction of the great herds and flocks of animals. To the native Indians it presented a demonic spectacle of apocalyptic proportions as they looked on bewildered and helpless.

But in modern times this triumph is increasingly seen to be Pyrrhic as the relentless exploitation of the earth brings the realization that this dynamic is unsustainable and potentially catastrophic for humanity. For not only is the commodification of nature for profit destructive of the planet, but urbanization has brought a detachment from nature that is increasingly proving destructive of human well-being. In reaction a new ecological awareness has now returned, seeking to reconnect humans to the natural world and identify with its rhythms; it is an understanding similar to that which the first people had with the environment of which they were an integral part. This is the new but ancient narrative of respect for the earth, a view expressed cogently by Sir David Attenborough at the recent Davos meeting of world leaders in 2018, that we are part of nature and depend on it for our survival. With this recognition comes the imperative that we must change the narrative of how we imagine ourselves.[19]

Clearly, narratives of identity—personal, national, racial, cultural—are of profound significance. But they in turn feed off a deeper and more embracive narrative of the nature of our origins and what it is to be human. Here, of course, we enter the domain of myth. Of their nature myths are graphic and compelling, embracive and definitive, but above all simple enough that all can understand their message. In doing so the myths we tell ourselves determine how we act. Think how Romulus and Remus, reared by the wolf and fighting to the death, provided the seminal image that would characterize and legitimize the blood-soaked history of Rome and the blood lust which would fill its amphitheaters with gore to the delight of the baying crowds. Or Pandora, not with a box as prudish Victorians liked to pretend, but the womb from which, Greeks imagined, all the world's evil and chaos flowed; for here an image of not what a woman had or did but what a woman existentially *was* provided the basis for one of the most profoundly misogynistic societies that has ever existed. It is an archaic mentality that still enjoys widespread appeal.

But more influential by far was the biblical myth—the story of the creation of the first pristine man, entire and complete, noble and serene from the outset, set apart and above all nature is compelling in its simplicity and potency. And it has become even more so through innumerable visual images. Who can think of Adam other than as depicted by Michelangelo in the Sistine Chapel or in the glorious portrayal by Lucas Cranach the Elder, now in the Uffizi? This is the figure destined to march through human history as civilization unfolded. Flawed perhaps but peerless in might and cunning, godlike in ambition and destiny. And then consider the very obvious assumption and message of how very white and European this icon appears. This is the underlying, unquestioned image—so crypto-Aryan white Caucasian, typical of the representation of biblical figures, even of God "himself"—that shaped the notion that white supremacy was the natural order of things long before any racial theories arose.

But all is not as it seems. In the original ur-myth Adam is not a male at all but an "it": a composite male/female figure. In "his" male configuration

---

19. *World Economic Forum Annual Meeting 2019* (website), "Conversation."

one will notice a flaw, often unperceived, that challenges the whole myth. Adam has a navel! More precisely, the belly button is an indication of a mammalian birth from a mother rather than creation ex nihilo. One could argue, as did Henry Gosse in his 1857 opus *Omphalos* (Greek for *navel*) that God provided Adam with a navel to stress his continuity with future men. The broader theme of Gosse, reflected in its subtitle—*An attempt to untie the geological knot*—that God endowed a pristine world with the appearance of an ordered history, disguising a more ancient past, so that the story told by Genesis could be literally affirmed. See the full story in paleontologist Stephen J. Gould's essay "Adam's Navel."[20]

One may believe this story—and many do—but over the last fifty years another, more compelling narrative has emerged. In 1953, Cambridge University scientists James D. Watson and Francis H. Crick announced that they had determined the double helix structure of DNA, the molecule containing human genes. Since then our understanding of human nature has been transformed. The subsequent sequencing of the human genome has allowed us not only to peer into nature's toolbox to identify the effects of specific genes and how whole organisms are constructed, but it has also opened a window onto our past. Our genome records our evolution over millennia.

Further developments over the last decade have given us even more revolutionary insights into our origins and identity. In 2008 a team of geneticists led by Svante Pääbo at the Max Planck Institute for Evolutionary Anthropology at Leipzig, Germany, achieved the astonishing feat of sequencing 60 percent of the Neanderthal genome from bone fragments forty thousand years old. Subsequent comparison revealed that it was 99.8 percent the same as the modern human genome. Then came another discovery which, as Pääbo records in his detailed account of his research, *Neanderthal Man: In Search of Lost Genomes,* was quite unexpected. Not only were the two genomes, Neanderthal and modern human, similar, but they shared genes of between 1.5 and 2.1 percent of the DNA revealed interbreeding.[21]

Still further research showed that this gene flow was characteristic of all non-African populations, and thus the most likely locus of this interbreeding was the Middle East—the same as that of the mythical garden of Eden! In modern-day Israel overlapping campsites have been found on the Mount Carmel range from the period when modern humans emerged from

20. Gould, "Adam's."

21. Pääbo, *Neanderthal.*

Africa some sixty-five thousand years ago. This suggests that interbreeding had taken place between different population groups, a view supported by the discovery of the first modern human bones in Europe at Oase in Romania in 2002. Dating from about forty thousand years ago these featured a skull top that seemed to have the gracile features of a modern skull, but the jawbone had some oddities, and the huge molars were more typical of a more archaic human. In other words they suggested an ancient hybrid.[22]

The common perception of our Neanderthal relatives is that of an apelike caveman. As the distinguished palaeoanthropologist Chris Stringer wrote, "No other group of prehistoric people carries such a weight of scientific and popular preconceptions, or has its name so associated with . . . the lingering traits of savagery, stupidity and animal strength."[23] Perhaps this long-held misconception reflects a subliminal fear of recognizing an ancestry from which we seek to distance ourselves.

The more we have learned about Neanderthals, the more apparent has become the scale of this gross misrepresentation. It is clear that over their half million years of existence they continued to evolve by developing effective hunting weapons, by making clothes and ornamentation, by caring for their sick and injured (indicated by healed bone fractures), by burying their dead with basic rituals (as at Shanidar Cave, in Iraq or at Es-Skhul, in Israel), and by developing basic language. Basic language facility is evident from the presence of the FOXP2 gene associated with speech, and from the presence of the hyoid bone in the neck, which anchors speech muscles. Neanderthals also made the cave art discovered at El Castillo, in Spain, and they even played music (indicated by a forty-three-thousand-year-old flute found at Divje Turk in Slovenia). All these emergent features are what we have until recently attributed uniquely to modern humans. But perhaps the greatest tribute to their intelligence and skill was that they survived in Europe for over two hundred fifty thousand years.

Contemporary analysis of the Neanderthal genome indicates that during this time they developed a very useful mutation on chromosome 9 that affects the gene associated with pale skin. The significance of this is that dark skin protects from harmful UV radiation in sunny climes but makes it harder to generate vitamin D in northern latitudes. Lighter skin helped to solve this problem for the dark-skinned humans coming from Africa. This Neanderthal mutation is now present in 70 percent of people

22. Roberts, *Incredible*, 64–69.

23. McKie, *Ape*, 150.

with European ancestry and absent in those with no European origins. Along with these we have inherited genes for red hair and susceptibility to the common cold. In short our "ape-man" ancestry has allowed modern Europeans to survive in Europe. One wonders what white supremacists may make of this, especially the AfD (Alternative für Deutschland), who claim Germans to be "an ethnobiologically homogenous people."[24]

And it is not only the Neanderthal genetic inheritance that lives on in us. In 2009 Pääbo's team delivered another piece of stunning research based on a small piece of bone recovered from a remote cave of Denisova in the Altai Mountains of central Siberia. Sequencing the genome revealed that this was not Neanderthal but a previously unknown sister group that had branched off from a common ancestor with modern humans some six hundred thousand years ago and separated from the Neanderthals about two hundred thousand years ago. Denisovans, as they were subsequently named, had migrated eastward to Asia, leaving the Neanderthals in Europe. Denisova itself was situated in a midpoint between the two population groups.[25]

Further gene sequencing on Denisovian fragments in August 2018 revealed that a finger bone was that of a girl about thirteen years of age whose father was Denisovan and mother Neanderthal, proof of interbreeding. Comparing hers to the modern human genome provided yet another surprise: not only were there shared genes, but in Southeast Asia these were as high as 4.8 percent. In other words, here was a previously unknown human group that had wandered widely over Asia for some four hundred thousand years and contributed to the DNA of humans, but of whom we had previously know nothing. This was particularly true in Tibet, where an inherited Denisovan gene, *EPSA1*, which is carried by 80 percent of Tibetans and helps people survive in high-altitude low -oxygen conditions. Other genes for cold tolerance were also found; and as if to show that this was not the end of the story further unknown "ghost" genes indicated the presence of yet another completely unknown human source.

From this brief sketch of a vast and growing body of research based on highly technical information a picture begins to emerge. It is far from simple, but it has fundamental implications for understanding what it means to be human and thus challenges both religious myths and scientific models of understanding. The image of a single pristine and unique human species

24. Moody, "AfD."

25. Pääbo. *Neanderthal*, 244–45.

disappears. In fact Pääbo refuses to use the word *species*; for him it is unnecessarily divisive and refers to the latest modern humans as "the replacement crowd"; the geneticist and phylogeographer Stephen Oppenheimer uses the term *races*—though perhaps instead of this loaded word the more neutral word *lineages* may be preferable. After all a species is defined by an inability to cross-fertilize. From that perspective, Pääbo writes, "we had shown that Neanderthals and modern humans were the same species." The same can be said of Denisovans and others.[26]

The startling discovery of evidence of early humans living in Morocco around three hundred thousand years ago was an indication that "modernization" was taking place much earlier than we thought and in different lineages. Throughout Africa population groups were changing in parallel rather than one small tribe becoming "modern human beings," taking over the continent and later the world. Once our human ancestors reached a certain level of development, interaction began to create selection pressures which in turn promoted the development of new faculties like language, genetic and fossil evidence for which (such as the presence of the hyoid bone necessary for speech) indicates an origin several hundred thousand years ago. Increased networking of brains improved our capabilities for example in tool making. This no doubt happened in different lineages in the phenomenon known as "gene-culture co-evolution" or "niche constructions."

What we are dealing with is a varied distribution of human populations that split from one another over a period of one and half million years, adapted to different environments and then periodically recombined and hybridized. The picture is of a vast web, mosaic, or jigsaw puzzle of formerly interlocking human groups unsatisfactorily referred to as "species." The title of geneticist David Quammen's recent work, *The Tangled Tree: A Radical New History of Life*, gives a clear indication of our changed view of evolution.

This in turn compromises the previously established picture of human evolution as one of a dominant emergent stem from which other hominin species periodically branched off and migrated out of Africa before the final ascendancy of modern humans. This is an understanding instantly recognizable in one of the most iconic scientific illustrations of all time popularly called *The March of Progress* (the most accurate title is *The Road to* Homo sapiens), in which the early relatives of humans lined up, starting with a chimpanzee. The artist, Rudolph Zallinger of the Peabody Museum

---

26. Roberts, *Incredible*, 102.

of Natural History, sketched them (in 1965) striding purposefully across the page, becoming more modern with every step and giving the impression that human evolution was a linear progression. This beguiling image, comparable to the many Renaissance paintings of Adam—and perhaps subliminally influenced by them—is almost impossible to dismiss from memory. Though it forms a prism through which we unconsciously view "the facts," it is little more than a myth, perhaps the ur-myth of modern Western civilization but one now seen to be a gross simplification entirely without foundation.

The "Out of Africa" model now needs to be replaced by a much more nuanced and complex picture of a global network of human groups developing different traits in different regions and recombining over a periods of hundreds of thousands of years. These traits embedded in the DNA of modern humans now provide the basis for such physiological and regional variations as white skin! This is particularly true of China where numerous fossil discoveries have provided what anthropologist Dr. Alice Roberts has termed "an unbroken line of descent from archaic humans that made it to East Asia over a million years ago"[27] in *The Incredible Human Journey,* the book which accompanied her fascinating BBC TV series. It is worth noting further that distinguished Chinese palaeoanthropologists such as Professor Xinghi Wu claim such modern Chinese features as the flatter face and prominent cheekbones to be typical of these ancient fossils and indicative of regional evolution.[28]

All this has profound implications for how we view ourselves as humans, for our concept of what it is to be human. No longer does *Homo sapiens* appear to be a dominant master race or even a distinctive species but rather the final survivors of a vast human family whose genetic identity lives on in us and of which modern humans, in all their variety, are the summation. As Alice Robert comments, we should view our ancestors with respect for "They were groups of humans that are no longer with us," not other, slightly inadequate species trodden underfoot by snootily superior *sapiens.*[29] These other hominins are to be viewed in terms of their own complete lives; they are not "a step" on the way to something else any more than First Peoples are to be view as on their way to civilization, a process that devastated them often to the point of genocidal destruction.

27. Roberts, *Incredible,* 181.

28. Roberts, *Incredible,* 180–84.

29. Roberts, *Incredible,* 102.

But this in turn must lead on to a yet more elusive question of what exactly are those features that have enabled the dominance of modern humans and that now distinguish us from our hominin ancestors. It is this which will be the next stage of genetic research and already Pääbo has identified ninety-six "functional mutations" that alter the protein produced by genes that are unique to modern humans. These genes will be crucial to understanding the very last stage of our evolution and the difference to our psychology, physiology and biochemistry. As Pääbo writes, "This will represent an essentially complete answer to the question of what makes humans 'modern,' at least from a genetic perspective."[30]

The already widespread agreement about the cognitive distinctiveness of modern humans is biologically based and substantial. In *The Prehistory of the Mind*, Steven Mithen talks of "cognitive fluidity" and the "capacity for metaphor" that arises from the ability to link brain activities and produce complex symbolic objects. It is this "poetic consciousness" that we see so dramatically expressed in ancient figurines, personal decoration and above all in stunning cave art of late Palaeolithic times.

In her fascinating research, the palaeoanthropologist Genevieve von Petzinger, of the University of Victoria, Canada, has focused not on the usual study of cave art—of the breathtaking bulls, horses, and bison—but the often overlooked smaller geometric symbols often found alongside them. From these she has discerned a consistent body of signs—just thirty-two in Europe—that form the basis of a human code used by various groups across the globe. Her research shows that modern humans were using two-thirds of these signs when they first settled in Europe. As she writes in her book *The First Signs: Unlocking the Mysteries of the World's Oldest Symbols,* "Our ability to represent a concept with an abstract symbol is uniquely human."[31]

What the symbols actually mean may forever elude us—though in his penetrating book *The Mind in the Cave: Consciousness and the Origins of Art* David Lewis-Williams has provided a brilliant insight into understanding them from a neuropsychological viewpoint—but what they do indicate is a key ability to record and share knowledge. For the first time a species did not have to be in the same place at the same time in order to communicate. Information could be stored and passed on to future generations. Together with language, it is such distinctive symbolic activity that gave humans the

---

30. Pääbo, *Neanderthal*, 213.

31. See von Petzinger, *First*, 263–68; see also George, "Hidden."

ability to cooperate and coalesce in ever more complex societies and thus enabled them to survive and outperform other groups.

Thus, as an image-making, symbolic species, we today find ourselves at a critical point where information technology and the sheer scale of human communication threaten to overwhelm us. "Fake news," "trolling," and internet storms of public anger have become all-too-common destabilizing features of modern society. And lest we be tempted to look back at our archaic ancestors with contempt for their lack of sophistication, we should remember that they survived in harmony with their environment for hundreds of thousands of years. Despite our vaunted superior intelligence, it is far from clear whether modern humans will be able to survive for anything near that length of time.

So what is the image or understanding needed today that humans should have of themselves if there is to be a future? One feature that has gained widespread acknowledgment is the need for respect, a wide-ranging deference to others, to those who may be different, and to all forms of life. Important though this is, I would suggest something else is needed, which for want of a better word I call *reticence*. By this I mean the conscious decision not to do all that is within our power to do, to draw back from what is possible. An example would be the nuclear nonproliferation treaties as a conscious decision not to use weapons of mass destruction: to follow the route of mutually assured destruction (MAD) would indeed be madness. But this is a global issue beyond the constraint of ordinary individuals whereas the reticence of which I speak is more personal; the willingness not to pluck a flower, kill an animal, cut down a tree would be examples. Also, the reticence to fulfill all our ambitions, such as the fanciful "bucket list" of unfulfilled wishes that is so popular, that dream new kitchen or world cruise. The planet is simply not able to bear the exercise of such expectation by so many; mass tourism destroys what it goes to see, as in Venice and with the Great Barrier Reef. This also is a form of madness in the face of which we must show reticence if there is to be a future.

Just as past behaviors have been legitimized by powerful myths and images, such as that of humanity having been made in the divine image or the march of progress, one wonders how reticence may thus be portrayed, and if there is a suitable image available. I would suggest there is already one at hand in the scriptural tradition of Judaism. The later part of this tradition expressed in the Kabbalah seeks to explain the relationship between God, the eternal and mysterious *Ein Sof* ("The Infinite"), and the mortal, finite universe that is God's creation. In this teaching the divine fire is seen to withdraw, leaving a shadowed earth. Crucially, the concept of *kavanah* (self-effacement) is used to explain how the infinite power of God withdraws to let others be; just as a parent may withdraw to allow a child to find its own living space, so the image of such divine reticence makes creation possible.

Prior to the development of this esoteric strand of thought, the Scriptures contained an even more graphic image of reticence, the so-called Songs of the Suffering Servant found in the book of Isaiah. These enigmatic passages have long been understood as the core of a messianic prophecy fulfilled in Jesus. Ultimately the sacrificial servant from Nazareth is presented as the king who refuses to exercise power. This is given even sharper relief in the early liturgical hymn recorded in Paul's letter to the Philippians (2:6–11), in which the Savior humbles himself and is emptied to the point of death so that others may live.

Such a *kenotic* self-emptying is the image in which I would root the concept of reticence. Such reticence is challenging to everything humanity instinctively understands of itself. Yet it is also a challenge that can be seen to be clearly rooted in those very Scriptures which have also been ab/used to legitimate the gross abuse of human power. And so it is that humanity, with the god-like powers it has now assumed, must withdraw to make future life possible. It is in such reticence that I would argue lies the hope for the future of humanity.

Part 2

A Conflicted Species

8

Homo Religiosus
The Place of Religion in Human Experience

When I lived in a monastery in Sussex, I would often meet the church warden from the neighbouring Anglican parish church in the lane. Invariably he would have some cryptic comment on the general state of affairs. One Christmas, as I was erecting the outside crib, he stopped and said, "You know, for me Christmas begins when I sit down and turn on the radio to listen to the service of readings and carols from King's College, Cambridge."

No doubt many would agree, but now we can go one better and watch it on TV—an experience not to be missed. As the camera pans down the *candle-lit aisle* to the elaborately carved choir stalls, and then up past the magnificent *painting* of Ruebens's *Adoration of the Magi* to the stained glass windows with the soaring *columns* fanning out into breathtaking stone tracery, it becomes clear that this is the perfect background for the exquisite *musical cadences and chanting that* drift with angelic effortlessness through the ethereal void and create an altogether *ecstatic sentience* of transcendental beauty. The result is a quintessential expression and example of religious experience.

Indeed, it is an experience that can be replicated in any number of the great medieval churches and cathedrals. On another occasion I remember showing a visiting priest from India around the sites of Sussex one Sunday afternoon. We called into Chichester Cathedral, and there, *stepping down* the short flight of stairs through the superbly carved portico of the Last

Judgement, we entered a transformed world and *journeyed up* the long nave with its overarching *columns* and the elaborately carved rood screen beyond which a *hidden* chorister had just begun to sing Mendelssohn's "O for the Wings of a Dove." We were transfixed. Where else on earth, I wondered, could one casually wander in from the street and be caught up in such an ecstatic sensation?

Or, walk down the aisle of Durham Cathedral, whose mighty columns inscribed with *zigzag, scrolled, and boxed lattice patterning* all but compel one toward the *distant* sanctuary. For me, Norman architecture is defined by those multiple *zigzag*, dogtooth arches, which as a child I recall my mother pointing out to me as that which distinguished them from mediocre Saxon structures. Even now upon entering a church I almost instinctively look for them.

Now scroll back the clock some four thousand years to ancient Egypt, with its monumental ritual landscape typified by the mighty temple at Karnak. Beginning in the court before the towering pylons, one enters and is overwhelmed by the *columns* of the colossal hypocaust hall that seem to reduce one to puny insignificance.

Impressive now, they were even more so in their original state when not only elaborately carved but *brilliantly painted* with messages beyond one's comprehension. Through the darkened, incense laden maze one *journeyed on*—if allowed thus far—to glimpse a yet further *inner sanctuary*, a forbidden area from whence the chanting of priests echoed through the *candle-lit* precincts. Perhaps a visitor from England might be aware of echoes from familiar ritual landscapes that have more than a few homologues!

Now scroll the clock back even further—some thirty thousand years— to the caves of ice-bound southern Europe, such as Lascaux, Chauvet, and Altimira. Again, curiously, one may approach a foreboding, darkened entrance before *creeping* into a long, rather frightening *passage, journeying into mystery*, to a space that suddenly opens up ablaze in flickering *candle-light* with magical paintings that seem to move in living concourse across rock faces and past columned stalagmites and stalactites, *columns* fanning out into breathtaking stone tracery, and find oneself surrounded by further patterns of stippled, *zigzag, scrolled and boxed lattice patterning* on the rock face.

In time these features would also become incorporated in the great Neolithic burial mounds such as that at Newgrange in Ireland. Here, after stepping over an elaborately carved curbstone with *zigzag, scrolled, and boxed lattice patterning*, one enters the mighty mound through a narrow *passage* that suddenly opens up to a great chambered space, an *inner sanctum*. Here once a year at the winter solstice, the sunlight penetrated for a brief moment to the back of the sanctuary wall through a skillfully placed window box. Even on the summer's day I visited with some other clergy on an international conference, the place was haunting; even more so in the past when shamanic priests laden with incense would enter under the *zigzag* patterned lintels (which do indeed bear a frightening resemblance to the teeth of a dog with open jaws ready to bite and swallow!) with solemn *chanting* that would be amplified and echo out along the passage as if the spirits were communicating from another world to the awed gathering of people beyond the outer sanctuary.

In the above narrative the italicized and repeated words are meant to be clues after the manner of one of my favorite TV personalities, Keith Lemon, and his hilarious show *Through the Keyhole*, where a panel has to guess the celebrity homeowner from the clues provided while visiting their property. But here they point not to the personality who happens to live in the building(s) but to what is going on in them. When we examine all these religious monuments, we see some remarkable similarities—columns, passageways, grand spaces, awesome artwork . . . There are far too many similarities, even in such minor details as the patterning, stepping and stooping down, and hidden inner spaces to suppose they are purely coincidental. Regardless of the actual content of the rituals enacted in these places, a structural homology seems to connect them over the vast reaches of time and space. What on earth *is* going on? Who "lives there"—and perhaps more important, where does all this come from?

I believe the answer is to be found in the brilliant insight of the South African paleoanthropologist David Lewis-Williams. Elaborated in his epochal books *The Mind in the Cave* and *Inside the Neolithic Mind*[1] is the proposition that neurological patterns of thought that came to typify *Homo sapiens* as an emergent species were replicated and imprinted on the physical landscape so as to become a ritualized means of understanding the world and our place within it. This is a vast and profound engagement related to the nature of human consciousness, the structure of the brain, and offers a neuropsychological model that helps us to understand ourselves.

Though we may tend to think of ourselves as being either awake or asleep, conscious or unconscious, in fact these are to a large degree a false

---

1. Lewis-Williams, *Mind*; and Lewis-Williams and Pearce, *Inside*.

dichotomy. In between waking and sleeping are such states of mind as day-dreaming, *reverie,* hallucination, flashbacks, and amnesia. Furthermore, different states of mind can be induced by a wide variety of means and experiences: fatigue, hunger, migraine, extreme pain, near-death experiences, schizophrenia, drugs, chanting, dancing, flickering light, and so forth. What recent neurological research has revealed is that altered states of consciousness come to be characterized by certain imagery and patterns that reveal themselves in recognizable sequences.[2] Indeed, as people enter deeper levels of altered consciousness they usually pass through three potential stages: *first,* a level of entopic phenomena (images generated in the optic system) typified by zigzags, sets of latticed lines, scrolls, whirls, dot clusters, and flecks; *second comes* the experience of entering a long, dark tunnel or vortex with the sense of floating to a distant, bright light; and *third is* the emergence into an ecstatic light with the experience of bizarre sensory hallucinations and shape-shifting with the sensation of acquiring extra limbs (polymelia), seeing and becoming animals (zoopia), hearing colors (synesthesia), and finally a sensory confusion that can lead to the dissolution of the self. Some of this may have a familiar ring to it.

From this description, as we look through "the keyhole" of consciousness, we begin to see what lies behind that strange world of ritual. The ritual landscape replicates the neurological experience. From the earliest times of humanity this hidden world has been thought to be the real world of spiritual power, a world that challenges us all and into which certain skilled "professionals" can lead us. These are the ones called shamans, saints, mystics, skywalkers, seers, lawmen, medicine men, witch doctors—different cultures have different names for them. Across the continents and cultures such spiritually powerful people not only are known and feared but become authorities who shape and even determine the life and fate of communities. Their appearance in prehistoric times introduced the first division into social structures so as to constitute an elite, a hierarchy or "priesthood" set apart. Their power derived from their skill in navigating the journey through the spiritual world—which is mirrored in our world by the ritual landscape created to enshrine its potentialities, and ranges from initiation ceremonies to the provisioning of life to the direction of the dead. This journey that embraced and traversed the cosmos in its tripartite division of heaven, world, and underworld, and constituted the context of all life and

2. Lewis-Williams, *Mind,* 126–30.

fate—an existential unity bound together by the *axis mundi,* world pillar or tree of life.

All this, I think, people of any belief or none would generally understand and describe as the world of religion—a vast and complex world, but one with certain common elements and defining features.[3] Amongst all these I would here take special note of but one: *the line.* On the entrance curbstone of the Newgrange barrow is a deeply inscribed line pointing to the tomb entrance. One follows the symbolic line through life, leading through the ritual landscape and ultimately death to the ancestral life. It is a journey of fate and fear, its end by no means assured, and with its many dangers and distractions indicated by those zigzag "teeth" (the "jaws of hell"). The nature of our journey is inscribed on the tomb lintels, the spirals and whirls that lead into the maze of life inscribed on the megaliths. This linear axis denotes a journey through this life that leads to the ultimate reality of the life to come, and provides the fundamental structural and symbolic plan of all temples, churches, and places of worship, for their cosmic orientations and processional routes are intended to lead one deeper and deeper into mystery, the inner sanctum, and ultimately into the presence of the divine.

This understanding of life as a transient passage through the world of illusions that are but mere shadows of a greater hidden reality was expressed in its most complete and sophisticated form by the greatest of philosophers, Plato, often hailed as "the father of Western thought." In its later Neoplatonist modality this view became the most decisive element in the matrix from which the nascent Christian theology would be shaped after the third century, and thus became constitutive of the worldview of the medieval civilization we know as Christendom.

Gathering all this vast picture together—from the Chauvet Cave to King's College Chapel—I feel impelled to sum it all up in one admittedly controversial and provocative word: *pagan.* Though this is commonly a pejorative term, I can think of no better, and use it simply to denote the world of religious experience that is at once innate, distinctive, and definitive of *Homo sapiens.* It is a world that has largely helped us to understand who we are and that is so deeply embedded in our minds that it feels 'natural' to us, and that therefore continues to endure and flourish with undiminished power. Forever mystical and transcendental, enticing and entrancing, it is also a world congenial and useful to governing authorities intent

3 Mithen, *Prehistory.*

on providing a backdrop for suitably impressive public rituals that bestow legitimation.

But it is not the only worldview, and I would now like to offer another: one defined not by *a line* of journey, submission, and distance, but by *a circle* of presence, companionship, and communion. This also is an ancient view, but not equally so, since it is one that emerged from the earlier cosmology some four thousand years ago with the advent of the first identifiable religious figure or "prophet," Zarathustra.[4] He also was a celebrant and priest in the vast ritual world I have been describing. But his "revolution" involved introducing a moral element. For him the success or failure of our journey through life would be determined not so much by respecting taboos, following rituals, or offering sacrifices as by the way we lived. And the end point would be a judgment of the balance of good and evil in our lives. Indeed, he saw the whole of history to be leading to such a final judgment or end point for everyone. An ultimate conflict of Good and Evil would be presaged by the warnings of a messenger ("messiah") that would lead to a Final Judgment presided over not by animistic and polytheistic spiritual entities, but by one supreme being, the God of light, *Ahura Mazda*.

For such disturbing and "heretical" views Zarathustra was murdered by another priest during a ritual celebration. But his thinking survived. Indeed, it might sound rather familiar to us! By some curious historical coincidences his views came to be absorbed by another religious group that happened to be exiled in the Zoroastrian sphere of influence at Babylon in the sixth century BCE. In fact so transformative did these ideas become that they became constitutive of the religion we now know as Judaism, as it mutated from a tribal ethnocracy into a world religion.[5] And thus, of course, they subsequently became determinative of Christianity.

Though I mention all this now, it is redolent of a discussion I had some forty years ago in the company of a group of rabbinical students led by Rabbi Lionel Blue around the table of a seder at the monastery where I then lived. If all this sounds a bit confusing, I can perhaps explain by saying that one of the more interesting things that happened in my life was when, by historical coincidence, Rabbi Blue used to bring groups of rabbinical students (both male and female) to our monastery as a break in the country from the stresses of London living so they could relax together for a few

4. Kriwaczek, *In Search*.

5. Sands, *Invention*, 130–53.

days. The fact that it was a monastery was perhaps incidental to its being largely empty and the accommodation cheap if only basic.

As a recently ordained priest I found not only their beliefs but their behavior a revelation. The cloistered monastic world, even though internally homogeneous, was still divided between the church as a place of worship and the domestic quarters of daily work, with the rituals of the two clearly differentiated. When Lionel came, the two worlds merged around the large refectory table and kitchen. The Friday seder was an informal hybrid of party and prayer during which we all gathered around the table, read prayers, sang songs, ate food, and generally had a good time in no particular order of service or even any order at all. It was in this context that I got into a discussion about the *massoud*/messiah!

One thing that stands out about Jesus—for indeed it was from this tradition that he came—is that he did not have much time for temples. As he is reported to have said to the woman at the well below Mount Gerizim, God is to be worshiped neither on this mountain nor any other mountain, but in spirit and truth (see John 4:21). And not only did he undoubtedly utter many such unorthodox doctrines, he actually lived by them. His brief life was typified by sharing meals in people's houses, and his teaching was characterized by stories of everyday events and often presented during meals, like the unforgettable parable of Dives and Lazarus (see Luke 16:19–29), which according to Luke he directed at his Pharisaic dinner companions (see Luke 16:14). The setting for his final testimony depicts him and his followers gathered around a table in a public house. One could say that his life was lived *in the round, in the circle* of his friends and followers. It is that *circle* that I believe defines not only his life and teaching but also how he is to be remembered. And that memory is incompatible with *the line* of paganism.

In fact Jesus himself implied as much when he blasted those hierarchical officials who at table and even at worship like to occupy the best seats and expect both obsequious titles and deferential treatment. He, on the other hand, advised his followers to serve unknown, and did so himself. The controversy of those who would be the keepers of his memory has rumbled on for the subsequent two thousand years; and however one may like to recount this history, it has been characterized by a conflict between the ritual line and the intimate circle—whether, one might say, it is possible to put new wine into old skins. Generally, the line has been triumphant.

Initially this was not the case. We know that like the seder they grew out of, the earliest eucharists or *agapes* were largely informal affairs around a table with a presider (either male or female), whose primary duties were to keep order and extemporize suitable prayers—but not too long lest people fall asleep! Snooty Roman critics like Celsus disdainfully observed that this movement had no temples, altars, priesthood, or rituals; but all this would soon change. Many theologians have, like Hans Küng, questioned whether the conversion of Constantine led to the Christianization of the pagan empire or the paganization of Christianity.[6] Certainly the growth of Caesaropapism created such a formidable landscape of ritual and sanctuary that within a few centuries the priest had literally turned his back on the congregation during liturgical celebration so that the ordinary faithful were increasingly excluded and disparaged. Communicants were thus demoted to onlookers, voyeurs of incomprehensible mysteries whose threatening power seemed to most little more than magic.

I vividly recall one Easter Sunday when I found myself at the priestly center of a solemn procession down the aisle of our impressive basilica, passing between the towering Romanesque columns, dressed in the finest gold embroidered silk dalmatic (once the height of fashion for young men of the fourth century), surrounded by candle bearers and the thurifer, whose incense filled the church with clouds pierced by sunlight streaming through the stained-glass windows, and all to the accompaniment of intoned chanting in Latin. The memory of other such holy places suffused my mind, and suddenly I thought to myself, "This is magnificent, and nothing has changed in millennia—but why am *I* doing this and what is the link to the original voice of the gospel?"

Though there were always "apostolic" movements that resisted the ecclesiastical juggernaut, they tended to be informal, evanescent, and domestically based—like the *fraterelli, humiliati,* and *poverelli*—meeting in homes for simple prayers and meals in imitation of the first days of the post-Pentecostal church when the apostles gathered in the Cenacle and shared all things in common. Movements such as those of Peter Waldo, Francis of Assisi, and the Brethren of the Common Life attempted to keep alive this original spirit. These movements, deemed subversive and heretical, were either brought *into line* or crushed by the ecclesiastical power of the Inquisition or the numerous crusades of what one may call the great

6. Brown, *Authority,*

"cathedral culture" of the time.[7] In fact, conformity became the overriding concern of orthodoxy. The corollary was, as the distinguished medievalist R. I. Moore expressed it in his groundbreaking work *The Formation of a Persecuting Society,* the creation not simply of a society where persecution took place, but one that was constituted "through deliberate and socially sanctioned violence."[8] This was to become a fundamental feature of the so-called Age of Faith that characterized Christendom at its apogee and is still glorified by traditionalists as its normative form. These same traditionalists tend to overlook or even deny this untidy element of church history even though it has come to characterize European society ever since, down to the tyrannies of modern totalitarianism.[9]

But not entirely! Just as Zarathustra's moral understanding emerged in the context of the preceding prehistoric worldview, so now a new trans-formative worldview began to emerge from the context of Christendom—secularism. A number of narratives have been proposed to explain this fundamental change, often with the intention of seeing it as some sort of antithetical countermovement to Christianity, and thus atheistic and repu-diating all religion. I believe this to be largely a mistaken understanding; rather, secularism is the consequence of Christianity, and has actually en-abled Christianity to rediscover its true original nature—that is, the histori-cal teaching of Jesus as distinct from hierarchical creation of Christianity.

It is too often forgotten that those who laid the foundations of mod-ern secularism were refugees from the Inquisition of sixteenth-century Catholic Spain with its demand for absolute conformity.[10] Notable among these was the family of the French author Michael Montaigne and the humanist *converso* Joan-Luis Vives—writers who in coming to terms with their trauma began to give priority to reason over faith, to be skeptical of absolute claims to truth, and to display an interest in the variety of human experience. In this their concerns converged with such other Renaissance humanists as Erasmus, whose *via media* offended traditionalists alike, and Pico della Mirandola, who in his *Oration on the Dignity of Man* sought to emphasize the positive values of humanity. These thinkers challenged dogmatic Christianity, and it was the *converso* doctor, Francisco Sanches, whose work *That Nothing Is Known* would provide the essential context

---

7. Moore, *War on Heresy.*

8. Moore, *Formation,* 4.

9. See Preston, *Spanish.*

10. Green, *Inquisition,* 256–83.

for Spinoza and Descartes. It is a delicious coincidence that Sanches's work was reprinted in Frankfurt in 1618, the year before Descartes produced his seminal *Discourse on Method* in the same town. Together these writers prepared the ground for a radical new way of thinking about humanity and thereby laid the foundations of what became the European Enlightenment, the matrix of modern secularism.

This great transformation of European thinking had several aspects and took different forms, but at its most fundamental level it was very simple: people begin to regard the world simply in terms of itself—it was not an illusion or shadow of some greater reality, but simply itself. In a sense this was another step in the journey begun by Zarathustra in emphasizing our moral responsibility and continued in the great transformation that revolutionized religious thinking in the sixth century BCE by discarding much of the ritualism attendant on polytheism. Now, in the seventeenth century of our era, a further step affirmed the integral and egalitarian nature of humanity and thus provided the inviolable basis of human rights.

Many choose to see this development as a threat to traditional Christianity in particular and religion in general, an acid that dissolves the very foundations of religious belief. In many ways it was. But it can be also seen as cathartic of Christianity, purging away the dross, for it reasserted the original humanitarian ethic of the historical Jesus. As Larry Siedentop has convincingly argued in his aptly named work *Inventing the Individual,* what really constituted the revolution of Christianity was its affirmation of the moral equivalence of everyone. Saint Paul put it most effectively by abolishing the differences between slave and free, Jew and Gentile, male and female.[11] Gathered around the table of celebration, all persons were now seen to be of equal worth. The Letter of James could not be more explicit when it insists that the nature of true religion is in the performance of simple acts of kindness: "to help orphans and widows when they need it and keep oneself uncontaminated by the world" (Jas 1:27, JB). One could compress this even further to "Don't be nasty"; or as Rabbi Blue once said to me, "We should try to be nice to people." It really is that simple—or difficult!

The appearance of what we now call secularism has enabled us to refocus on what had been the most challenging and subversive element of the life of Jesus: the radical and indeed subversive nature of his moral teachings that had been obscured by the demands of a ritualized Christianity that was concerned with the nature of his personality and embellished by a

11. Siedentop, *Inventing,* 353.

Neoplatonist theology. This shift of focus has enabled us to rediscover the intrinsically humanistic nature of the teaching of Jesus. And in the process, as Don Cupitt has noted in his *Ethics in the Last Days of Humanity,* a curious paradox has been revealed: as the church-based religion of Christianity is increasingly discredited and marginalized, the Jesus of history has become truly cosmic and eschatological.[12] His prophetic teaching set the standard by which we now judge all religious and secular behavior—*hesed,* humaneness.[13]

Looking back, we can now see that the secularism of the Enlightenment has enabled us to rediscover what was truly revolutionary about the teaching of the historical Jesus; namely, the degree to which he emphasized the purely humanitarian basis of ethics. His radical demand that we should not only love our neighbor as ourself but also love our enemies and do good to those who hate us have rarely been adhered to, yet they are the touchstone of his teaching. And his moral system referred not to some supernatural destiny but to the nature of everyday life.[14] The distinctive characteristic of such living is its internalized morality, which is independent of authority and respects the dignity of all others. This challenging but noble ethic has in our secular age become the basis of our modern understanding of human rights.[15]

As a counterpoint to my brusque summary of ancient religion as "pagan," I would now like to epitomize this second, almost equally vast scenario with the word "prophetic." Though we often use the word *prophetic* as with a view to the unfolding of future events—"down the line," so to speak—in fact its more proper meaning is seeing into the significance of the circle of present events. The alternative word *seer* refers to the power of insight to see what changes we must make now to our lives if there is to be a future. It seems that what kick-started prophecy in ancient Israel was a sense of outrage at the gross discrepancy between public ritualized behavior associated with the temple cult and the personal (im)morality of those involved in it. And ever since then the two have rarely been reconcilable. One sees this, for example, in Vladimir Putin's Russia in the promotion of Russia Orthodoxy as an icon of nationalism, while Putin's political

12. Cupitt, *Ethics.*

13. See Luke 1:78

14. Dodd, *Parables,* 21.

15. Geering, *Christianity.*

regime is characterized by mendacity, murder, and ruthless indifference to individuals and human rights.

So has it ever been. Though many would try to reconcile the line and the circle, others would dismiss the difference between the two spiritual modalities as wholly contrived and artificial. Surely religion can encompass both the pagan and prophetic. And in a sense, it does, or rather has long done so, though today we have entered a new period typified by a secularism that simply dismisses the whole lot. But this too is deficient. The prophetic need for morality in public life still exists, as we see in such movements as Not in Our Name and Occupy. We can begin to recognize that the teaching of Jesus—the parables of the kingdom—had the unique potential to bring forth a new humanism that would set new standards by which we understand life. Indeed, what was once the sacrilege of questioning religious doctrine and practice has become our new religion, and much of what was once religion has now become superstition.

In this narrative we see the triumph of *the circle* over *the line*! The humanitarian circle of human companionship and care, of person and presence, once again challenges the formal line of ritualized submission to an overbearing metaphysical abstraction. The humanitarian ethic, basic to the ethic of Jesus celebrated in the Sermon on the Mount—a celebration of the humble and lowly, an affirmation of the individual worth of even the poorest, a call to aid the sick and oppressed whatever their origin—is now the only credible ethic for humanity. By capturing the spirit and truth of all true religion, of what it means to be human, this ethic sets the standard by which we now judge all other beliefs and practices. In our century it defines *homo religiosus*.

9

A Clash of Minds

Conflicting Styles of Thinking

Mentioning styles may well bring to mind the fashion industry, for which the constant introduction of new fashions is a driving force. The almost limitless possibilities that result mean that most people now have an ample choice of clothes with which to express their feelings and personality. Though perhaps it is not so widely recognized, the same is true of thinking. To be sure, many people are well informed and highly knowledgeable, but not everyone uses these attainments in the same way. And just as with one's clothes, one's thinking tends to change with age and circumstances.

Regardless of your opinion of him, one of the greatest and surely most influential thinkers of all time was Charles Darwin. One of his less famous works written towards the end of his life, *Recollections*, provides a fascinating insight into how his way of thinking changed—or better yet, evolved! As he put it, circumstances had altered "the tone of one's mind." This is particularly true of the passages in which he reflected on his religious beliefs, noting that "disbelief crept over me at a very slow rate"—so slowly, in fact, that he hardly noticed it happening until it was thoroughly ensconced. The same was true of the more general change in his thinking, whereby "I discovered, though unconsciously and insensibly, that the pleasure of observing and reasoning was a much higher one than of skill and sport." As life changes, so does one's thinking.[1]

The same is true of cultures. In modern times it has become axiomatic that we are all part of a wider cultural stream of consciousness, a modality that is never static but shapes our thinking as it moves on without our full awareness until some disruption makes apparent its previously covert influences. Such, for example, was the case of the Reformation, which split Europe into northern Protestantism and southern Catholicism, with the former soon manifesting a very different way of thinking that led to a scientific revolution and the Age of Enlightenment.

But for centuries before this occurred, subtle changes of thinking and perspective had been emerging. The incendiary issue of indulgences grew out of such significant differences as the northern rejection of purgatory and confessional practice.[2] This in turn seems to have reflected a difference in temperament already expressed in such meditative and "inward" pietistic movements of the north as the *devotio moderna*, the Brethren of the Common Life, and the semimonastic Beguines, all of which preceded and shaped the Reformation.

And these cultural and conceptual changes fed into the seventeenth-century Enlightenment. The standard narrative of this "seminal moment" in European history has often been presented as a reaction to and rejection of the claims of the church, drawing inspiration from the Renaissance and its roots in the classical world of antiquity, thus paving the way for a newborn secularism that closed the door on the clergy-ridden world of the Middle Ages.[3] In fact nothing could be further from the truth; for when we look more closely at the historical roots of the Enlightenment—with its affirmation of individual rights, emphasis on critical thinking, and promotion of science—we see all these elements slowly arising out of the culture of the Christian Middle Ages, particularly after the thirteenth century.[4] For example, in the anniversary year of Magna Carta, we were again reminded that this pivotal document opened the door to a new understanding of the rights of the individual and the nature of the state—for both the words

1. Darwin, *Autobiographies*, 49–55. These quotations are all found in this section, called "Religious Belief."

2. MacCulloch, *History*, 551–58.

3. Law, *Philosophy*, 34.

4. Siedentop, *Inventing*, 333–48.

individual and *state* entered into common usage in fifteenth-century English and French before being taken up by Enlightenment thinkers.

It should also be recalled that in the early modern period fundamental changes in attitude toward the self and the world accompanied changed styles of religious thinking across northern Europe. In addition to the popular religious and mystical movements emphasizing "innerness" was the more "scholastic" academic debate derived from the new style of the English Franciscan William of Ockham. His critical approach to Aristotle's physics led to a view of the world that by relying on observation began to point out anomalies in speculative theories. "Ockham's razor" did away with a stifling collection of needless assumptions, abstruse rationalizations, and antiquarian obfuscations. As Steven Weinberg notes in *To Explain the World*, his study of the discovery of modern science, "The precocious scientific revolution that began in the fourteenth century was largely a revolt against Aristotelianism."[5] Yet the roots of this revolution are so deeply embedded in the clash of thinking styles that the later emergence of the scientific revolution would have been impossible without them.[6]

The close etymological and existential association of "science" and "con-science" is an interesting but often overlooked feature of the new style of thinking. The sixteenth century's scrupulous attention to "movements of the spirit" and intuitions of divine purposes, clearly rooted in earlier confessional practices, led to the keeping of meticulous "spiritual journals" and diaries for further reflection.[7] This style of thinking not only became a distinctive feature of seventeenth-century Puritanism and later Methodism, but also provided the matrix for a scientific method dependent on a similarly scrupulous observation and recording of natural phenomena that enabled understanding. Thus it was that spiritual illumination both pointed the way and gave way to cerebral enlightenment, for this whole style of thinking would have been impossible without the long tradition of monastic asceticism that traced its origins to the Dark Ages of premedieval western Europe.[8] In all this we can see the emergent nature of an altered "tone of mind" that in turn would have significant consequences for traditional religious thinking.

5. Weinberg, *To Explain*, 28.

6. Whitehead, *Science,* 14.

7. Foucault, *History.*

8. Cupitt, *Meaning,* 94–101.

I mention all this not just as some arcane reflection, but because of its very real significance in the conflicted world of the present. Once again, as at the Reformation, many parts of the world are convulsed by new challenges to established patterns of thinking, particularly from Islam. What we see here are two very different cultural worlds suddenly thrown into a collision from which there seems no escape: a clash of two very different styles of thinking. But is this entirely true? Or is there a prequel that offers further explanations?

This conflicted situation has grown as much from what these two traditions of thought originally had in common as from their differences. Indeed, the two can be viewed as different points on similar trajectories that have similar origins: each has evolved from a common source of biblical and classical antiquity; each was originally dismissive of purely natural or worldly knowledge; each began to flourish in the context of an all-pervasive monotheism; and both Christian and Arabic scholars contributed to the revival in thought in eleventh-century Europe—so much so that Ibn-Rushd (known in Europe as Averroes) has been called "the founding father of secular thought in Western Europe."[9] There is no intrinsic reason why both cultures should not have continued to evolve in a similar way.[10] But it was only in the West this evolution took place. Why?

This issue is at the heart of current controversy. Whereas some Islamist fundamentalists—like Boko Haram—reject everything implicit in Western education and culture, others affirm that much of this conflict is a consequence of misunderstanding, inasmuch as some elements of Western thought (such as science) have a proud place in the history of Islam. This same thesis led the BBC in 2009 to run a major TV series on Science and Islam, expounding the extraordinary scientific revolution that between 700 and 1500 CE took place in the Islamic world.[11] The scientific advisor to this series, Ehsan Masood, argued in his tie-in book to the series that the decline of Islamic science after the eleventh century was a Western myth, for it played a vital role in enabling Europe's own scientific revolution. While this may in part be true, it is far from being the whole story, and it remains something of a revisionist myth that tends only to confuse things further.

In fact, one of the keys to understanding this cultural conflict lies in the recognition of deeper context of thought and what exactly is meant by

9. Weinberg, *To Explain*, 113.

10. Russell, *History*, 390–97.

11. Masood, *Science & Islam*.

"Islamic science"—that is, if there ever was such a thing. This may seem an outrageous disclaimer statement, but for a number of significant reasons it will illuminate the controversy. One is linguistic. During the period claimed for Islamic science, no such word or concept corresponding to what we now understand of science existed. In its Latin origins *scientia* was simply "knowledge," and until the fourteenth century remained very general in its usage—as in the so-called liberal sciences (also, confusingly, called the liberal arts) of grammar, art, astronomy, and so forth.[12] Only with the advent of the Enlightenment in the seventeenth century did science begin to be distinct from the arts and to involve a special style of thinking.

One may regard this as mere semantics and argue that Islamic cultures had their own equivalent in the Arabic word *ilm* (plural, *ulum*), which also means "knowledge" and can pertain to both the natural world and religious matters. This is true, but quite unlike its usage in the West, this ambivalence remained; and it was only in the nineteenth century that the Ottomans, in their drive for modernization in an attempt to catch up with the scientific advances of the West, introduced a more specific word for scientific techniques, *fen*. And in any case, this term was not taken up in the wider Islamic world, which continued to understand mundane knowledge ("science") and religion as simply two variant forms of knowledge (*ulum*), with religion as the dominant denotation. For example, one enduringly influential work, *Fatihat al-Ulum* (*The Beginning of Knowledge*), by the influential eleventh-century scholar al-Ghazali (regarded as the greatest and most influential theologian in Islamic history), stated the traditional view that mundane knowledge—the sciences—was like wine: not only was it forbidden by Islam but, by implication, it led to a loss of reason. Besides, many of the thoughts it led to raised "the fear that one might be attracted through them to doctrines that are dangerous."[13] Allah could not and should not be "chained" or constrained by human rationality.

By way of contrast, Europe of this period saw theology, the "queen of the sciences" gradually being upstaged by her handmaidens; and by the seventeenth century a new and specific methodology or style of thinking began to take shape. This ultimately undermined the earlier hybrid nature of science as "knowledge" and gave rise to the secularism that resulted from critical reflection based entirely on observation and experimentation. As Weinberg says, "It is essential for the discovery of science that religious

12. Williams, *Keywords*, "Science."

13. Weinberg, *To Explain*, 103–23.

ideas be divorced from the study of nature."[14] And despite opposition from church authorities, religious objections did little to halt the momentum of new thinking. Thus we can see how words chart the process of transformation in styles of thinking, a process that in Europe continued to evolve, but in the Muslim world was frustrated by cultural forces.

Two significant factors explain why this is crucial in understanding present conflicts. One is that many of the great scientists of the Muslim world were from Persia and the Mediterranean lands, which drew on an ancient, diffuse, and sophisticated tradition of learning. The great historian of the Mediterranean civilizations, Fernand Braudel, characterized this as one great dynamic culture.[15] None of this was "Islamic" in origin, though the spread of Islam did provide a unifying force for this disparate world, one that extended to the equally great civilization of India with its outstanding achievements in mathematics, astronomy, and medicine. For all of this learning the Islamic world provided a conduit to the west. Furthermore, many of the great Muslim scholars of this period may have deferred to Islamic teaching in public but were often privately skeptical. They endured an uneasy relationship with religious authority which, apart from periodic intermissions, remained hostile.

This hostility, the second crucial factor in the decline of "Islamic science," culminated in al-Ghazali's famous denunciation in his *Incoherence of the Philosophers*. This was a full-on broadside against "the heretics of our times" who "have been deceived by the exaggerations made by the followers of these philosophers" (Socrates, Hippocrates, Plato, Aristotle, and so forth), so that "their excellent intelligence justifies their bold attempts to discover the Hidden Things by deductive methods; and . . . they repudiated the authority of religious laws."[16] For al-Ghazali this was blasphemous, implying as it did restrictions to God's omnipotence; for since God could do whatever he wanted, there was really no such thing as a "natural" order. Neither was there any point in imagining the existence of "laws" that needed investigating, for everything depended on the divine will. Such "consequentialism" was devastating to the development of such concepts as natural order or scientific thinking. Purely scientific speculation was at best unnecessary.

14. Weinberg, *To Explain*, 44.

15. Braudel, *History*.

16. Quoted in Weinberg, *To Explain*, 121.

The effect of such an attitude on the subsequent history of thought in the Muslim world was catastrophic. From a list of seventy-two great Islamic scholars provided in Jim Al-Khalili's study of Arabic science called *Pathfinders*, almost half were from the two centuries immediately after the Arab conquests and only ten lived after the twelfth century.[17] As suspicious mullahs exerted increasingly greater control over cultural life, the freedom to speculate diminished. One indication of the growing hostility to science came in 1013, when the fanatical Almoravids from North Africa (think Isis or Boko-Haram) destroyed the great library and palace at Medinat al-Zahra outside Cordoba, one of the greatest centres of Islamic scholarship. Later, in 1194 the *ulama* (religious scholars) of Cordoba burned all the medical and scientific books they could find.

Such intolerance became the norm. In the very year books were being torched in Cordoba, jihadists at the other end of the Islamic world entered India under the direction of Sultan Muhammad of Ghor—celebrated as *Jahanzos* or "World Burner"—where they systematically destroyed the greatest seat of learning in Asia, the Buddhist *Mahavihara* or "Great Monastery" at Nalanda. It was burned to the ground, and contemporary observers reported that for a period of months the smoke from burning manuscripts hung like a pall over the low hills of Bengal.[18] In other words, whatever one may think of the concept of "Islamic science," the evidence clearly shows that it was frustrated and ultimately overwhelmed by the zealots of Islam itself, which became increasingly intolerant of learning: No voices or movements like those in Europe proved capable of challenging "orthodoxy"; and as a result Islam never progressed in its thinking as did the Christian culture of Europe, particularly after the sixteenth century.

Meanwhile in Europe a quite different narrative was unfolding. Perhaps the decisive events in the development of European thought came in 1325, the year marking the climax of an esoteric controversy that embroiled the universities of Europe, the papacy, two of the most influential religious orders (the Franciscans and Dominicans), and the greatest minds of the time, if not of all time![19] Prior to this the works of Ibn-Rushd (Averroes) had been the means of reintroducing works of Aristotle to the new universities of western Europe, where their rational principles of thought were eagerly taken up and applied to the Christian tradition by such influential thinkers

17. Al-Khalili, *Pathfinders*, 271–87.

18. Allen, *Asoka*, 5.

19. Hannam, *God's Philosophers*, 86–104.

as Albert the Great and Saint Thomas Aquinas, both Dominicans. But in the 1250s opposition to this emphasis on reason in religious thinking grew under leadership of Saint Bonaventure, who as a Franciscan represented something of a "rival" religious order, and who emphasized the freedom of God's will, which could not be "chained" by natural laws.[20]

This was exactly the position of al-Ghazali with regard the Aristotelian style of thinking; and in 1277 the bishop of Paris, who stood at the epicenter of the controversy, condemned 219 propositions of Aristotle and Aquinas, an action that was confirmed by Pope John XXI. But this pontiff was succeeded by John XXII, who had been educated by the Dominicans, and in 1325 he wholly annulled the condemnation of the articles. He did not come down on one side or the other but chose not to pass judgment "because we neither approve nor disapprove of these articles but leave them for free scholastic discussion."[21] Not only did this momentous decision avoid taking the side of either party; perhaps more important is the fact that it affirmed academic freedom of debate. In doing so it opened the door to the possibility of further discussion and the development of thinking.

A further decision in 1341 led to the formulation of an oath to be taken by masters of the University of Paris that they would teach "the system of Aristotle and his commentator Averroes, and of other ancient commentators."[22] While the Muslim world burned the works of Averroes, the Christian world adopted and praised them! The die had been cast; the door to the exploration of the natural world had been opened in Christian Europe, whereas in the Islamic world it had been closed.[23]

The consequential debate then took an unexpected turn. Ironically, it would be Franciscans—in particular the Englishmen William Grossteste (Bighead!), Roger Bacon, William of Ockham, and the Scotsman Duns Scotus—who would be the most influential figures in using nominalism to undermine Aristotelianism conceptually. In a sense this could be seen as a sort of "revenge" for the previous reversal of 1325, but it was achieved through scholastic argument using the academic freedom this reversal allowed. And above all, it paved the way for the new form of rational discourse that became empirical science and thus provided the foundation of

20. Dodd, *Parables*, 21.
21. Weinberg, *To Explain*, 130.
22. Weinberg, *To Explain*, 130.
23. Gilson, *Unity*, 31–60.

a new nature-based methodology to which another Bacon, three centuries later, would give new momentum.[24]

A further crucial aspect of this new style of thinking was its ability to admit error. This does not come easily to humans in general and is particularly problematic for academics and "authorities" with a vested interest in certain ways of understanding. It has been found, for example, that the higher people rise in the ranks of management or a profession, the more they are likely to cover error with blanket excuses. This is also true of those possessing religious authority based on supposedly revealed truth. In contrast, the great figures of the scientific revolution—one thinks of Galileo—were characterized by the willingness to look again at the data and learn from mistakes. As Matthew Syed has noted, "To put it starkly: the dawning of science, one of the great watersheds in history, occurred because they started to do something they had resisted for centuries: learn from mistakes."[25]

As has so often been the case in the history of science, this is a convoluted story in which unexpected twists and unintended consequences led to many counterintuitive conclusions. What it confirmed was the crucial importance of the critical thinking and freedom of academic thought that had come to characterize European culture. In time the further disputes of the Reformation and the division of Europe into Catholic and Protestant zones of influence enabled northern Europe to become an area where naturalistic thinking and science would thrive; this was where Galileo's "subversive" writings would be sent for publication after being smuggled out of Italy. Ultimately, Aristotelian thought came to be seen as essentially misleading in the pursuit of understanding the natural world, and it was at last rejected in the seventeenth century to allow a truly scientific method to emerge.

The new style of natural philosophy would from then on grow in confidence, and by the nineteenth century it was strong enough to counter ecclesiastical restraint of its own accord. In *The Meaning of the West*, Don Cupitt has described with great clarity and cogency how modern secularism emerged almost seamlessly from its very specific Christian roots.[26] This is equally true of science as a whole. Clearly the Christian West, unlike the Muslim East, had found ways of accommodating new knowledge.

24. Dampier, *Shorter History*, 37–45.

25. Syed, "Blame"; see also Syed, *Black*.

26. Cupitt, *Meaning*.

Not only were many of the early scientists clergy—as was the case with the foundation of the Royal Society, the world's oldest scientific fellowship—but the very nature of scientific thinking can be seen to have emerged from a specifically Christian matrix. Henceforth, as the philosopher Karl Popper noted, true ignorance would not be the absence of knowledge, "but the refusal to acquire it."[27]

But this narrative has yet a further twist. The new secular or worldly way of thinking that accompanied the emergence of the modern world has now brought the modern world to the brink of catastrophe as a result of treating the natural world simply as an expendable externality.[28] The further irony is that this is happening just as the conflict between Western and Islamic styles of thinking is also causing an ancient controversy to be revisited. Suddenly, globalization has thrust the two worlds into each other's domains, first by the imperialism of the West and more recently by immigration from the East. Would two worlds that had developed very different styles of thinking be able to live together?

Today our world again stands on the brink of one of those decisive moments in the seemingly never-ending conflict between styles of thinking. The title of the current best-selling book by Naomi Klein really says it all: *This Changes Everything*. The looming issues of climate change and environmental destruction demand a completely different way of thinking about the world and a different lifestyle if we are to survive.[29] The Western lifestyle based on consumer- or turbo-capitalism is unsustainable. More important, perhaps, is that the style of thinking that underpins it needs to change.

What humankind now needs is a new and greater sensitivity to the natural world, a new way of perceiving it, and the recognition that we are all part of what ecologist Thomas Berry called an "Earth community" of Life.[30] We need a style of thinking that acknowledges that we are to be more than semidetached occupants of a natural world, that sees respect for the natural order as the basis for any sustainable way of life, that places nature's rights ahead of ours, that requires our appetites for both consumption and procreation to be restrained. Just as the purely critical rationalism of the Enlightenment was succeeded by Romanticism, we now need to replace an

---

27. Quoted in Syed, *Black*, ch. 11.
28. Schwägerl, *Anthropocene*.
29. Klein, *This*.
30. Berry, *Selected Writings*.

exploitative secularism with a new kind of emotivism that will balance our rational ambitions with respect for the environment.

Just as the story of recent millennia can be seen to hinge on the evolution of different styles of thinking, so we urgently need a new style of thinking if we are to survive as a species in this new age of human dominance. The modern secular way of regarding the earth as an "externality" or commodity at our disposal has proved disastrous. It is a mental distortion that has arisen from the scientific way of thinking—the unfortunate habit of regarding all things as objects for investigation, or subjects for experimentation—usually to meet our commercial and social needs. Perhaps the *ash'ari* and Franciscan thinkers were right to distrust the unaided powers of reason and to defend their vision of the world as a sacred space. In regarding the natural world as merely a commodity to be exploited—or as Francis Bacon put it, to have her secrets wrenched from her—we have allowed our actions to become detached from any valuation of nature in its own right or from some other coherent system of values that will recognize this right. Just as Islam destroyed "Islamic science" through religious intolerance, so the secular West could now destroy itself by paying unqualified devotion to a science that is indifferent to values.

10

Respect and Radical Religion
Religious Extremism and
the Challenge of Radical Theology

Recently I was talking to my neighbor, a Sikh. He had just had a dispute with another member of the temple (*gurdwara*) fundraising committee over the wording of a publicity leaflet that someone suggested should include appropriate words of wisdom from the Guru Granth. One of the committee vehemently opposed such a suggestion on the basis that a leaflet might be dropped on the floor and trodden on, an occurrence that would result in the desecration of a text from Holy Scripture and thus constitute an intolerable lack of respect.

Respect is a word increasingly being called upon in the multitude of discordant discourses that characterise contemporary society. From footballers (soccer players) being racially abused, to ethnic street gangs demanding—in the terminology of Ali G—'respek,' or reporters picking up on Islamophobia or anti-Semitism, the demand for *respect* is so all-pervasive that we even have a political party going by that name. After all, to be disrespectful of difference not only undermines the multicultural civilization to which we now belong but also reopens the door to the inequities of fascism that in the last century led to unprecedented barbarity. *Respect* is a word that patrols the frontiers between two states of being—savagery and civilization.

But it is also something else. The demand for *respect* has the capacity to close off discussion with a nonnegotiable demand: "Keep your hands off my beliefs." Such a *noli me tangere* is not only a defensive parry to offensiveness or criticism but also a powerful counterthrust. Such was the position my neighbor found himself in. But he was having none of it. For him the purpose of Holy Scripture was to promote positive behavior and human fellowship, and if this was what a particular initiative achieved then that was all that was important. I was reminded of Jesus' saying that the Sabbath was made for man, not the other way around (see Mark 2:27). The test for *respect* should be the quality of human interaction it fosters, not simply its justification of difference.

This wider perspective can easily be lost sight of, so much so that the passionate defense of difference has now become a challenge to social cohesion as the reification of different traditions replaces aspirations of global harmony with a new tribalism. Demanding *respect* for incompatible and even unacceptable practices is common; but whatever the cultural justification, are not child marriage and female circumcision to be regarded as abusive practices? In a highly interactive world the search for personal identity and cultural rootedness is understandable, but the regressive potentiality of religious difference has been growing in tandem with modern global culture for over a century, and now it acts as a powerful obstruction to social harmony.

During the nineteenth century whole blocks of humanity began to be consigned to particular ethnicities or races, and their beliefs to all-inclusive isms.[1] Whereas previously there had been fluidity and ambiguity, a sort of cultural transhumance, an imperial centralization demanded clear boundaries and ordered definitions of peoples, languages, and beliefs. Thus were created such new entities as Hinduism and Buddhaism; and since Sun Yat-sen felt that China needed a morally authoritative religion that could stand tall among other nations, Confucianism was concocted out of what had been merely collections of disparate precepts in an attempt to represent the religious "essence" of the Chinese people. Such "essences" were required to create "entities" with distinguishing structures. To this end, early in the twentieth century the Catholic hierarchy promulgated a code of canon law at about the same time American Baptists were defining the "fundamentals" of their beliefs so that people would be in no doubt about what they stood for. Similarly, in the 1930s Sikh scholars were defining the fundamental

1. Bayly, *Birth*, 325–63.

tenets of Sikhism in the modern world, just as had Islamic scholars of the immensely influential Deoband movement. This formalization of belief and practice was to reassure the faithful in the face of a multiform modernity, replacing whatever former fluidity of beliefs had obtained with unambiguous clarity. The world was defining itself by creating different neighborhoods—and thus opening itself to potentially disastrous consequences.

Reflecting on his experience of Nazism, Martin Niemöller offered a searing indictment of sectarian isolationism:

> First they came for the socialists, and I did not speak out—
> Because I was not a socialist.
> Then they came for the trade unionists, and I did not speak out—
> Because I was not a trade unionist.
> Then they came for the Jews, and I did not speak out—
> Because I was not a Jew.
> Then they came for me—and there was no one left to speak for me.[2]

Even those with whom we may feel we have little in common and with whose beliefs we do not agree nevertheless share with us something much more fundamental and important—humanity. This insight should be the lodestone of *respect,* a precarious modality that sounds laudable, but whose challenging demands can be extremely threatening to traditionalists.

Those who remember the genial cosmopolitanism of Rabbi Hugo Gryn will also perhaps remember what motivated his outlook. He had grown up in a small Czechoslovakian town where the Jewish community kept itself to itself and took little interest in its neighbors. This changed only when members of the community began to be rounded up and put on railway wagons, never to be seen again. With hindsight he recognized the potentially disastrous consequences of communities cocooned in social isolation, keeping to their own traditions regardless of their neighbors. His ecumenical outlook was born of the realization that we cannot afford to live in ignorance of our neighbor, for *respect* demands interaction and a shared sense of humanity.[3] Like many other religious leaders of the time, Pope

---

2. This rendering of Niemöller's famous words appears in the United States National Holocaust Memorial Museum. See the museum's *Holocaust Encyclopedia* website, listed in the bibliography, for more information about Niemöller's words.

3. This material comes from the TV documentary *Chasing Shadows,* directed by Naomi Gryn.

John XXIII also recognized that things would be different in a world that needed to practice openness and modernization (*aggiornamento*).

Thus, we enter our contemporary world, which is shaped by on the one hand globalization and increasing interconnectedness, but on the other by cultural entities defined in contradistinction to their neighbors by radicalized religion. A phrase that has begun to appear with ominous regularity is, "He seemed to be quite ordinary and then began to become more religious." Of the 2013 Boston Marathon bombers, Tamerlan and Dzhokhar Tsarnaev, friends said they seemed like ordinary Americans, "just like one of us"; similar things were said of the principal London July 7, 2005, bomber, Mohammed Sidique Khan, and of the 9/11 bomber Zacarias Moussaoui. His mother asked, "How could he be involved in such a thing? ... I could understand if he had grown up unhappy or poor. But they had everything."[4] In all of these cases something changed, and individuals began "to become religious," entering into the hermetically sealed world of religious traditionalism or fundamentalism that defines itself against everyone else, and that obliterates the ties of common humanity by sectarian rage. *Respect* disappears in such a poisonous atmosphere.[5]

One of the greatest contemporary cultural challenges is to reexamine those great systems of belief to which so many give uncritical allegiance and for which they demand unequivocal *respect,* for their polemicists are wont to arrogate to themselves not only proprietary claims of noble ideals and principles but also authority to enforce absolute demands that control the minutiae of people's lives. In like manner, Jesus was content to proclaim ethereal beatitudes while the Catholic hierarchy is more concerned to legislate about what goes on between the bedsheets; and the prophets of Israel preached a universal ethic of justice, whereas modern Israelis want fortified settlements on land stolen from their neighbors. And Mohammad may have been the poet of a sublime vision for humanity, but many contemporary mullahs demand blind submission to draconian and misogynistic laws. Though many may be reassured by totally prescribed ways of life, the greater need is to discriminate between what is culturally relative and what is essential to humanity.

It is the sort of realization that Saint Peter came to in the house of Cornelius when a dream revealed that the distinction between pure and impure foods—what is permitted (*halal*) and what is forbidden (*haram*)—is

4. Quoted in Solomon, "One Mother."

5. Wood, *Way.*

entirely without validity. Though he later seems to have reneged on this all-too-threatening bit of inspiration, it was a step towards a more inclusive vision of humanity renewed. When compared to such precepts as feeding the starving or doing good to one's enemy, the minutiae of dietary regulation become at best nugatory. Though hierarchies tend to see the touchstone of orthodoxy in such details of daily living—since they demand respectful conformity or when necessary provide the grounds for outraged sensibilities—in fact these petty regulations are more often covert expressions of control and intolerance. When civilization lacks enlightened scrutiny and discrimination, the world threatens to become a hostile battleground of rites and rituals, fear and ignorance.

This became apparent in the recent sacking of Timbuktu by Islamists.[6] What could be more bizarre than the wanton destruction of ancient Islamic texts in the library of this ancient seat of Islamic learning by Islamist religious zealots? For them any education, not just Western education, is forbidden—*boko haram*—which is also the local name of the Islamic fundamentalist movement. For such extremists all learning and all knowledge not circumscribed by a specific text, even all historical memory, must be obliterated. And this is why the Wahhabist government of Saudi Arabia has destroyed many of the ancient sites associated with the origins of Islam, for like the iconoclastic Calvinists of the sixteenth century it insists that nothing must be allowed to compromise the incontestable word, the *sola scriptura*, that they authoritatively proclaim. This "truth" alone deserves *respect*. When historian Tom Holland tried to delve into the historical background of the prophet Mohammed and the composition of the Qur'an, he was denounced for lack of respect and Western arrogance; but more than that, as others have done before him, he literally risked his life.[7]

It is difficult to see a way forward, and not only in countries of extreme intolerance like Saudi Arabia where even those who, like Raif Badawi, may want to reconsider the place of faith in the modern world are silenced. In Britain, when moderate Muslims like Manzoor Moghul of the Muslim Forum suggest that "The Muslim community in Britain is somewhat backward in its thinking . . . refusing to change its old habits," they are immediately shouted down as attacking "our religion."[8] Even modest proposals from scholarly voices, such as that of the jurist Dr. Usama Hasan suggesting

6. Jones, "Destruction."

7. This is my own summary of news. See also Sim, dir., *Islam*.

8. Quoted in Gosden, "David Cameron."

that the fasting laws of Ramadan should be amended to take into account the length of northern summertime, are denounced as subordinating God's will to the "desires" of human beings, even though seventh-century Arabs had no awareness of "lands of the midnight sun."[9] It is an argument that the traditionalists and extremists always win by claiming the more severe version is most "authentic." But in doing so, as Tehmina Kazi of British Muslims for Secular Democracy points out, they are "failing to see that one of the highest virtues is actually reason."[10] This is also precisely why this conflict, between reason or respect for other traditions, is now such a thorny problem for Islam: the intransigence of tradition makes no concessions to modernity or critical thinking, and then feels threatened by any who suggest it should. The result is an increasingly vicious circle of accusation and paranoia, for as Kazi rightly notes, "This is born of an insecurity."

Just as romantically inclined nationalists of the nineteenth century fought to resurrect putative histories with revolutionary zeal, so today religiously inspired *jihadists* fight to resurrect medieval mirages of theocracy and *caliphate*. The past is always potent. Strangely, one of the most contentious subjects is archaeology. Nowhere is this more true than in Israel, where no consensus can be reached between those who read the archaeological evidence through the prism of biblical belief and secularists, who accommodate the Bible to the evidence of archaeology. To the former group, King David founded Jerusalem, thereby giving it mythic, eschatological status; to the latter he was merely a hill-country bandit whose achievements were appropriated from the apostate king, Omri. In the eyes of many, mythical history legitimizes the modern state even as the demand for *respect* of belief clashes irreconcilably with *respect* for evidence.

This scenario encapsulates a larger conflict over the understanding of truth. Regardless of belief, reality also demands respect. When Galileo invited his inquisitors to look through his telescope they declined his devilish deception. "But they do move" he insisted of Jupiter's moons, demanding *respect* for the evidence—but to no avail. Today science presents overwhelming evidence that demands *respect* for many generally accepted facts that contradict religious tradition: that species are not created but evolve, that the world is not a mere six thousand years old, that contemporary humans are but one surviving subspecies of numerous previous human variants, that women are not defective males, that homosexuality is a natural

9. See Kazi, "Ramadan"; see also Hasan, "Fatwa."

10. Kazi, "Ramadan."

condition, and so on. Religious beliefs based on previous cultural understandings of reality now seen to be contrary to scientific evidence have no unequivocal claim to *respect*, even if they may be tolerated as interesting historical anomalies, and often controversies are really about the deeper epistemological basis of knowledge. As the Oxford church historian Diarmaid McCulloch has noted, "The disputes which currently wrack Western Christianity are superficially about sexuality, social conduct or leadership style: at root they are about what constitutes authority."[11] The contest for the soul of Christianity in the West relates to the deeper question of how Scripture, claiming divine authority, relates to such other sources of human understanding as observation, experience, and critical reflection.

In a recent controversy on the issue of what to tolerate in religion, the well-known atheist Sam Harris went still further by insisting that just as some religions are less credible than others, not all are mistaken to the same degree. So Mormonism is less credible than Christianity, for "It is mathematically true to say that whatever probability one assigns to Jesus returning to Earth to judge the living and the dead, one must assign a lesser probability to his doing so from Jackson County, Missouri."[12] Similarly, some deserve closer scrutiny because they pose greater threats. For example, the core of Jainism is nonviolent even if extreme in some of its practices, whereas Islam has "a dogmatic commitment to using violence to defend one's faith," and this incites extremists to acts of such appalling brutality as the murder of drummer Lee Rigby.[13] A belief that entails the brutal killing of innocent individuals, as for example the human sacrifice of the historical Aztecs or terrorist attacks by modern Islamists, cannot be tolerated in a modern society and certainly cannot claim *respect*.

In all walks of life, *respect* is earned by generosity of spirit and noble behavior. Religion, as the philosopher A. C. Grayling recently wrote, is "the belief system of our remote ancestors who knew little about the universe, and made up stories to explain themselves." These stories may be venerable and persuasive, they may contain profound insights, but they remain stories. The degree of *respect* one has for a belief is never without reservations; it cannot be absolute, but necessarily varies according to its credibility and the degree to which it promotes human welfare as we now understand it. For those who yearn for the certainty of a belief system, the security of an

11. MacCulloch, *All Things*, 319.

12. Harris, *End*; Taylor, "Atheist."

13 Quoted in Taylor, "Atheist."

impregnable -ism, modernity possess a formidable and threatening challenge, for the best we can do to achieve a common standard of humanity
is by consensual dialogue, reflection, and experimentation based on the
totality of contemporary understanding and experience.

A recently published bestselling work by Ayaan Hirsi Ali, *Heretic:
Why Islam Needs a Reformation Now,* articulates this challenge perfectly.
The template of Ali's presentation is a division of Muslims into three broad
categories, which she calls Meccan Muslims (the overwhelming majority
who practice their faith peaceably, as did Muhammad in his early days of
revelation at Mecca), Medina Muslims (who enforce their beliefs more
violently, as did Muhammad at Medina and in the later years of his life),
and the modern Reformers (a small number of marginal dissident voices—
"heretics"—arguing for change in response to the challenges of modernity).
Her thesis is that the Medina Muslims create the headlines to the exclusion,
but with the connivance, of the passive majority, and that if there is to be
change the West must start to give more support to the minority of oppressed voices calling for freedom from intimidation and recognition of
human rights.[14]

The solution, according to Ali, is that the monolithic world of Islam,
because it is immune to historical change and critical reflection, needs a Reformation like that which took place in Europe. Instead of Luther's Ninety-
Five Theses she proposes a more modest five: reassessing the semidivine
status of Muhammad and the Qur'an, challenging the cult of life after death,
easing the strictures of Sharia and the expectation of individuals to enforce
Islamic law, and abandoning the imperative to wage jihad.

But apart from the fact that no reform movement has ever succeeded
in the Islamic world, championing the precedent of the Reformation may
not be all it seems. Apart from the immediate consequence of the violent
fragmentation of Christendom, decades of unspeakable savagery were
resolved only by temporal powers that separated individual belief from
public policy based on rational principles and human rights—in short, by
enacting the leitmotiv of the Enlightenment. Accompanying this after the
time of Spinoza was the reformulation of our understanding of God, transforming monotheism to monism, and relegating beliefs to states of mind
rather than objective reality.

Rather than the intended "reform" of Christianity, the real outcome
of the Reformation is an outcome reflected in the radical theology of the

14. Ali, *Heretic,* 13–23.

last century such as that of the Sea of Faith network.[15] Such a theology recapitulates the inevitable and final expression of the Reformation: God and religion are seen as human creations in which wisdom is not supernaturally dispensed from on high but is inseparable from the poetic genius of humanity. It is this "radical" theology that is the real challenge to modern "radical" fundamentalisms, for it takes up the task of critical thinking and separating what are undeniably commendable ethical values and cultural traditions from their traditional, tribal, and theological underpinnings.

This is the sort of post-Christian thinking that has been so brilliantly charted by Don Cupitt in such works as *The Meaning of the West* and his recent *Ethics in the Last Days of Humanity*. In the former he presents Christianity as a utopian cultural movement, which, "emerging as and when it did, had in the short term to take the form of a religion, but which eventually burst out of its religious chrysalis and became the modern world."[16] Its essential spirit is humanitarian, an ethos that has recently emerged from a specifically Christian matrix and is now expressed in the modern humanitarianism of the welfare state. An organization such as Britain's National Health Service, while being inspired by Christian ideals, now expresses those ideals in a secular form far more effectively and inclusively than was possible in a religious context. Paradoxically, while the church-religion of Christianity is consumed by ever-increasing controversy, the spirit of the "Jesus of history"—the posttheistic Son of Man—has become ever more influential as the standard by which we judge all other beliefs.

And surprisingly it is this that Graeme Wood also found in his conversations with jihadists. As the supporters of ISIS look back to the idealized time of their forefathers they find, for example, that slave-owning and the use of slaves for sex was quite acceptable. Yet despite this, Wood found that his interviewees were often forcing themselves to believe in this monstrous aspect of life: "They are coming from cultures where the idea of human ownership of other human beings or sexual enslavement is sickening and there is a deeply instilled instinct of revulsion."[17] It is this "instilled" humanitarian instinct that they have to overcome in order to rationalize the often spectacular brutality of their cause.

In the modern world it is respect for the individual that, as Greenfield writes, "is the pre-eminent form of experience and expression in much

---

15. Greenfield, *Introduction*.

16. Cupitt, *Meaning*, viii.

17. Whitworth, "The Man."

Radical Theology."[18] This is the expression of religion as a social phenomenon in a time that Dietrich Bonhoeffer described as one when mankind is understood to have come of age and must cope without the security blanket of the old man in the sky. Instead, as Don Cupitt notes, the "word God does not designate a distinct metaphysical being; it is simply Love's name."[19] For others it is the symbol of the highest values we strive to live by.

Ultimately, as my Sikh neighbor said to me in our conversation, "If your religion doesn't help to make you into a better human being, it's a waste of time." This is an ongoing endeavor, a perpetually unfinished work that is by no means limited by the past. Rather, it opens out to a different future, for that is also essential for the renewal of religious belief if it is to become anything other than a fossilized relic. To be sure, this is a thoroughly pragmatic approach, but it mirrors the way that ancient wisdom emerged from the assortment of human experience—the very process that is anathema to religious zealots and acolytes of other worlds. In the end it is not religious belief but Life in all its forms that is alone worthy of *respect*. We respect life and this world because in the end that is all we have.

18. Greenfield, *Introduction*, 170.
19. Cupitt, "All."

II

Against the West
Crosscurrents in Hostility to the Idea of the West

The twenty-first century has thus far been characterized by increasingly violent forms of terrorism. The war on terror launched by the United States, the world's greatest military power, threatens to become a war without end. In the minds of many, this conflict epitomizes the polarity of two amorphous entities: the West and Islam. Unfortunately, that antithesis is as vague as it is misleading.

For one thing, neither is a true entity. The West is not a place but a metaphor for a certain (equally vague) way of life—putatively godless, materialistic, and to a considerable degree amoral. Against this secular entity is pitted a faith-based world, *dar ul-Islam*—"the domain of faith"—a land under Sharia, wholly based on religious observation. Of course, this latter exists more as an aspiration than a practice—or better, perhaps as a mirage that constantly beguiles religious zealots but is never quite achieved. Both polities exist only in the imagination.

Rage and resentment further obscure any attempt to define these worlds. For example, the Facebook page of Anis Amri, the Berlin Christmas Market murderer, expressed his indiscriminate hatred: "Slaughter the pigs." And rage against the West came to characterize the writings of the founding father of al-Qaeda, Sayyid Qutb. Fueled by an irrational attachment to antiquated religious texts, Qutb, like other Islamists, saw the fall of the Ottoman Empire as a humiliation for all Muslims that must be expunged by reclaiming the zeal of the seventh century together with its scimitar-edged certainties and purity. But an equally indiscriminate conviction inspires many Christian fundamentalists. In the name of Western values, George W. Bush, a self-declared born-again Christian, pursued his war on terror—a sweeping action initially termed a crusade until the diction was recognized to be too incendiary.[1] Still, it was fully supported by the powerful Christian fundamentalist lobby that has no such reservations, and that equally rages against the godless, materialistic, amoral society that characterizes the West.

Other Christian groups were not far behind. In fact, the situation could not have been expressed more plainly than by Cardinal Ratzinger, later Pope Benedict XVI, when as head of the Holy Office, he said that "the most urgent task facing Christians is that of regaining the capacity of nonconformity . . . to oppose many developments of the surrounding culture." In short, he called for confrontation within Western society. This theme of the church as a countercultural force was also dear to the heart of his predecessor, Pope John Paul II, who had so little time for the contemporary culture of Europe that he glibly dismissed the European Union as a fascistic organization that should be opposed.[2]

But the polarization thus becomes confused. What we find in both the West and Islam are common elements that make them appear to have common views about a common enemy—the liberal, secular, permissive lifestyle of the modern West. This situation was highlighted during the 1994 United Nations Conference on Population and Development held in Cairo when the Vatican and various Islamic factions found family planning, abortion, and women's rights equally anathema, and they secretly colluded to frustrate any resolutions on such matters.[3] Was this an example of Ratzinger's nonconformism at work? Later, after a visit to the Vatican in 1999, President Khatami of Iran commented that one outcome of his meeting with the pope, was the "hope for the final victory of monotheism and morality," as if the latter were somehow predicated on the former.[4]

---

1. For reflection on Bush's use of the term *crusade*, see Carroll, "Bush"; and Suskind, "Faith."

2. John Paul II, *Memory*.

3. See Martino, "Statement."

4. Quoted in Sengupta, "Iran President."

Reflecting on the situation, John Wilkins, then editor of the Catholic weekly *The Tablet* put the whole issue in a wider context: the conflict at Cairo was not simply over sexual ethics, he wrote, "It is over Western values, specifically the values of the European Enlightenment." He added that Cardinal Ratzinger was "explicit in his criticism of the Enlightenment"—or the "so-called" Enlightenment, to use Pope John Paul's withering dismissal of the great cultural metamorphosis that shaped the foundations of modern secular society.

If the Enlightenment was to be so problematic for the churches of the West, it is hardly surprising that it should be even more so for the Islamic world. For Muslims, such concepts of inherent human rights, freedom of thought, critical thinking, and a religiously neutral civil order did not arise within the matrix of their faith but had been thrust upon them by an oppressive imperialism. Democracy and all else that came with modernity represented a *kufir* (infidel) imposition.

Indeed, this is exactly what was said by the radical Wahhabi *ulema* of Saudi Arabia in echo of the eighteenth-century founder of the movement, Abd al-Wahhab.[5] Even if some things—such indispensable modern technological wonders as automobiles and computers—have since slipped through the net of prohibition, the fact remains that ever since the origins of the *Scienza Nuova* in the sixteenth century, such European imports as empiricism and rational thinking, new inventions and ideas, and unsettling investigations in physics and metaphysics have been inextricably linked in the Muslim mind.[6] So it remains. And the increasing flow of technological innovation results in an ever-rising tide of new things that in turn spread new thinking. Modern autocrats and theocracies must now fear those who have learned to tweet on mobile phones.

And any attempts to separate things from ideas and desire from denial on the basis of religious conviction necessarily lead to a schizoid state of constant instability—desiring the things the West has to offer but denying their intellectual provenance.[7] This is, of course, similar to the case of Christian fundamentalists, who might well accept DNA profiling in a court of law but deny the biological context of evolution and concomitant coherence of life. A more difficult impasse faces Islamic fundamentalists who

---

5. Allen, *God's Terrorists*, 42–68.

6. Appleyard, *Understanding*, 30.

7. Ali, *Heretic*, 16.

seek to establish a true Islamic identity and state of *dur al-Islam* but declare intellectual accommodation to be apostasy. In Saudi Arabia it is a crime.

It is interesting to note that *the West* is neither a term invented in or by the West nor one of self-description, but a coinage that originally reflected a perception of "otherness."[8] The non-West invented the West; oriental annals, particularly Chinese, contain the earliest mentions of the exotic lands to the West, across the far horizons of the setting sun. In the late fourth century a Syrian bishop, Severian, stated that the garden of Eden was placed in the East so that "just as the light of heaven moves towards the West, so the human race hastens towards death."[9] This view of non-Europeans was confirmed by the fact that the inhabitants of the West were white—in Asia, the traditional color of death. When conjoined with the spectacle of ruthless white conquistadores, it produced a fearful presentiment: the West is the place of death, to be feared and avoided.[10]

But the idea of the West remains amorphous. What it now stands for cannot be restricted to the belief in rational secularism and progress that characterized the Enlightenment, or to the utopian uniformity that its thinkers assumed to be the destiny of humankind. Equally important was the Romantic reaction in the eighteenth century, which developed a much more individualistic and pluralistic view of the world. Of this revolutionary change, Isaiah Berlin, the historian of ideas, notes that, "the history of ideas offers few examples of so dramatic a change of outlook as the birth of the new belief . . . in the value and importance of the singular and unique, of variety."[11]

The new humanitarian spirit of philanthropy that arose in the nineteenth century reflected the new priority of the humane over every other consideration.[12] Perhaps more than anything else it is this reverence for the human spirit that has come to typify the distinctive Western view of things. Its pluralistic view is perhaps best seen in the UNESCO program of preserving world cultural heritage sites. The dramatic destruction of the historic Buddhas of Bamyan by the Taliban in Afghanistan or of the palaces of Palmyra and Nimrud by ISIS typifies the contrary but much older and traditional view of the world that sees things entirely from the perspective

8. Bonnett, *Idea*, 5.

9. Quoted in Bonnett, *Idea*, 5.

10. Bonnett, *Idea*, 5.

11. Berlin, *Crooked,* 56.

12. Williams, *Keywords,* "Humanitarian."

of a single-minded and even blazing intolerance. And this is the perspective that the monotheistic faiths share, and which ironically makes them so intolerant not only of each other but of every "other." As Berlin correctly explained, "No doctrine that has at its heart a monistic conception of the true . . . can allow variety as an independent value to be pursued for its own sake."[13]

With individualism came an interest in individual histories and the distinguishing features of different historical epochs, characteristics we find in the stories of Sir Walter Scott. By coincidence this new romantic interest in the past developed at the same time as colonial expansion gathered momentum in the countries of the Orient. Imperial collectors, like the curators and exhibitors at the Great Exhibition, gloried in portraying the diversity of human societies; and this fascination with the cultural differences uncovered by imperialism prompted romantic antiquarians to extend their explorations yet further. In India, for example, they rediscovered the forgotten world of Buddhist civilization.[14]

The vast cornucopia of coexisting cultures and spiritualities, together with a new historical perspective that framed the genesis of each, brought with it an implicit challenge to the monistic mentality of conformity to a single vision. In the late eighteenth century imperial administrators in India—the so-called White Moguls—began to accommodate their lifestyles to the native culture. Until, that is, a new breed of evangelical Christian missionaries appeared, and sought to impose a rigid idealism and uniformity that ran counter to the native beliefs and customs. In this way they demonstrated the more traditional approach of Western monotheists to the so-called devil worshipers of the East.

But the result was not quite according to plan. As historian C. A. Bayly comments in *The Birth of the Modern World*, "Perhaps the most important point was that Asian religions rapidly took up Christian missionaries' methods of preaching and evangelization."[15] With native religious leaders learning to speak authoritatively for cohesive communities, religions like Islam began taking on more organized institutional forms, following the lead of the imperial powers' preference for dealing with organized bodies. And thus the lines of demarcation between previously amorphous and

13 Berlin, *Crooked*, 59–60.

14. Allen, *Buddha*.

15. Bayly, *Birth*, 343–51.

blurred religious entities became ever more starkly defined, often delineated as an ism.

This may have pleased imperial bureaucrats, but its ominous potential appeared when the organization of clandestine resistance to the West began to accelerate. Islamic leaders wanted a cohesive pan-Islamism with which to oppose imperialism. In his study of the roots of the modern jihad, Charles Allen charts how extremist Muslim groups in the nineteenth century anticipated in almost every detail the present activities of al-Qaeda.[16] Concerning the appearance of a new, radicalized Islam he writes, "The end result was a seismic shift in the Sunni Islam of South Asia, which became increasingly conservative and introverted, less tolerant and far more inclined to look for political leadership to the madrassah (religious colleges)."[17]

We are now living with the consequences of that shift. In particular one may note the Deoband Madrassah, which was founded in the small village of Deoband to the north of Delhi in 1857 by Muhammad Qasim and Rashid Ahmed, two failed jihadists of the Indian Mutiny who sought to continue the struggle by other means. Its explicit purpose was to rid India of British and Western values. Qasim had firsthand experience of the British-backed college system and determined to use his knowledge and skills for the benefit of Islam by creating an educational system that would teach and enable ordinary people to resist Western values. The intention was not unlike that of the Jesuits of the Catholic Counter-Reformation in creating an educational system that could provide, as Allen writes, "a distinctive, politicized leadership. . .who could compete to advantage against all others, [and] outshine critics in public debate."[18] The consequence, as Allen notes, was "a closed, introverted, tightly-knit society of young males approaching or in the throes of puberty, taught to regard their sexuality as innately sinful and women as weak creatures incapable of self-control and easily tempted, therefore best kept in subjection."[19]

Now a century later this movement is one of the dominant forces in the Muslim world and shows its powerful influence in mosques throughout the United Kingdom.[20] Since its UK center is at Dewsbury, it is perhaps no coincidence that it was from here that the July 7, 2005, bombers of the

16. Allen, *God's Terrorists,*185–211.

17 Allen, *God's Terrorists,* 210–11.

18. Allen, *God's Terrorists,* 210.

19. Allen, *God's Terrorists,* 209.

20. *Daily Mail,* "Report."

London Underground came, and whence subsequently a number of jihadists and families have suddenly disappeared to support ISIS in Syria. This is in perfect accord with the Deobandi philosophy that a Muslim's first duty is to his religion; his only community is the world community of Islam, and his sworn duty is to defend Sunni Islam. In 1993 an associate of Osama bin Laden, Masood Azhar, toured Britain, visiting Deobandi mosques, preaching "the elimination of the oppressive and infidel system by the blessings of jihad" and explaining how a significant proportion of the Qur'an was "devoted to murders for the sake of Allah." His view of Britain was that any dog "that spent some time in a decent place" would be "embarrassed by the [UK's] debasement of humanity." Azhar's sermons were warmly received by packed congregations, embraced by the leadership, and have now been identified as the root cause of a long list of terrorists' atrocities.[21]

Given this background it seems astonishing that political leaders should be surprised by the way radicalization takes place and should profess to be at a loss to understand how it happens. They prefer to see it as some mental aberration or the consequence of political or social stress rather than the very obvious outcome of a well-embedded and distinctive community way of life from which extremism quite predictably arises. Needless to say, these same communities deny all knowledge of and commitment to extremism. But then, as Azhar said, "if seeking glory for the name of Allah is fundamentalism and terrorism, then we were fundamentalists and terrorists yesterday, we are fundamentalists and terrorists today and will be, god willing, tomorrow."[22] In contrast to befuddled politicians seeking to placate moderate Muslims, Muhammed Qasim was clearly not so much a failed jihadist as a very perceptive long-term strategic thinker whose initiative has succeeded beyond his wildest dreams.

Throughout the nineteenth century Muslims under the European imperial yoke not only came increasingly to consider it a religious duty to fight against Western influences, but also began to sense a need to return to spiritual roots, the *salafi*—"following of the forefathers." This was accompanied by a nostalgia for the glories of the past—of the Moguls, the caliphate, and particularly the kingdom of Andalusia—for the time when Islam overawed Europe. All these formed part of what Allen calls a "great leap backwards" when Muslims turned their backs on progress in favor of

21. Norfolk, "Muslim Leaders."
22. Norfolk, "Muslim Leaders."

the past.[23] Such were the eulogies of the influential poet Mohammad Iqbal, whose work gained political expression in parties like the *Jamaat-I-Islam* (Party of Islam) and ultimately culminated in the creation of Pakistan. This would be, in Jinnah's thinking, a "land of the pure," the necessary *dar ul-Islam* from which to confront the West. The Taliban are simply the "scholars" of this new orthodoxy, and the central aims of ISIS are not only to restore the caliphate but, according to their newssheet *Dabiq*, are "to bring division to the world and destroy the grey zone everywhere," thus completing the demarcations of earlier imperial bureaucrats.[24]

As if anticipating what would happen in the Islamic world, the nineteenth-century Gothic revival offered the West its own escape into the past. Those disturbed by the new age of squalid industrialization felt a similar nostalgic yearning for the kinder lifestyle of an imagined past, a mythical middle age that once flourished between ancient classical and modern times. The term *Gothic*, coined specially for the occasion, became the powerful expression of this nostalgic counterflow. The numerous architectural creations (mostly churches and monasteries) of Augustine and Edmund Pugin epitomize the attempt to re-create a mythical age of triumphant Christianity that was in fact no more than a Disneyfication of the past, a religious fantasy that offered an escape—Marx called it an "opiate"—from the reality of a heartless world.

In this same vein a resurgent ultramontane Catholicism sought to restore the glory of the church. One dearly held objective was the conversion of England to the true faith of old, perhaps even to fly the papal flag above Downing Street (not unlike the future many Islamists now imagine for their own mercerized banners!). But that too was a form of fundamentalism that spurned the tepid prevarications of Anglicanism. To the celebrated Oxford convert John Henry Newman conversion offered a chance to be reassured by timeless certainties; to others, like Lawrence of Arabia, the empire offered a means of escape from the tedious drudgery of modernity. As David Cannadine noted in his illuminating study *Ornamentalism*, the empire was promoted by romantics "seeking to escape from the travails of industrialization, democracy and the big cities." Sir Edwin Lutyens aptly expressed it when he said that going to India made him feel very "pre-Tory Feudal."[25] Lawrence fully supported what he found in the dashing exoti-

---

23. Allen, *God's Terrorists*, 205.

24. *Dabiq*, "Extinction."

25. Cannadine, *Ornamentalism*, 131.

cism of the Wahhabite House of Saud and helped to secure its ascendancy in the twentieth century.

Indeed, throughout this period the puritanical Wahhabis had set about consolidating "the reign of God" in a manner remarkably similar to the way in which the Calvinist fundamentalism of *sola Dei, sola scriptura* had inspired Christian evangelicals in post-Reformation Europe. In July 2014 Abu Bakr al-Baghdadi, the leader of ISIS, declared himself leader of a new caliphate, and the proclamation sent shock waves around the Islamic world. But the photo that in many papers accompanied the news, one of al-Baghdadi preaching jihad in the Grand Mosque of Mosul (his only public appearance) was even more interesting; for apart from the microphone, it resembled in eerie detail pictures of John Calvin preaching in his Geneva pulpit. And the similarity was not only visual; each preached a return to the purity of his revered scriptural text uncorrupted by tradition and historical accommodation, and each drew a stream of ideologically motivated followers. When one reads a modern ecclesiastical historian writing on John Calvin's achievement in repudiating the traditional leadership of such a major city as Geneva—"and in the confused aftermath . . . [of] a religious Reformation, violently destroying much of the past in the process"[26]—it is difficult not to think of what was happening in Mosul.

An interesting modern development of this theme is that a number of writers have expressed Islam's need for reformation, most notably Ayaan Hirsi Ali, the prominent and provocative Somalian refugee-cum-political activist.[27] It is with regard to this process that Islam has such a problem. As the case of Raif Badawi in Saudi Arabia (who was sentenced to one thousand lashes for promoting a website discussion) so clearly indicates, even those who might wish to reconsider the place of faith and fear in the modern world are silenced. Moderate Muslim voices are immediately shouted down, as was Manzoor Moghul of the Muslim Forum (of Great Britain) for suggesting that "The Muslim community in Britain is somewhat backward in its thinking. . . refusing to change its old habits." One must not attack "our religion."[28] Even modest proposals from such scholarly voices as that of the jurist Dr. Usama Hasan, who suggested that the fasting laws of Ramadan should be amended to take into account the length of northern summertime, are denounced as subordinating God's will to the "desires" of

26. MacCulloch, *All Things,* 59.

27. Ali, *Heretic.*

28. Gosden, "David Cameron."

human beings.[29] Of course, seventh-century Arabs had no awareness of the phenomenon of the "land of the midnight sun," but the traditionalists and extremists always win such arguments by claiming the more severe version is most "authentic." Unfortunately, as Tehmina Kazi of British Muslims for Secular Democracy points out, by doing so they are "failing to see that one of the highest virtues is actually reason."[30]

This sentiment points in a slightly different direction than Ali's thesis; rather than reformation, it proposes that the primary need is space for the ongoing process of cultural osmosis and rational discourse through which different traditions can find accommodation. Here the precedent of the Reformation may not be too helpful, for that confrontational divide merely led to the violent fragmentation of Christendom and decades of unspeakable savagery. It is within the crosscurrents of a much broader cultural process of political change and religious evolution, one stretching back millennia, that we should locate present religious polarizations. We tend to forget that what we call the Judeo-Christian tradition—one of whose branches is Islam—comprises a vast evolutionary development that is still ongoing.[31] The Bible itself is witness to the process. This vast assembly of texts still bears testimony to the way a tribal, henotheistic religion evolved into a magisterial monotheism and ultimately to an almost worldly secularism. It must be clear to any but the most superficial reader that the sapiental skepticism of Qoheleth bears little resemblance to the emphatic certainties of Pentateuch.

This evolutionary pattern of belief is mimetic of the changes in institutional religion. After its encounter with Zorastrianism, postexilic Judaism emerged from Israelite religion, and Christianity emerged from Pharisaic Judaism, Mohammad picked up echoes of this monotheistic tradition in creating Islam, and finally Christendom provided the context for the emergence of the secular humanism of the Renaissance, from which emerged both the Reformation and Enlightenment. As a consequence of this and the insights of Spinoza came the reformulation of our understanding of God, transforming monotheism to monism and relegating beliefs to states of mind rather than objective reality. And this is the real challenge to Islamic reform: the need to separate undeniably commendable ethical values from their archaic theological underpinnings. This is the sort of post-Christian thinking espoused by the Sea of Faith network and represents the real

---

29. Kazi, "Ramadan"; see also Hasan, "Fatwa."

30. Kazi, "Ramadan."

31. Geering, *Christianity*.

consequence of the Reformation. God and religion are now to be seen as human creations in which wisdom is not supernaturally dispensed from on high but is inseparable from the poetic genius of humanity.

To this vast cultural flow over millennia the Islamic world made crucial contributions between the eighth and twelfth centuries, after which it lapsed into a reactionary traditionalism hostile to rational exploration and critical thinking. Therefore, we should look for inspiration not so much to the Reformation as to the Enlightenment, which resolved religious conflict by enabling temporal powers to separate individual belief from public policy by employing criteria based on rational principles and human rights—the leitmotif of the Enlightenment. This has left us with a fundamental dilemma facing all religious traditions over what constitutes authority. In his conclusion to a fine study of Richard Hooker and the Anglican tradition the ecclesiastical historian Diarmaid MacCulloch articulates this dilemma with prefect precision: "The contest for the soul; of the church in the West rages around the question of how a scripture claiming divine revelation relates to those other perennial sources of human revelation, personal and collective consciousness and memory; whether, indeed, there can be any relationship between the two."[32]

But perhaps the decisive innovation of the Enlightenment was insistence on the simple recognition of facts, or what we now call data. When Galileo tried to persuade his inquisitors to look through his telescope at the moons of Jupiter—something they refused to do on the grounds of diabolical deception—he was merely seeking to challenge authority with fact. Looking through what is often regarded as perhaps the most monumental scientific work of all time, Newton's *Principia Mathematica*, one is struck but the vast collection of observational detail in factual tables. The same is true of the records of Lavoisier's experiments in chemistry and Dalton's daily notes on meteorology. It would be the factual observation of nature—the hallmark of the European *scienza nuova*—that would gather increasing momentum after the time of Galileo. It would lead so often to counterintuitive theories that pitted the true understanding of reality against common sense and common beliefs.

Surprising as it may seem to us now, facts were "invented" only in the seventeenth century when this new word came into circulation as a way of verifying experience through observation. It was in this century that a whole array of fact-based sciences came into being: neurology, chemistry, optics,

32. MacCulloch, *All Things*, 319.

geology, and so forth. Strictly speaking facts (from *factum*—"something made") arise from or are constructed out of data (*datum*—"things or that which is given"), another word that appeared in the seventeenth century. This empirical tradition has made possible the dazzling array of techno-logical artefacts that has now captivated the entire population of the planet regardless of one's spiritual beliefs. Until this point it was "truth" that mat-tered, determined by authority and ultimately confirmed by an appeal to God. Now we construct our own truth in virtual worlds. But by buying in to the technology we also subscribe, whether knowingly or otherwise, to the implicit epistemology. It is this that many still find threatening, and that is increasingly challenged by the arbitrary affirmations of belief.

The insistence on seeing the world empirically gave rise to another important facet of the Enlightenment, historical consciousness. Prompted by the seminal works of Giambattista Vico, people no longer saw the past as normative, as an expression of reality to be accepted passively. In what Vico saw as a "New Science," history becomes a collective social experience unfolding in time through perpetual creative activity, endlessly probing and questioning.[33] With a willingness to cast aside the past in the pursuit of innovation, the West now stood in contradistinction to Europe's preced-ing civilization, Christendom. The growth of an empirically based *scienza nuova* unleashed a technological whirlwind, and from it emerged a new creation—a secularized and industrialized civilization. This post-Christian West, shaped by its scientific, secular, and liberal outlook, has now become a distinct civilization even though it is rooted in its Christian origins.[34]

Christian fundamentalism has remained as iconoclastic of "supersti-tious" historical pieties as it has been dismissive of the new reality of the biblical history revealed by modern archaeology, which often challenged the narrative of the Word of God.[35] Islam has been equally insistent that any historical context presents a potential threat to the sovereignty of the Qur'an, and by extension to the authority of the mullahs who proclaim it. In areas controlled by ISIS, as elsewhere in Muslim lands, history must be not only suppressed but obliterated, lest any historical associations with the Prophet compromise or qualify the sovereignty of the textual word; and this policy continues under the current Wahhabite Saudi government. For example, the site of the house where Mohamed's first wife lived in Mecca

33. Berlin, *Vico*, 25.

34. See Cupitt, *Meaning.*

35. See Finkelstein and Mazar, *Quest.*

has now been turned into public toilets.[36] If the "revealed" past does not quite coincide with the real past, then in the interests of established beliefs it is better to destroy the evidence—if necessary by explosives, as happened with the Mosque of Jonah in Mosul.[37]

Many who adhere to the Christian and Islamic traditions continue to deny the transformation of understanding that has taken place over the centuries and thus has formed the basis of what is commonly called the progressive or liberal view of the world. One does not need to look as far away as the *madrasahs* of the Middle East to encounter the contempt for such thinking. It is notable in members of the U.S. Republican Party and especially those of the "alt-right." Many who have an almost pathological hatred of "liberalism" and the empirical/evolutionary view of the world find no difficulty in espousing fervent evangelical Christian beliefs. For Tea Party activists, the word *liberal* is a pejorative term. In this contempt they show a remarkable similarity to the lunatic fringe of Islam, whom they despise, yet with whom they share a deep hostility to Western values. Both groups view Liberalism—that cult of open-mindedness, individuality, freedom, and generosity that emerged in the early nineteenth century and became a defining characteristic of the new industrial bourgeoisie—as a weak and sentimental construct that lacks intellectual coherence. Both have contempt for this defining feature of the modern West.

We can now begin to see the true lines that delineate the West from its Muslim and Christian antagonists. The two mentalities are polar opposites. For the religious fundamentalist freedom lies in submission to the past—in one case, *sola scriptura*, in the other, *aslama*, Islam; for both renewal is simply a return to the past, to the time of the founders, or it is nothing. As William Palgrave, the first Western visitor to Riyadh observed, the prevailing Wahhabism was "incapable of true internal progress . . . and in the highest degree intolerant and aggressive, it can neither benefit itself nor better others."[38]

Not that any of this matters to zealots of either faith, for both belief systems were born of an apocalyptic mentality, in which the end is always imminent. To the innumerable millenarian movements of Europe—including the Crusades—the Final Coming is always at hand, and a better world always beckons in the beyond. Similarly, each of the innumerable uprisings

36. Power, "Saudi Arabia."
37. Davies, "Shocking."
38. Allen, *God's Terrorists*, 234–37.

of various mahdis over the centuries announced the final destruction of the infidels and a new messianic age. And even as "born-again" Christians await the rapture (which, it is believed, will sweep the faithful up to heaven), the Islamist zealot-cum-terrorist proactively poses with explosive vest on the threshold of paradise. Each now confronts the other at the gates of Armageddon, and temporal inconvenience is irrelevant .The similarities are brought into sharp relief in the life of Anders Breivik and the thought processes that led to his killing spree in Norway. It instructive how confusing the news was initially: that events had all the hallmarks of jihadists (and were actually claimed by such) but then turned out to be the work of a man who described himself as a Christian fundamentalist. In his fifteen-hundred–page manifesto one finds a crazy-quilt range of ideas—gender-segregated schooling, restrictions on abortion and divorce, criminalization of homosexuality, limits on freedom of speech, censorship of the media . . .[39] And while all of them have a long Christian pedigree, they could also characterize an Islamic theocracy. Though some dismissed Breivik as insane, the same could be and was said about Bush's crusade or war on terror. In fact, what all these views have in common is opposition to what has become the Western way of life.

The struggle for hearts and minds goes on. What is clear is that ordinary men and women across the great cultural divides share common aspirations characterized by what countless migrants who now seeking to enter Europe desire: a better way of life. That way of life is called Western. As for its future, the West urgently needs to address many negative consequences of its own lifestyle, for it has created a scenario that is becoming increasingly apocalyptic. And yet solutions that suit everyone's interests may be possible through cooperation. What is equally clear from any reading of history is that there are no predetermined outcomes. The polarizing elements are minorities whose constricted thinking is a dangerous caricature of a cultural diversity that has evolved during a long clash of civilizations. What we urgently need to address is the festering hostility that unites *both* Christian and Islamic fundamentalists against the West.

---

39. See Wikipedia, s.v. "Anders Behring Breivik," https://en.wikipedia.org/wiki/Anders_Behring_Breivik/.

12

The New Crusaders
New Wars, New Heresies—Old Mentality

Those who remember the late 1980s after the collapse of the Soviet Union will recall that a remarkable sense of optimism seemed to suffuse the landscape of global affairs. Like a sunburst penetrating the parting storm clouds came the hope of a better future: the "evil empire" was no more, ideological polarizations had collapsed as surely as the Berlin Wall, and everybody could now work together for a better future. The expectant mood was captured by the appearance in 1992 of Francis Fukuyama's book *The End of History and the Last Man*. If somewhat hubristic, its claim that we had reached an "end point of mankind's ideological evolution" seemed both apposite and persuasive to many.[1]

How wrong they were! Before the brouhaha over this book had died down, a more somber sounding title appeared on the bookshelves: Samuel Huntington's *The Clash of Civilizations and the Remaking of the World Order*.[2] According to its stark message, the storm clouds were regathering without a break on the horizon; ideological distinctions between people may have disappeared, but insuperable cultural differences have replaced them, and the future will be dominated by these powerful entities grinding against each other like vast tectonic plates each intent on the subduction of

---

1. Quoted in Fukuyama, *End* (2006), xi.
2. Huntington, *Clash*.

the other. Once again, many demurred. Things didn't have to be like that; no Manichaean inevitability certified the need for conflict.

Or did it? One fly in the ointment of optimism was the massive arms industry that had built up during the Cold War. This multibillion-dollar colossus dominated the economy of the world's remaining superpower (the USA) just as it had dominated the world. A major employer and promoter of scientific research, not to mention a source of great national pride, there was no way this juggernaut was simply going to grind to a halt, declare "Job done," close shop, and let everyone go home. No, an "enemy" was needed— some clear and present danger to galvanize and justify business as usual. And it would not be long before one presented itself, on 9/11.

Before the dust of the Twin Towers had settled and President George W. Bush had managed to get his tongue around "al-Qaeda," he declared there would be a "crusade" against those responsible. The choice of that word created such shock waves as it reverberated around the media studios of the world that it was quickly withdrawn and never used again. But this indiscrete Bushism—or was it a Freudian slip?—made crystal clear what was intended and what was going to happen. The rephrased catchphrase "war on terror" was less provocative, but everyone got the message: an openended, perhaps unlimited exercise of military might would be necessary.

The rest is history—history as deja vu! Soon Prime Minister Tony Blair was wading in. In his keynote Sedgefield constituency speech of 2004, he outlined his global vision for a new type of war.[3] Gone are the restraints of the long-standing Westphalian order of national boundaries that had created a semblance of order after the cataclysmic wars of seventeenth-century Europe; gone are the restrictions of international law in cases when unilateral humanitarian intervention might seem necessary; gone is the Cold War precautionary restraint in favoring self-defense over preemptive strikes. In comes the war of right against wrong, good against evil, civilization against barbarism, belief over ignorance. Suddenly in vogue was the politics of the medieval ballade *The Song of Roland*: "we were right and they were wrong"—and Americans loved it. In the end it all came down to belief, as Bush and Blair acted on faith and did not hesitate to say so. Like true medieval Crusaders, they *believed* above all else that they were right.

What was not noted at the time was an ominous coincidence: 2004 was the eight-hundredth anniversary of the Fourth Crusade. Lest this seem an arcane datum, let us recall its significance. The "collateral damage"

3. Blair, Speech.

resulting from this holy war devastated Byzantium, which was perhaps the greatest beacon of Christian civilization that has ever existed. It forever associated the word *Frank* (or *Westerner*) with *barbarism*—and rendered the two terms synonymous among both the Christian and Muslim nations of the East. And like a virus the memory of this terrible event has lingered on and metastasized across the centuries. Not only did it critically weaken Byzantine civilization, but as recent studies have reminded us its greater impact was to redirect history in unexpected ways. Whatever the initial intentions of the crusaders, "policy decisions, each with unforeseen outcomes," arose from a "mixture of idealism, pragmatism, confusion and opportunism."[4] This may be an apposite summary of the recent debacle that has similarly embroiled the region in unexpected ways.

Even more important, perhaps, is the revelation of a mentality that has become the default position of European or Western thinking. Even if its origins have been forgotten, the Fourth Crusade was an affirmation of Christendom that provided both an outlet for ideological zeal and a useful application of surplus military potency—particularly among the feuding feudal nobility. Though the term *crusade* was not coined until their significance had begun to decline in the fourteenth century, the Crusades were never just military campaigns against a distant enemy; they were the affirmation of an apocalyptic mentality that saw the world in terms of imminent danger of collapse and terminal destruction.[5] And equating the enemy with the forces of barbarism required the affirmation of a society that saw itself as the special bearer of Christian providence whose duty was to convert the contemptible heathen.

This first became manifest in the Carolingian Empire and the subsequent Holy Roman Empire, which came to define our understanding of Christendom. As the great medievalist Friedrich Heer made clear, "The Carolingian gospel was a lordly doctrine and a doctrine of lordship . . . It speaks not of the suffering Christ, the 'poor' Christ, the Christ of the 'destitute' but of the God-Christ, the King of noble lineage."[6] Just as the Eastern emperors saw themselves after Constantine as "external" bishops responsible for the "orthodox" imperial church, so we see Charlemagne at the Council of Frankfurt in 793 acting with a similar understanding. It is a view, as Heer, notes, "which has had tragic, if not lethal, consequences for

4. Le Goff, *Birth*, 93.

5. Armstrong, *Holy*, 1–53 (first three chapters).

6. Heer, *Holy*, 17.

Europe."[7] The belief that values and "truth" could and should be imposed by violence was as little questioned as the current view that cruise missiles can be used to impose, or at least clear the way for, democracy.

This understanding shaped Europe's history both in the suppression of dissent (all too easily labeled "heresy") and the expansion of its borders. An example is the Great Northern Crusade, which spanned most of the medieval period. Under the ruthless leadership of the warrior monks of the Order of Saint Mary (also known as the Teutonic Knights), all of the Baltic lands were gradually reclaimed for Christendom. In fact the operation was little less than a merciless land grab that enabled colonization by the great Benedictine and Cistercian monasteries. It was much like the actions of today's multinational consortia, though perhaps the nearest contemporary equivalent is Israel's expropriation of the West Bank. The twelfth-century chronicler Saxo Grammaticus writes of the iconic Bishop Absalon of Roskilde, "he deemed it vain to foster religion inwardly, if he let it founder outwardly, and he acted the pirate as much as the prelate, for it is no less religious to repulse the enemies of the public faith than to uphold its ceremonies."[8] Here in contrast to the sublime idealism of Jesus's Beatitudes we have such a grotesque distortion of "Christendom" that one can hardly be surprised at the groundswell of "heresy" that dissented from this view.

The outcome of this crusading mentality was the expansion of Christendom in a way that was to have continuing repercussions. Again, the Prussian state exemplifies this malign inheritance in its cherished values of religious fervor; robust masculinity expressed through duty, order, and hard work; and unfailing vigilance in its defense of the fragile frontiers that separated *Kultur* from barbarism. With the Prussianization of Germany under Bismarck's chancellorship, this crusader mentality took on the added dimension of an aggressive nationalism, culminating in what would be a final crusade. It is worth recalling that Hitler's Operation Barbarossa, named after the great German crusading emperor, was intended to crush once and for all "the threat from the East" of barbarism/Bolshevism. Under the black cross of the Teutonic Knights, with the motto "Gott mit uns" (God with us) on their belt buckles, these latter-day brothers of the sword adopted not only the crusader modus operandi that spanned the centuries, but also the special kind of viral thinking that shows utter contempt for everyone and anything different. It was completely in character that during the invasion

7. Heer, *Holy*, 17.
8. Christiansen, *Northern*, 61.

of Poland, the stereotypical junker Claus von Stauffenberg (later to lose faith in Hitler and attempt his assassination) portrayed the enemy as "this unbelievable rabble . . . which is surely comfortable under the knout."[9] No wonder Churchill wanted a "clean sweep" that would forever remove the memory of Prussia from the face of the earth.

It is a tragic irony that what was portrayed as a crusade to defend civilization led to the destruction of everything civilization stood for, and its incongruous apex was marked by one of the pivotal battles of this great war/crusade—the siege of the ancient monastery of Monte Cassino. Not only had this place been the cradle of Western monasticism, but its myriad European offspring had been the key agents in shaping Western civilization. That the monastery was utterly destroyed in this so-called "war for civilization" is surely symbolic of the futility and self-destructiveness of the mentality and values that drove it. The war of *Kultur* against Western civilization no doubt discredited the whole concept of the crusade.

Or perhaps not! The war on terror now provides a new incubator for this particular virulent way of thinking. Just as the Crusades were, so the war on terror is underpinned by an ill-defined fear of heretical enemies who, like terrorists, never clearly reveal themselves. In medieval times, heretics were feared because they were deemed to be part of a clandestine league seeking to contaminate and destroy the "good society" of Christendom. Such fear was well expressed by the thirteenth-century bishop William of Auvergne when he wrote—referring to the gospel parable of the wheat and tares—that "we have the certainty that these tares turn the wheat into tares; for it is incredible with what ease they subvert, by their cunning, the simple and the unlearned." (It was this parable, related in the Gospel of Mark 4:1–9, that ends with the gathering of the tares for burning that provided the justification of sorts for burning heretics, though it was the third-century Roman emperor Diocletian who first set the precedent by ordering burning for the new synthesis of monotheistic belief known as Manicheism.[10]) "Heresy" then reflects not something clearly defined in itself, but the projection by the powerful of their fear of those enemies who would subvert that power.[11]

The "enemy," whether Muslims, Jews, heretics, lepers, homosexuals, was seen as a front for a putative demonic agency of unsleeping malice

---

9. Egremont, *Forgotten*, 193.

10. MacCulloch, *All Things*, 80.

11. Rounding, *Burning*.

that has continued to haunt the European imagination ever since. In her seminal study of the Cathars of Languedoc, '*Inventer l'heresie*,' Monique Zerner showed how the bogeyman of Catharism, far from being an inevitable threat, was a construct of the minds of the hunters and inquisitors.[12] The clue to this mentality lies in the double meaning of the word *inventer* meaning both "to invent" and "to discover": what Crusaders and heresy hunters discover is what they need to invent! The witch hunt will always find its "witches"—Cathars, Manachees, Communists, Islamists; as with McCarthyism, the net will always be sufficiently wide and arbitrary to catch some unsuspecting victim. Beliefs, not objective criteria, define the enemy; the medieval Manachee was almost entirely a fabrication of the inquisitorial imagination.

Taking up the revisionist insight of Zerner, the historian R. I. Moore has recently reevaluated a lifetime's academic study of the Middle Ages in *The War on Heresy*. His thesis is that the violent, extreme, and massive campaigns against "heresy" that began abruptly in the eleventh century were the reflection a new mentality that came to define medieval Christendom. This arose through the innovative ecclesiastical reforms of the Gregorian era, the overall thrust of which was to emphasize the difference between clergy and laypeople and to centralize ecclesiastical power and clearly identify religious properties in order to protect the church's material wealth.

Only after the Third Lateran Council of 1184—which lumped together disparate groups opposed to these reforms as "heretics" and inaugurated the Inquisition to pursue them—did mass burnings start in previously undisturbed cities such as Verona.

Reflecting on this same period before the Second World War the distinguished Oxford historian H. A. L. Fisher wrote of Pope Gregory VII, "To this stern and implacable idealist we may principally ascribe the spread through Europe of a theocratic philosophy as menacing to the nascent state life of the eleventh century as in our own times is the communism of Lenin."[13] Had he been writing today he would surely have mentioned the self-proclaimed Islamist caliphate as a more apt parallel, for it is the theocratic conviction of divine inevitability that underlay the Investiture Controversy that tore apart medieval kingdoms which also motivates the contemporary jihadist assault on the democratic states of the West. But it should also be remembered that the church's assault that led to Crusades

12. Moore, *War*, 289.

13. Fisher, *History*, 199.

on its own members was every bit as ruthless as the current assault by so-called Monotheistic Brigades (affiliates of ISIS) on the ordinary Muslim citizens of the Middle East. The fact that the events of the twelfth century were unprecedented in the previous thousand years of Christianity should alert us to the fact that something new was at play. In a similar way the sudden appearance of the suicide bomber in our own time after one and half thousand years of Islamic history indicates more than a reaffirmation of traditional belief. Though in both cases the overt religious context seems the primary factor, it disguises deeper social changes that led to hitherto unprecedented stresses. In the eleventh century this is clearly reflected in the fact that weavers became closely associated with heresy just as new trades and towns were beginning to flourish again after the Dark Ages—a phenomenon particularly noteworthy in the lower Rhineland, an area with extensive international links. The invention of the new, larger looms required workshops and thus enabled groups of workers to discuss such issues of concern as the disparity of wealth and clerical simony, issues fed the desire for social reform and promotion of an idealized view of the apostolic life described in the Acts of the Apostles (Acts 2:44–45) when "all things were held in common." Among the first burnings for heresy were those in Arras (the center of the cloth industry) in 1025 but the ideas rapidly gathered momentum and spread to the South of France.

In our own time the pressures of globalization threaten traditional ways of life, creating vast disparities of wealth to which the ideal of the Islamic caliphate and universal brotherhood offers an attractive and potent alternative. In both cases "heresy" and "terror" are not alien imports from elsewhere but the expression of an "antimodel" that emerges seamlessly from the very nature of the society it opposes, with its practitioners from dislocated, disturbed, and even criminal backgrounds. Ultimately, the crusade and the war on terror are attacks that Europe (now the West) launched on itself.

Despite the Lateran Council identifying Albi as a center of "Catharism"—a name previously only used for some Rhineland groups of laity seeking to live purer lives—there was no more evidence of any such groups existing there than there was of al-Qaeda groups in Iraq before the Gulf War, though this too was used as an excuse for armed invasion. As Moore points out, the so-called Albigensians were simply those who sought a more idealized or spiritual way of life. Often the widespread attitude or philosophical outlook of Neoplatonism, derived from such spiritual classics as Boethius's *The Consolations of Philosophy*, was by far the most influential source of such ideas.[14] But it was in the interests of both a power-hungry clergy and the nobility to treat religious dissent as the expression of a vast and sinister clandestine movement of organized subversion which, like today's putative "terror networks," could justify a crusade of extreme violence. What the Third Lateran Council achieved was to transform a generalized but amorphous concern into a specific and universal threat. As a result, Moore concludes, "Denunciation, arbitrary arrest, imprisonment without charge, judicial torture, and burning alive became ordinary features of European life."

One may care to pause here and read that last sentence again in the context of the yesterday's news. With the exception of "burning alive" we have all the elements of the current war on terror. Even the title of Moore's book, *The War on Heresy*, has a curiously contemporary resonance; certainly much of its narrative echoes events of the present. However it may be defined, 'the war on terror" both reflects an indelible tradition of European/ Western thinking and expresses a remarkably consistent pattern of paranoid suspicion—what Norman Cohn has called Europe's "Inner Demons." When at last Khalid Sheikh Mohammad and other coconspirators were recently brought to trial at Guantanamo Bay, the proceedings swiftly devolved into farce. On the first day, one member of the public in attendance neatly summarized the general view: "Their values are not our values. They have complete contempt for all we believe in." It could have come straight out of *The Song of Roland*—life is a struggle of us against them.

But what exactly are "our values"? Rugged Republicans like one-time presidential hopeful Mitt Romney understand them to be Judeo-Christian values. This ponderous affirmation of "Judeo-Christian values" commonly functions like a battleship's broadside salvo—an effective way to blow the enemy out of the water with no further questions asked. But exactly what "Judeo-Christian" ever was or is, the foundations of American success equally included the institution of slavery and the extermination of the native inhabitants along with the expropriation of their territory. And this was achieved by convinced "Judeo-Christians" inspired by the sacred texts that they fervently believed legitimated and even demanded such behavior. That Mitt Romney should have made his fortune by stripping companies of their assets and throwing the redundant workforce on the scrap heap of economic misery while dodging taxes himself is presumably to be seen as a

14. Moore, *War*, 67.

part of this rich tapestry of Judeo-Christian values: the modern crusader as corporate raider. It was exactly such sentiments of the grotesque distortion of what Christianity was really about that prompted the protest of John Wycliffe in the fourteenth century, who argued, in *De Civili Dominio* that power or "dominion" is founded on grace, and that authority disappears in the absence of virtue. Ideas that would lead to the Reformation.

Curiously, the medieval Crusade in southern and central Europe was aimed at a supposed veiled conspiracy (Manicheism) thought to have been smuggled in from distant lands to threaten Christendom. In fact, that distant land was Bamyan, in Afghanistan, where the third-century Persian prophet Mani stayed for several years formulating his ideas. The modern war on terror replays the drama: a conspiratorial network (al-Qaeda) based in the caves of the Tora Bora mountains of Afghanistan, where Osama bin Laden formulated his evil plans that threaten us all. In the Middle Ages this was an unimaginably distant place and the Manichean connection entirely speculative—even the word *Manichee* was used as a noun though it is in fact an exclamation. (After Mani's martyrdom his followers exclaimed, in Aramaic, *Mani Khia!* "Mani lives!"). Today this is still a largely distant and exotic land beyond the comprehension of ordinary people, but they are increasingly less inclined to believe in the speculative threat it poses. The real threat to society, both medieval and modern, is one woven into the fabric of the society we have created.

Like the medieval "War on Heresy" (a.k.a. the Crusade), the war on terror is all-consuming and all-embracing. As the expression of a fixed mind-set, it becomes both the defining purpose of state policy and the cover for other ambitions, and it can be ended only by a radical change of understanding. The crusades against heresy ceased only when the concept of heresy was replaced by a vision of society as a pluralist forum where individual rights are respected. To be sure, the emergence of this view required repeated and sustained confrontations, and a good indicator of where today's society stands in relation to this paradigm is its treatment of minorities, women, and gender variants—that is, its values. When the monolithic state returns, as it did under the various tyrannies of the twentieth century, so does the crusade.

Underlying Bush's war on terror was the unquestioning assumption of the superiority of "our" values. This was the essence of Fukuyama's central thesis that "the logic of modern natural science would be seen to dictate a universal evolution in the direction of capitalism." This grand Hegelian view of history also assumed that Christianity was an "absolute religion," more "evolved" than other faiths and therefore of superior moral standing. Again we hear the echo of the conviction clearly enunciated in *The Song of Roland* that "we are right and they are wrong." Combine all this with the unquestioning self-belief of an unrivaled military superpower, and we have all the elements of a new crusade.

The ideology of this overbearing colossus of military self-righteousness necessarily led to what Tariq Ali called a "Clash of Fundamentalisms."[15] The new crusaders—with their polarized view of the world based on ignorance and suspicion, biblical evangelism, and self-righteous conviction—conform exactly to the mentalities of their predecessors. Driven by apocalyptic (and apoplectic) rhetoric, religious conviction serves to cloak the workings of shallow minds with a mantle of respectability. In response, opposing faith groups like Boko-Haram ("Western education forbidden") spring up like dragons' teeth, denouncing all that the West stands for. So the spiral of confrontation escalates without clear military objectives, becoming a struggle for global domination, cultural exclusivity, and the elimination of difference. This is how it was in the Middle Ages, and how the Crusades got going in the first place. Welcome to the modern world!

15. Ali, *Clash.*

13

The Apocalyptic Mentality
The Strange Story of the "Prophet" John Wroe

The story of John Wroe, a rather obscure nineteenth-century "prophet" and visionary, centers on the small Lancashire mill town of Ashton-under-Lyne, situated on the edge of Pennines. Its former industrial character of mighty cotton mills overshadowing innumerable rows of grimy terraced houses has now largely vanished, though it remains the center of the Metropolitan Borough of Tameside and has some claim to fame as being one of the most efficiently administered boroughs in the country. But this is as nothing compared to what John Wroe prophesied for it: this was to be the New Jerusalem, foretold in the book of the Revelation—the place of the second coming of Christ, where the kingdom of heaven would begin. As I live nearby, I can assure readers this has not yet happened.

John Wroe was a woolcomber who was born in Bradford, just over the Pennines in West Yorkshire, in 1782.[1] A difficult and abusive childhood left him partially crippled and with a stammer. During an illness in 1819 he took to reading the Bible, and like many people who do so under oppressive circumstances he began to feel himself consoled and specially directed with "illuminations" or private revelations. These made clear to him that he must learn Hebrew, join the Jewish faith, and gather together the lost tribes of Israel in readiness for the imminent end of the world and second coming

---

1. Green, *Prophet*.

of Jesus. In due time he became the leader and prophet of a movement known as the Christian Israelites.

At its peak in the 1830s, thousands flocked to hear Wroe's message and be baptized in the local river, the Medlock—presumably the nearest equivalent to the River Jordan. A sumptuously furnished sanctuary was built for worship in the Ashton town center at the then-phenomenal cost of £9,500, which was twice the cost of the town hall. But this was just the centerpiece of his visionary messianic city, for on Ashton Moss near the outskirts of the town he bought a house—since demolished for the building of a highway—that would become one of the "gatehouses" of the New Jerusalem as it was depicted in Rev 21. I remember it as the old folks' home that it later became. Other "gatehouses" of the citadel later became pubs, and perhaps appropriately, the field in which he prophesied to large crowds the light that would shine forth "to enlighten the Gentiles" would finally become the site of a gasworks to provide street lighting for the town.

If all of this is beginning to sound rather improbable, it may be reassuring to know that in the long history of Europe's millenarian movements, John Wroe's was nothing if not typical.[2] Inspired by enigmatic biblical prophecies, he drew much of his support from a similarly inspired group who were followers of Joanna Southcott, another visionary and millenarian prophet who preceded him by a decade. She had also received special divine communications that she recorded in a book appropriately named *The Strange Effects of Faith.* Published in 1801, it brought her widespread national fame. The centerpiece of her revelations was that she would bear a son who would be conceived of the Holy Spirit and would usher in the messianic age.

After a phantom pregnancy, the only notable result of which was to intrigue the medical world of the day, she died on December 27, 1814. Her numerous followers immediately declared her to be "the woman clothed with the sun" mentioned in Revelation, whose child had been snatched back to heaven for safekeeping. In a manner that shows how faith can never be disappointed, her followers declared that Joanna's "son" would soon return—on October 14, 1820, to be precise. When this did not happen, word went out that God was testing people's faith but would not disappoint them. It was at this point that John Wroe saw his opportunity, declaring before a meeting of Southcottians that he had received a vision in which he was

---

2. Knox, *Enthusiasm.*

commissioned to be their prophet; and thereupon he assumed that leadership role and renamed the movement the Society of Christian Israelites.

Though much of this story may seem bizarre, it is not without a wider context and significance. The revolutionary age in which Wroe lived has often been taken to mark the beginning of modern times, and as such produced dramatic changes on many levels. The French Revolution caused massive political upheaval across Europe just as the Industrial Revolution was bringing about economic changes that destroyed traditional lifestyles, uprooting and marginalizing a whole new social cohort that drifted into new industrial towns like Manchester. The vast and lurid paintings of John Martin (1789–1854) depicting biblical scenes in works such as *Belshazzar's Feast* (1820) and *The Destruction of Sodom and Gomorrah* (1852) were hugely popular and tapped into the anxieties and apocalyptic fantasies of the period. To the poor and dispossessed masses millenarian and apocalyptic thinking had a particular appeal.

In *The Small Sects in America*, Elmer Clark summarized the situation succinctly: "Pre-millenarianism is essentially a 'defence mechanism' of the disinherited; despairing of obtaining substantial blessings through social processes, they turn on the world which has withheld its benefits and look to its destruction in a cosmic cataclysm which will exalt them and cast down the rich and powerful."[3]

In fact, Wroe's movement of British Israelites can also be located within a larger national and international context. According to seventeenth-century antiquarians who sought to unravel the origins of Albion's ancient inhabitants by using the Bible as a window on the ancient world, the most plausible explanation seemed to be that they had arrived here after fleeing from the flood. In short, our ancestors must have been none other than the remnants of the lost tribes of ancient Israel! In his *Britannia Antiqua Illustrata* of 1676, antiquarian Aylett Sammes has a detailed map of the journey taken by the ancient Britons across Europe from Ararat to England. He argued vigorously that the island of Britain had been providentially set aside for the safety of these people in a land that "abounds in all things, both for the necessary delight and support of Man . . . a distinct World, by it self."[4]

So now we have moved from a supposed providential design for a North Country industrial town to one for a whole nation. It is a view that

3. Quoted in Green, *Prophet*, 28.
4. Quoted in Piggott, *Ancient*, 19.

became widely held in the eighteenth century. In fact, so persuasive was the feeling of special election that it became a fundamental element of the optimism underlying Britain's imperial expansion—the British Empire, a chosen instrument of God for the advancement of mankind. Thus, for example, the first professor of geology at Oxford University, the Reverend William Buckland, could proudly proclaim that the great mineral wealth of the nation was "no mere accident of nature; it showed rather, the express intention of Providence that the inhabitants of Britain should become, by this gift, the richest and most powerful nation on Earth." At the end of his lectures he would invite the audience to sing, "God save the Queen!" This conviction of Britain's manifest destiny was admirably symbolized in a contemporary *Punch* cartoon showing Queen Victoria handing a Bible to an Indian maharajah with the caption, "The secret of our success."[5]

And the story does not end there. In his book *Chosen People*, the former religious affairs correspondent of the *Times*, Clifford Longley, shows how this concept has morphed into a central element of modern global politics.[6] A sense of "chosenness," based on a reading of the Bible, was central to the self-understanding of the first English settlers in America, and many of the colonists who followed them to New England were, like John Wroe, biblical visionaries and idealists. Aboard the *Mayflower*, William Bradford and his companions dreamed of founding a new "Godly Kingdom," and it was the first governor of Massachusetts, John Winthrop, who proclaimed a vision of creating a godly "city on a hill." (Apparently cities on hills have something inherently messianic about them!)[7] Not only had these settlers the prime motive of establishing a more perfect, biblically based Christian kingdom, but they also had the driving conviction that they were "chosen" for this task.

The conviction of divine destiny became a defining characteristic of the American psyche and includes its own peculiar historical narrative: after smiting the latter-day Jebusites (native Indians), God's chosen people went on to overthrow Magog, the false king (George III and the Hanoverian dynasty); and with the eventual demise of the British Empire, the United States of America has become the leading repository of the idea of sacred destiny. And even now this vision is standard fare on powerful media networks in the United States that daily broadcast impassioned televangelists

5. Clark, *Shadowed*, 76.

6. Longley, *Chosen*.

7. Hill, "God."

expounding biblical themes of predestination and imminent apocalypse, and that give influential political commentators like Glenn Beck a platform to expound their inflammatory brand of Christian Zionism.

And their message is still essentially that of John Wroe: the Bible's dramatic call, the imminent end, the possibility of salvation, the reappearance of Jesus with the chance of being "raptured" up to heaven—and of course the opportunity to fund "the Lord's work" and invest in its rewards through support of the "prophet." How John Wroe would have envied the formidable power of the modern media to reach into people's lives—and pockets! Still, it is cruelly ironic that his sanctuary in Ashton later became a cinema for popular entertainment.

And now the enigmatic story has come full circle from George Washington's claim of "a "special providence" to the world's only superpower fostering the resettlement of the original chosen people (the Jews) in the original promised land. Even the biblically based reasoning for the colonial land grab of the "Wild West" is eerily reminiscent and anticipatory of that now going on in the West Bank—a program specifically encouraged by the Christian Zionists, who see this as a decisive preparation for history's final consummation in a modern Armageddon and the second coming. Thus, the visionary's narrative of chosen election continues to shape our world. Like John Wroe, our contemporary visionaries never become disillusioned with their interpretation of the world: one way or another the vision filters the world in such a way that some further "evidence" will always be found to support it.

When probing the origin of this manner of thinking, neuroscientists such as Paul Fletcher, trace it back to the nature of the brain itself. His work on delusion and hallucination indicates that forms of belief, like conspiracy theories, arise from the natural functioning of the mind. "The brain—our minds—have an impossible task of making sense of a world that is noisy and ambiguous. We have to take short cuts. We have to add our own evidence rather than being a passive receptacle of the world."[8] So though the majority of our beliefs may be useful, they do not provide a facsimile of what is out there. Instead they are attempts to craft an explanation of the world. But they are also more than this. Far from being passive attempts at description, they also bestow a sense of agency to those who may feel impotent in the face of forces they cannot control.

8. James and Thibault, "World," 24.

A further corollary of this would seem to be that the more disturbed and unsettled the mind or the times may be, the more urgent the need to exert some control, and the greater the likelihood of the appearance of an assertive or "prophetic" voice. So to understand the visionary impulse we must also look into the dynamics of the wider cultural environment and its psychological effects. Times of significant social change and uncertainty—such as those in which John Wroe lived—create widespread demand for some directional voice. Cognitive scientist Merlin Donald provides a further insight into this phenomenon when he likens human culture to "a gigantic search-engine that seeks out and tests various solutions to the many cognitive challenges faced by people."[9] Where confusion reigns, the visionary steps forth as both the creation and prophet of his culture, and articulates the kind of solutions which, as Donald notes, are "ultimately products of our own attempts at self- governance."

We have no reason to think that John Wroe set out to deceive others any more than he may have thought himself to have been deceived. People listened to him because, like him, they were profoundly disturbed by the times in which they lived, and found reassurance in a clear, decisive message delivered with conviction.

Studies on the functioning of the brain have thrown further light on the etiology of the visionary's world and why only some assume the role of prophet. This also has to do with states of mind. As neuroscientist Gerald Edelman has pointed out, consciousness is not a single, unitary state.[10] Rather it is a spectrum of modalities ranging from focused attention to reflectiveness and reverie to meditative states and on into the dream-world. These states can vary according to degrees of emotion or stress, physiology (such as epilepsy and schizophrenia), or environment. But the information conveyed in these different states of mind is no less real to the cognitive subject; in fact, dream-like visions can seem even more real than normal rational comprehension. For this reason, they may give rise to the impression of special revelation and become treasured as insights into a deeper reality than that of the everyday world. It has often been noted that in times of personal or social stress such visions and revelations not only increase in frequency but also more readily find wide acceptance.

If, as Donald says, the search engine of human culture provides the necessary solutions for people to construct a meaningful world and live

9. Donald, *Origins*.

10. Edelman, *Bright*.

ordered lives, the corollary is that in times of cultural upheaval the need for visionary reassurance becomes paramount. And so we find a common thread running through the previously mentioned eras: the early Industrial Revolution through which Wroe lived, the Reformation and English Civil War, during which the American colonies were seeded, and the current era of globalization and clashing cultures. The supporters of the ISIS in Syria reckon the caliphate of Abu al-Bahgdadi with its total imposition of Sharia law to offer all the reassurance they could wish for. Puritans whether of the seventeenth or twentieth century have the same mentality regardless of denomination. The "prophet" provides the necessary reassurance of an end to turmoil and better times ahead—whether as a utopian vision for this world or as an apocalyptic vision of the next. All that is required is allegiance and submission to the prophet's word.

And so the prophetic voice and visionary message become both an attempt at self-governance and a tool for the manipulation of others. For no prophet is ever content to stay silent on the mountain—or as in the case of Wroe, in the bed where he received his visions. The immediate vision may be real or simulated (a spying neighbor caught Wroe, while reputedly in a twelve-day trance, sitting up in bed eating pickled cabbage and oat cakes). But it is nothing if not communicated. This in itself brings rewards, as willing devotees provide the power and privileged status that become a self-sustaining intoxicant to the visionary.

Eventual disillusionment with Wroe's message resulted from other more mundane events. After a missionary tour in 1830 with his seven elected virgins—who, it had been revealed, should accompany him at all times—two of them charged John Wroe with "indecency and things not fit to be spoken." This caused shock waves throughout the movement. After a trial that resulted in his acquittal, a riot arose in the sanctuary in Ashton, and Wroe barely escaped with his life. He fled the country but continued his missionary career in America and Australia, where he founded other Christian Israelite communities, some of which still survive to this day. But any biblically minded prophet will perceive a lingering paradox: for while the written word of the Bible can provide the basis for a restorative vision, all too often the very proliferation of printed words, the ideas they convey, and the books that contain them lead to disturbances. In our own time, for instance, chaotic and torrential floods of information can be overwhelmingly confusing. The visionary grasps and clings to particular texts like a drowning man to straws; absolute conviction may draw strength from the biblical text, but as numerous millenarian and fundamentalist movements have shown, the Bible can teach anything that is demanded of it. Its ambiguity can be applied to address any eventuality. In the quiet of one's room its voice becomes almost another personal presence.

And so it was for John Wroe. Whether pondering Scripture on his sickbed or listening to the voice coming from the second bar of the fire grate, he found the persuasiveness of the message immediate and forceful. In his solitary musings, he felt illuminated and inspired to share with the world his "message." Of course, it was not simply "his" message but also the message that had been given to him—or so he was convinced. And so it is with every visionary and prophet. We will never be without them—or free of them. In the meantime, Ashton-under-Lyne awaits its destiny.

14

Remembering the Secular Age?
A Question of Evolution

I must begin with an apology for plagiarism. My title is that of an article by Michael Novak, a prominent American Catholic philosopher and journalist, that a friend of mine recently passed on to me.[1] It has something of a Proustian ring to it—an echo of *The Remembrance of Times Past*—a tone that nicely captures the tenor of the article's adumbration that the secular age has passed. Indeed, Novak quotes favorably the opinion of the eminent German philosopher Jürgen Habermas that we now live in "the post-secular age," a time characterized by the resurgence of religious belief, even bellicosity. I have, however taken one liberty: to Novak's title and thesis I have added a question mark.

Not that he is lacking in persuasive conviction and argument. After all, as he writes, since 91 percent of Americans say they believe in God and 82 percent identify specifically with Christianity, the paltry 3 percent of atheists and agnostics are a rather rare, if not irrelevant, breed. In Britain the figures are substantially different, for only a little over half the population do not identify with any particular religious belief—the highest percentage in Europe. But it's not just about percentages. Novak quotes approvingly a remark by Irving Kristol, once dubbed "the godfather of neoconservatism," that two major turning points in the history of the twentieth century are the death of socialism and "the collapse of secular humanism . . . as an

---

1. Novak, "Remembering."

148

ideal." Was it ever more than an eccentric aspiration? This is also the view of Habermas, who sees secularism as the persuasion of a fairly small minority in a sea of rising religious commitment—a view heartily endorsed by his friend, former Pope Benedict XVI.

In contrast to the angry brigade of militant atheists like Dawkins, Hitchens, Harris, and so on, Novak adopts a more benign, paternalistic, and even condescending advocacy of reasoned argument and mutual conversations as a guide for how to come closer to the truth. After all, civilization is constituted by reasoned conversation, claims Novak: "Civilized humans converse with one another . . . Barbarians club one another." In this he is undoubtedly correct, as he is in another aspect of his thesis; namely, that secular culture owes much to Judaism and Christianity, indeed cannot be understood outside that context, for "Even without sharing in Christian faith, secular persons ought in all fairness to give due recognition to intellectual indebtedness."

This was also the theme of Nick Spencer's recently published book, *The Evolution of the West: How Christianity Has Shaped Our Values.*[2] Brilliantly written and argued, this work goes a step further to affirm that we cannot even understand the present without an awareness of our Christian past, which has served as both catalyst and context for virtually everything we understand to be modern, including secularism and atheism. This has become an increasingly persuasive thesis; the new look *apologia* for the twenty-first century.

I acknowledge all this, for obviously there is much truth in this thesis, but I fear that it is not the whole story. In fact, I am not even persuaded that it is the right story. In particular, I question—in fact clearly reject—the premise from which the argument proceeds; namely, that there is some quintessential quiddity called Christianity. Such a view would have us believe in a clear, objective view of truth and provide us with an essential narrative of meaning for our lives. And that such a quiddity has interacted with various cultures over the past two millennia as an unalloyed good without which we become morally confused and have no future hope. I would argue, on the contrary, that it is precisely because Christianity has never been "one thing" but has constantly searched for its identity and coherence—always in a state of fission, and with constant renewals seeking to recapture some lost charism—that it has provided the catalyst to its own evolution and that of the West.

2. Spencer, *Evolution.*

To my mind this is where the debate really gets interesting. And it is founded on the relationship between what Christianity became and the actual personhood and message of the historical Jesus. The work of scholars such as Geza Vermes and of the Jesus Seminar has revealed not only the powerful influences of Jesus' historical context, but also how his teaching was being amended and "interpreted" even before the gospels were being written. Indeed, many assumed *ipsissima verba* are now seen as no more than *theologumena* (later interpolations).[3] We can now begin to see that even at this early point Christianity reflects the working out of beliefs in specific social and changing cultural contexts. What we have assumed to be an immutable essence involving a defined persona and creed is no such thing.

This point is well made by John Dominic Crossan in his recent book *How to Read the Bible and Still Be a Christian*.[4] Among other examples, he considers the teaching of Saint Paul on slavery in the context of his corpus of letters, which Crossan divides into three groups: those certainly written by him, those probably not, and those certainly not. In the first group of letters is that to Philemon commanding him to free Onesimus the slave. Here Paul reveals the radicality of the Christian message centered on the belief that Christians have died to the values of Rome and live for the new life of God. Yet in Colossians, a later letter that was probably not written by Paul, we read a different directive: "Slaves, obey your earthly masters."

From this example Crossan concludes that a post-Pauline, pseudo-Pauline, and even an anti-Pauline vision has evolved to contradict the vision of the apostle. In this trajectory the radicality of God is announced and subsequently domesticated and integrated into the normalcy of civilization. And since *both* elements can then be cited as being from the mouth of God and the pen of Paul, we are forced to recognize that Scripture can seldom if ever be given a univocal reading but rather is bipolar if not schizophrenic. As Crossan concludes, "It is as if the Biblical Express Train runs on twin parallel but very dissimilar rails."[5]

The flaw in the thesis of both Novak and Spencer is precisely that they see Christianity as "one thing," an evolutionary force, benign and sustained, even providentially guided like Newman's "development" of Christian doctrine. Such a "development" can also be seen in the growth of monasticism,

3. Crossan, *Power*.

4. Crossan, *How*, 22–27.

5. Crossan, *How*, 28.

for it was clearly a key force in shaping Western Christendom, but this owes as much to the Greek tradition of hesychasm (solitary, contemplative prayer) as it does to the Gospels. Early monks were contemptuous of the ordinary life of the Christian community and were told, shun bishops as you would women. They often bordered on the psychotic, with a fanaticism feared by many and worthy of ISIS jihadists and expressed most notably in the burning of the library of Alexandria, the greatest repository of worldly wisdom in antiquity. Clearly this would in time change beyond recognition—but that is the point!

We now understand evolution to be characterized not only by slow developmental processes of stratification but also by dramatic and sometimes catastrophic leaps that leave nothing unchanged. For Christianity there have been a number of such occasions: the failure of the eschaton, the switch in focus from the message of Jesus to the cult of the *Christos,* the "conversion" of Constantine, the monasticization of ministry (complete by the eleventh century), and the Reformation. The result has been that Christianity—as a hierarchically structured, liturgically based cultic community—came to bear little resemblance to the original vision of Jesus. It is noteworthy that reformers were constantly harking back to how different things were in apostolic times.

One may further review this process at work in the corpus of moral teachings in the early church, as the distinguished scholar of classical antiquity Peter Brown has done in such masterly books as *Through the Eye of a Needle* and and *The Body and Society.* As the first Christian communities clearly expected the parousia within their own lifetime, they gave little thought to such trivial issues as marriage (don't bother) or wealth (just give it away). When the parousia didn't happen, church authorities became increasingly desperate to provide some sort of moral guidance. Culled partly from the Old Testament and contemporary philosophical thought, much of this came to sound remarkably like Stoicism. Further dramatic changes, such as the conversion of Constantine, brought a seismic shift in understanding as the massive edifice of Caesaropapism began to take shape; nothing more remote from the life of the Nazarene carpenter is possible to imagine. Of this transformation one sentence of Peter Brown has become inextricably lodged in my mind: "When the 'governing elite' of this officially Christian empire presented themselves to themselves and to the world at large, as being ' in truth governing,' the 'set of symbolic forms' by which they expressed this fact owed little or nothing to Christianity."[6]

A process of Christianization then? Brown thinks that Christianization, "if it happened at all, must be a slow process." In his *Pagans and Christians* another distinguished classical scholar, Robin Lane Fox, describes such a process more floridly as "that state which is always receding, like full employment or a garden without weeds."[7] It is a process that has taken us further and further from the ideals of the founder. An example of such change is the rise of the universities, undoubtedly a major agent of cultural formation and change distinctive of the Christian West. As the monastic cloister school mutated into the college quad, it remained an all-male zone. This was in clear contravention of one of the most distinctive features of primitive Christianity—that there was to be no place for discrimination in its inclusive worldview, as Saint Paul made clear to the Galatians: "There are to be no more distinctions between Jew and Greek, slave and free, male and female" (Gal 3:28, JB). It is only within recent memory that the bastions of male privilege have been breached by secular values, which paradoxically have turned out to have much in keeping with the original vision of Christianity.

That this process of Christianization is both fitful and partial one may glean from observing the 82 percent of Novak's fellow citizens who claim to be committed Christians. One may wonder, for example, what became of one of the most clear and unambiguous demands of discipleship: "If you wish to become a follower of mine, sell all you have and give it to the poor" (see, e.g., Matt 19:21; Luke 14:33); for these faithful followers live among some of the most deprived people in the Western world, and many are rabidly opposed to any form of universal healthcare, although caring for the sick was another of those challenging dominical demands! This may begin to sound like socialism, which Irving Kristol assures us has also had its day, but while we find no parables about building walls to keep people out, several call for us to bring people in. All of this leads to the inescapable conclusion that though Christianity may have shaped an evolving society, it did so in a way that radically and unambiguously distorted its own nature.

One of the most insightful chapters in Nick Spencer's previously mentioned *The Evolution of the West* is titled "The Secular Self"; in it he analyzes the secularization of the West over the last five hundred years, a story

---

6. Brown, *Authority*, 11.

7. Fox, *Pagans*, 21.

he colorfully likens to an "intellectual striptease act."[8] By this he means the mistaken assumption that simply by stripping away all such ideas as a supernatural realm, cosmic justice, immortality, and so forth, we are left with the modern secular self in all its naked glory. Using Charles Taylor's *A Secular Age* as a guide, he charts a more complex story of how "the final human good" lay in seeking a *summum bonum* that was immanent and self-referential. Unfortunately, however, in doing so the secular self-inverts the natural order of how our identity is shaped through relationship with others. By focusing entirely on the self, it normalizes an individualism that leaves us bewildered and isolated. And it is this state that Novak and others believe has now had its day as people increasingly realize their mistake.

Novak quotes Habermas in his favor, as agreeing that the liberal state is coming to an end and that a new inclusiveness will mark the postsecular age. Why? Because the liberal state expects its citizens to split their identities into public and private versions, insisting on the secular monopoly of the public square. But this is not quite the same conclusion as that of Spencer, who insists "that we are just at the beginning of a new age of religious searching" in which God is not pushed out of the picture altogether, but rather towards the periphery of people's lives where he remains lurking in the undergrowth. Thus, he observes, "there remains a palpable sense that the secular self isn't enough, that it doesn't satisfy." To support his claim, he quotes research he did on people visiting cathedrals where even self-identifying secular tourists of no particular religious convictions admitted not so much "to sloughing off their spiritual weeds" as to wriggling out of their secular selves.[9] In other words, a large proportion of modern secular people still admit to spiritual needs even though they do not evince any recognizable religious faith.

And this seems to be the true tenor of our age. As Spencer concludes, "it remains self-consciously in tension with, almost opposition to, religious faith, pivoting on the central and unquestioned importance of choice."[10] For religious traditionalists this supermarket approach to religion is anathema; for Novak it is at the root of our moral disarray, for in his view our moral codes should be guided by "the wisdom of our forefathers."[11] But this harking back to the past is hugely problematic, as can be seen from

8. Spencer, *Evolution*, 138.

9. Spencer, *Evolution*, 150.

10. Spencer, *Evolution*, 152.

11. Novak, "Remembering," 36.

the nineteenth-century religious reaction to the rationalism of the Enlightenment, and the perceived cross materialism of the industrial age went by the name of the Gothic Revival. As it happens I live near and often visit one its most notable products, Edmund Pugin's Gorton Monastery, now a UNESCO world heritage site. Yet the very title of "monastery" for this pseudo-Franciscan edifice (pseudo because the Franciscan movement and its friaries were a reaction *against* the monasticization of the church) is the giveaway for what was no more than a fanciful rendition of an imagined world that was a total travesty of the historical reality. Its abandonment and subsequent restoration as a secular space is testament to a further phase of Christianity's evolution.

This new situation is exactly what the great prophet of our present predicament, Dietrich Bonhoeffer, had in mind when he wrote of a religionless Christianity that has come of age.[12] As he pondered in his cell, the question that kept coming back to him was, "what *is* Christianity, and indeed what *is* Christ for us today?" His answer was that Christianity plunges us into many different dimensions of life simultaneously; that "Life is not compressed into a single dimension, but is kept multi-dimensional and polyphonous."[13] This may seem similar to the argument of Novak (quoting Habermas) that a new inclusiveness will mark the postsecular age. But this reactionary view is rather different from that of Bonhoeffer, who wrote of "the western pattern of Christianity as a mere preliminary stage to doing without religion altogether."[14]

This is similar to the conclusion of Spencer, who insists "that we are just at the beginning of a new age of religious searching."[15] The difference is that now we are on our own—or "come of age" in Bonhoeffer's phrase—and so must grow up and face our responsibilities. For all their lauded potency, the opiates of the past were no more than that. Novak argues that a "regulative idea" or a moral compass is dependent on God as if that alone enabled reasoned argument. On the contrary, the concept of God has too often been used as a club with which to beat dissenters into submission, creating a persecuting society like that of medieval Christendom. More often in the contemporary world God has become a "god of the gaps" who supplements gaps in our knowledge or our natural deficiencies. But this is no longer

12. Bonhoeffer, *Letters.*
13. Bonhoeffer, *Letters,* 103.
14. Bonhoeffer, *Letters,* 91.
15. Spencer, *Evolution,* 151.

persuasive for a time in which we find that sense of purpose and meaning, which the term God embodies, in what *we* do rather than the gaps. So let us rather deploy reasoned analysis and generosity of spirit in striving to achieve a full realization of human potential and fullness of life.

Looking back, we can now see that secularism, whatever its roots and trajectory, has enabled us to rediscover the real underpinnings of Christianity in the authentic teaching of the historical Jesus and in the degree to which he emphasized the purely humanitarian basis of ethics expressed in such radical sayings as "The Sabbath is made for man, not man for the Sabbath" (see Mark 2:27, my translation). This was a theme explored by Don Cupitt in his most recent book, *Ethics in the Last Days of Humanity*.[16] The distinctive characteristic of such living is that it reflects an internalized morality that is independent of authority and respects the dignity of all people. In a curious, rather paradoxical way, it is secularism that has enabled us to rediscover this "pearl of great price" that is now the basis of our modern understanding of human rights. The radical injunctions not only to love one's neighbor as oneself, but to love and do good to one's enemies have rarely been adhered to, let alone seriously demanded. And yet these epitomize the distinctive quality of the teaching of Jesus. The perennial challenge that confronts us all is how to create a better society. We have not been too successful in the past, but once more we can seek to do so as we "re-member" our secular age.

16. Cupitt, *Ethics.*

Part 3

A Ravaged Earth

15

So Is This It Then?

The New Ecological Awareness
of the Twenty-First Century

A decade ago the distinguished naturalist E. O. Wilson asked whether humanity is suicidal. He observed that we are carnivores who happened upon intelligence, and the evidence of our destructiveness is all around us in what amounts to an environmental holocaust. And having in the twentieth century finally accepted, though not fully understood, the possibility of holocaust, we are now haunted by another specter of our own contriving—extinction. As with ex-termination, it is the finality of that little prefix *ex* that is the chiller, if not killer.

One thing that the species whose life was once portrayed as "nasty, brutish and short" rarely doubted was its survival, either in this world or the next. True, there was always the possibility that a divine fiat could pull the plug at some unexpected moment; but this was tempered by the sly suspicion that by keeping a few godly heads down and knees bent we would get by, that in the end everything would be fine. Again, one recalls U.S. Republican senator Jim Inhofe's self-serving rant declaring it blasphemous to imagine that we mere humans could change the earth's divinely controlled climate. Behind such talk is the apocalyptic mentality that God's will and actions control all things. A 2004 poll of American opinion indicated that 60 percent believed the prophecies of Revelation were accurate and the end of time was imminent, and that how we treated the planet was of little significance.[1]

Though a religious awareness of catastrophism has been an element of many civilizations[2] from the ancient Israelites and Maya to the nineteenth-century discovery of vanished geological worlds, the assumption has always been that humanity was an unwitting and even innocent victim. Current versions of asteroid impacts and supervolcanoes (expect one any minute, even if only at a cinema near you) are representations of ancient fears for a scientific age; it was much the same fear that, as the Roman poet Lucretius wrote, "was the first thing on earth to make gods." But however inclined we were to think of ourselves as the Lord's creation—or lords of creation—it was hard to imagine things going on without us. But that is true no longer.

For now our understanding of apocalypse has changed from what is done to us to what we do to ourselves. A way of life has now developed that is so destructive and unsustainable as to make the very survival of our species—perhaps of any species—unlikely if not impossible. Ironically, this our guilty species of hominids has long had the conceit of describing itself as *sapiens,* intelligent. But then, as Wilson went on to reflect, "Perhaps a law of evolution is that intelligence usually extinguishes itself." For the first time in our planet's history a real future possibility is the organically induced destruction by one species of the biosphere—that precious membrane of life that clothes the earth.

This awareness has slowly crept upon us only in the last few decades. In 1966, paleoanthropologist Richard Leakey's *The Sixth Extinction* popularized the understanding of the "Big Five" catastrophes that have threatened the survival of life on the planet and could do so again.[3] To these have now been added a sixth very different extinction. The difference lies in the fact that its source is not a dramatic external event, but human activity—a small internal factor that has grown so exponentially as to threaten the biodiversity of the planet. Anthropogenic destruction, though often less obvious, is more damaging than a sudden event because it is sustained and cumulative. *Homo sapiens* is the first species in the history of the planet to become a geophysical force and to be caught between the combined threats of first-world over consumption and third-world overpopulation, Mother Nature will soon be exhausted.

1. Wilson, *Creation,* 6.
2. Diamond, *Collapse.*
3. Leakey, *Sixth.*

According to Wilson's latest work, *The Future of Life,* the critical threshold was crossed in 1978.[4] Using the concept of ecological footprint—the capacity of the land to sustain the human population—he argues that this was the point at which humanity exceeded the capacity of the earth to sustain it. Since then, ever-rising levels of population and consumption have overpowered the planet's ability to restore the damage already done. From that point on the larger species of fauna begin to dwindle and at length disappear. Environmentalist Bill McKibben has estimated that meeting the current needs of the human population would require the combined resources of two and half earths;[5] to enable the present population to enjoy a lifestyle like that of the United States would take four planets.

Despite this, Wilson remains remarkably sanguine that humanity has the ability to change its lifestyle by devising such policies as massively endowed natural parks in order to save the planet. I wonder! Since the track record of campaigns to change people's attitudes and lifestyles is not encouraging, a new Puritanism of survival is hardly likely to be more successful than the old Puritanism of salvation. For environmental change to be effective, the number of those sufficiently concerned and willing to change their lifestyles would have to rise from the present level of 10 percent to 90 percent. Such a dramatic change in human behavior would be without historical precedent. As a delegate to a recent Biodiversity Convention gloomily noted, "After ten years of these meetings there is no impact I can discern on slowing the destruction of the natural world." Indeed, every international conference seems to get cornered into postponing a decision until the next one.

Anyhow, it is too late—the system is in free fall. At least, this is the view of Michael Boulter in his recent book *Extinction: Evolution and the End of Man.*[6] The study of the fossil records by Boulter and his team shows that extinction is an integral part of evolution. What happens is explained by the concept of "self-organized criticality," which may be illustrated by observing grains of sand falling in a pile; there comes a critical point at which one more grain causes the pile to collapse with a period of quiescence until the process starts again. This helps us to envision how repetition of the same act can come to a point of finality—like the proverbial straw that broke the camel's back. It also explains how the loss of a key species

4. See Wilson, *Future,* ch. 3 (pp. 42–78).

5. McKibben, *Eaarth.*

6. Boulter, *Extinction.*

can trigger the collapse of a whole ecosystem. Of course, the converse is sometimes true: the reintroduction of a key species, such as the wolf in Yellowstone Park, can regenerate a whole ecosystem if the collapse has not gone too far. And it is the larger species at the top of the food chain that are most critical and now most vulnerable. Something very like this process now threatens to engulf us.

But life goes on. Given one hundred million years or so, a new ecosystem will evolve. The earth as a superorganism (think of James Lovelock's Gaia) will rejuvenate itself after correcting the cause of its own perturbation. It will be the ecologically adaptable and undemanding organisms that will inherit the earth—surely the echo of a beatitude! And the consummate irony is that this is what happened after the last great extinction, that of the dinosaurs, when small nocturnal mammals were given their chance and ultimately evolved into the not-so-wise primates presently at the top of the chain. The good news for the new species as yet unborn is that we will no longer be around to destroy them.

Our problem seems to be that our heedless and destructive attitude toward nature is part of the Paleolithic heritage hardwired into our brains. For millions of years our ancestors survived solely through the short-term exploitation of natural resources available to their immediate family groups. How painful must be the paradox that these very survival instincts now threaten our survival as a species. Though most of us still trudge numbly on, it is obvious that we can no longer indulge the tribal impulse for immediate advantage.

Contrary to much current nostalgia for primal cultures, it is clear that many of these were prodigious in their destructiveness and waste of natural resources. Massive faunal collapse always seems to coincide with the appearance of humans. Strenuous attempts have been made to discount the theory that this is what happened some fifty thousand years ago in Australia, but the evidence is now compelling.[7] Similarly, the extermination of the larger fauna of New Zealand by the Maoris reveals a similar story—one that has been repeated in modern times, as evidenced by the collapse of the cod stock thanks to New England and Newfoundland fishermen. It appears that humans are the only predators who cannot resist destroying the food sources on which they depend. And the problem grows ever more acute, for now whole shoals of tuna can be spotted from a helicopter and the sea swept clean in one fell swoop. Centuries ago, men with handsaws

7. Leakey, *Sixth.*

confronted mighty trees, today with chain saws they attack fragile forests. Our hardwood window frames and garden chairs come at a cost; but the ultimate cost is not the forest's destruction, it is our own.

It is sad, but perhaps not surprising, to note that primal instincts have long been reflected in and reinforced by traditional value systems. The ecologist Thomas Berry, a Roman Catholic priest, has been particularly critical of the failure of traditional religious leaders to grasp what has been happening. He identifies the cause of the problem as the lack of "an understanding of the developmental (evolutionary) character of the universe."[8] Because this has been particularly true of Christianity, he reminds us that "The present disruption of all the basic life systems of earth has come about within a culture that emerged from a biblical-Christian matrix. It did not arise out of the Buddhist world, or Hindu or Chinese or Japanese worlds or the Islamic world, it emerged from within our Western Christian-derived civilization."[9] The Judeo-Christian view of creation as an "externality" for our use and disposal is at the root of our present malaise.

Just as Berry did, Wilson seeks a way beyond this debilitating mentality in an impassioned appeal written in the form of an extended letter to a pastor calling for the preservation of creation.[10] He expresses the conviction that "If religion and science could be united on the common ground of biological conservation, the problem would be solved." However, he goes on to confess his puzzlement as to why, "so many religious leaders, who spiritually represent a large majority of people around the world, have hesitated to make protection of the Creation an important part of their magisterium."[11]

But there is no need for puzzlement. Biblical theism encouraged the exploitation of the earth. By presenting "man" as distinct from the animals and possessing domination over them, the Bible depicts "man" as created in the image of an absolute God and sharing "his" dominating power. As the historian Arnold Toynbee wrote, "Some of the major maladies of the present world—in particular the recklessly extravagant consumption of nature's irreplaceable treasures . . . can be traced back to a religious cause, and this cause is the rise of monotheism. . . . Monotheism, as enunciated in the book

8. Berry, *Selected Writings*, 69.
9. Berry, *Selected Writings*, 106.
10. Wilson, *Creation*.
11. Wilson, *Creation*, 5.

of Genesis, has removed the age-old restraint that was once placed on man's greed by his awe."[12]

A salutary difference in perspective is found in Zen Buddhism. In his study of primatology, *The Ape and the Sushi Master*, Frans de Waal suggests that the seminal contribution of the Japanese ethologist Kinji Imanishi to our understanding of primate behavior grew from a culture that lacked a human-animal dualism: "The smooth reception of this part of evolutionary theory—the continuity of life forms—meant that questions about animal behavior were from the start uncontaminated by feelings of superiority and aversion to the attribution of emotions and intentions that paralyzed Western science."[13] From this sense of interconnectedness of things he also developed the view that organisms possess a species identity and form a species-level society that affects individual behavior and evolves in response to need, and that therefore Life is one indivisible phenomenon.

The New Zealand theologian Lloyd Geering has pointed out yet another irony: that in this increasingly secular age we are called upon to make decisions (as in the case of genetic modification) that we had previously thought to be the sole prerogative of God. But he sees this as part of the fundamental change in thinking that has come with secularization. Whereas people once believed in a glorious future shaped by God—the *parousia* or second coming of Christ—for which they could do no more than wait and pray, now a different mentality is required: "Secular futurists today, however, know that the world's future is, as never before in human history, dependent on us humans."[14] This is part of the wider understanding of the world that theologians like Dietrich Bonhoeffer have for decades characterized as a time when human beings have "come of age" and must take adult responsibility for themselves and the world.

The new state of environmental awareness now emerging may be an expression of such a reality. Perhaps it may also be seen as a further proof that beliefs are evolutionary products that reflect our relationship with our environment. But in his biography of the living earth, *The Ages of Gaia*, James Lovelock cautions that any such new theory of the earth too easily becomes anthropocentric. Our future depends much more on our respect for the whole living organism of the planet (Gaia) than on the "never

12. Toynbee, "Genesis."

13. Waal, *Ape*, 110–19.

14. Geering, *Christianity*, 142.

ending drama of human interest."[15] He is skeptical that animals prone to tribal genocide could, by taking thought, change their natures: "It takes a lot of hubris even to think of ourselves as stewards of the Earth when in practice few of us can take care of our own bodies."[16]

But if this is it, if our mandate is really all over except for the shouting, then is there any further point to worrying? Why not go out in one last orgy of self-indulgence like the Roman emperors of old or as some modern U. S. Republicans claim the Lord intended? The only responsible response is that it is never too late to try. Though future generations are certainly destined to live in an impoverished landscape, many remarkable ecological initiatives show what can be achieved by collaborating with the amazing resilience of nature. But it would entail real changes of lifestyle, developing a Jain-like sensitivity to even the smallest organisms, and so deep a respect for life that no species is willingly allowed to die. As a remarkable Christian Aid poster once put it: "Live more simply, so that others may simply live." And of course these 'others' include generations yet to come. This should be seen not so much as a matter of hope for the future as a plan of action for today—for otherwise there will be no future!

15. Lovelock, *Ages*, 13.
16. Lovelock, *Ages*, 228.

16

The Context of Survival
A New Attitude toward Planet Earth

A friend of mine recently underwent hypnotherapy to overcome a life-long addiction to smoking. Some might think this an extreme measure, but intimations of mortality called for radical action. When we get doctor's orders in the last chance saloon, we are prepared to try anything!

The therapeutic methodology is both simple and intriguing: "Are you sitting comfortably? Then we will regress . . ."—and in stages one is taken back through memories and associations that are remembered then "re-membered," disconnected and restructured. Though these may initially be about smoking habits, something deeper is going on: a lifetime of experiences and even one's sense of identity are being remolded to provide a stronger and more congenial self-concept.

The implications of this technique suggest that behavioral patterns are intimately linked to both our personal history and the way we see ourselves. To change our behavior is not simply a matter of changing habits; we have to change our self-understanding, our view of ourselves. This means not just developing stronger willpower or resolve but becoming able to see ourselves in a new light. As my friend said, he could come to terms with losing a few toes—the result of his smoking—but when it came to further amputations and being pushed around in a wheelchair, well, "I can't quite get my head round that yet."

In a world of multiple addictions, the applications of this technique are also multiple. Whether we are hooked on junk food or suffer from a petroholic addiction to the instruments of mobility demanded by our global society, we need not only resolve, but a new sense of identity. The crux of the problem is discovering how to choose to be something that presently we are not even though it is not clear what this "something" is. A lifestyle without smoking? Possibly. A totally different lifestyle? Well, now . . .

The problem is compounded by the sheer pace and scale of life. Consider for example the staggering fact that between 2011 and 2014 China mixed as much concrete for building as did the USA in the entire twentieth century![1] We give too little thought to the implications or consequence of such "achievements" and shrug off such palpable dangers as air pollution. While London chokes on the smog of its frenetic lifestyle, and courts rule that for the sake of human health its carbon emissions must be reduced, politicians and businesses demand the expansion of what is already the world's busiest airport in order to sustain the ease of travel that our lifestyle demands. Clearly some contradictions need to be resolved.

But wondering about where everyone is rushing to—and why—is not something the average lemming has much time for. Anyway, the dazzling power and wealth that our economy can generate is beguiling beyond measure and hard to resist. But then, it was not initially clear to the fabled King Midas how more gold could possibly be a bad thing. That realization began to cause alarm only when the situation became life-threatening.

As we noted earlier, such can be the case for whole societies and civilizations as they embark upon a suicidal agenda of unsustainable economic growth. This seems to be happening now, for we have become aware that the ground on which we walk is not a theater of endless dreams but a planetary life support system of limited capabilities, and the power is gradually being turned off. But in the surreal world we inhabit, it is we who seem determined to flip the switch!

At least a few gurglings of dissent might well have been expected. Jared Diamond's *Collapse*, a starkly titled study of human behavior and past civilizations, is one.[2] James Lovelock's *The Revenge of Gaia* is another.[3] Perhaps the most incisive is Ronald Wright's *A Short History of Progress*.[4] His theme is that humankind is so bent on increasing its numbers and levels of consumption that it overlooks the limitations of its environment. And

1. Swanson, "How."
2. Diamond, *Collapse*.
3. Lovelock, *Revenge*.
4. Wright, *History*.

of course the inevitable "progress trap" leads to civilization's spectacular collapse.

As an archaeologist, Wright is in a good position to elaborate on the global record of such predicaments. From the first civilization in Sumer to the Maya and Khmer, civilizations have repeatedly fallen into that deadly maelstrom. Sir Leonard Woolley, the original excavator of Ur, wondered why the capital of a great empire, a city that once stood in the midst of a vast granary, should now be the center of a desert wasteland. The answer was, of course, unsustainable environmental exploitation in an attempt to provide for overpopulated cities, and accumulating saline deposits resulting from the irrigation that made that granary possible eventually destroyed it.

Sound familiar? One may substitute phosphates for salt in the modern drama that makes our food supply sustainable: the overuse of phosphates is now not only unsustainable but environmentally destructive. To be sure, ours is a very different situation from that of Ur, for heretofore no civilizational collapse has been final because all civilizations have been local or regional affairs and there has always been somewhere else to move on to. Until now. For the first time, we are part of a global civilization that embraces the entire planet, and we have nowhere else to go. We have entered the final phase of the 'progress trap,' the denouement of our epic tragedy, the end!

So what's to be done? As with giving up smoking, the problem lies in thinking of the alternatives, even the seemingly impossible—like life without a cigarette And as if that were not hard enough, imagining a whole new lifestyle is even harder. Recently, a feature writer in the automotive field who was reviewing the capabilities of new cars, admitted that until a reader challenged him he had never even thought to consider the planetary impact of such vehicles as SUVs. The pope is now writing an encyclical letter asking all people to reconsider their attitude toward the earth.[5] The fact that the Church resolutely opposes any form of birth control—which might help to address the central problem of an exploding population—is one more of those contradictions that seem to frustrate any solution.

The surgeon standing with poised scalpel over the foot of my friend is perhaps the sort of necessary incentive to meaningful action. But in the context of planetary disaster, what would the alternative look like? Again, the long view of the archaeologist may be of help. Dramatic changes in human lifestyles—when humanity has embarked upon a hitherto uncharted

5 This has become the encyclical *Laudato Sí*. See Francis I, *On Care*.

course—have taken place before, most significantly in Neolithic times. Lest this seem a rather remote regression, consider that in many ways we are still living in Neolithic times. Insofar as we depend on agriculture (both crop cultivation and the domestication of animals) the Neolithic is not past but present, for no new crops or domestic animals have been introduced since then. This 'revolution' was what enabled the first civic communities and intrinsically dynamic societies with burgeoning populations—such as ours—to thrive and prosper.

But what was truly revolutionary about this new lifestyle was the mentality that lay behind it. As David Lewis-Williams writes in his study *Inside the Neolithic Mind*,[6] the real revolution lay in the transformation of cosmological myths that had sustained a passive acceptance of natural phenomena. Humans began to tame and control the environment. In *The Anatomy of Human Destructiveness* the noted psychoanalyst Erich Fromm goes so far as to say of this newfound capability, "It would not be an exaggeration to say that the discovery of agriculture was the foundation of all scientific thinking and later technological development."[7] In the new lifestyle that evolved, the world became our instrumental resource. It is this mentality that has brought us to where we are.

The change that we must now undertake is equally all-encompassing, and the nature of the transition in that seemingly remote time offers a clue to the necessary remedial action. Even then the taming of 'the wild' led to its partial destruction: it was no accident that in the several continents the great faunal species disappeared with the appearance of man.[8] Even then, having driven the last herd of woolly mammoths over a cliff, humans seemed incapable of grasping the implications of their actions. The context of our survival must involve not only a rediscovery (or better, a recultivation) of respect for the natural world, but also a newly chastened sense of the vulnerability of the wilderness from which our life sprang and on which it still depends. Only in the presence of this 'other' can human identity be understood and sustained.

The ecologist Thomas Berry spent a lifetime elaborating and exploring this theme and provided us with many valuable insights into what such an 'Earth Community' would look like.[9] What saddened him most was that

6. Lewis-Williams and Pearce, *Inside*.

7. Fromm, *Anatomy*, 210.

8. Leakey, *Sixth*.

9. Berry, *Selected*.

humankind had become a devastating presence on the planet. Though humans may never have had a comprehensive understanding of the mysteries manifest in the world about them, at least in former times their religious traditions had "a capacity for being a creative presence within the ever-renewing sequence of life upon Earth. In the closing years of the twentieth century and the dawn of the twenty-first, we seem to have lost this capacity."[10] For Berry, the pathos of the present is that humanity has lost its capacity to interact creatively with other elements of the biosphere and has not come to recognize that all life systems are part of an immense complex that may exceed our full comprehension.

The scope of our survival strategy now becomes clearer. The simple steps of regression take us back deep into the primal traditions of humanity and the roots of our malaise. In the course of this sociocultural hypnotherapy, the choices and changes we have made will define the nature of the pathology—will, as it were, show how adult addiction followed youthful indiscretion. Only in remembering of all those previous steps will we come to understand the genesis of our present behavior and the points at which it needs to be "re-membered."

The elements of such a new lifestyle may be unclear, but an overwhelming urgency demands that we at least focus our attention on discovering the mental state that must underlie it. The recognition that something was radically wrong with our grasp of reality was already apparent in the last century to writers like Fromm, for whom the distinction between 'having' and 'being' was crucial. It had become clear that possessions can become an addiction, though they do not always produce a greater sense of satisfaction or well-being. Buying more clothes from Primark just because they are cheap can be no less addictive than buying four-by-fours or yachts or beachfront summer homes. In either case, only a systemic change can break the fetishism of unsustainable economic growth that presently both feeds and destroys the world. If we fail to heed Fromm's valedictory warning—"in the nineteenth century God was dead, in the twentieth century man is dead"[11]—we may well have to add, "In the twenty-first century, nature is dead."

Ultimately, the choices must be both individually and collectively ours, for change can come about only through a tectonic surge of ordinary behavior, through what Hannah Arendt intuitively called the personalization

10. Berry, *Selected*, 97.

11 Fromm, *Sane*, 360.

of politics. The small issues of our life are the large issues. And here is another point in the 're-membering' of the so-called Neolithic Revolution: it came about as a result of manipulation by elites who exercised great power. As early as 8,000 BCE Jericho needed a defensive stone tower eight meters tall and of immense strength. Today, change will come about only when ordinary people challenge the vested interests of elites.

This may seem a hopeless predicament, but paradoxically hope is no longer an issue. The surgeon who stands by the bedside expressing pious hope for a better future is at best irrelevant, at worst a deadly coconspirator. What humankind needs is skillful, decisive action that will bring about a different future. Hope is no more than a plea that something we have not even imagined might turn up, and thus can be a fatal illusion. Only well-focused and concerted actions will change things for the better. And even when our mass hypnotherapy is complete, the need for resolute action will remain. Herein the prophet and therapist concur: we must wake up and begin to cure ourselves!

16

This Life on Earth

The Tragic Chronicle of Life on a Small Planet

Life on earth is a strange, infinitesimally small part of something much greater—a cosmos that is not just a thing, or even everything, but a dynamic whole whose miraculous self-expression embraces everything that is. Having no past, no future, nor boundaries, Life is always and simply *present*, holding "everything" in its vast embrace.

This earth is a fragment, a 'specimen,' within the vast cosmic incubator of life that is constantly bringing all things into being. It is composed of scarcely imaginable physical forces whose energy has the ability to generate mass—not only as formless abstraction, but as shape. Even the vast amorphous nebulae are shaped mathematical structures in which chaos gives rise to unlimited possibilities. And therein lies the secret of life: a self-generating and self-organizing system of energy that expresses itself in endless forms most beautiful. This earth is simply one small part of this awesome process of creativity.

But wait! How can I know this? I can because of an even more amazing quality perhaps unique to this life on earth: consciousness. Yes, in the course of its endless thrusting and thriving diversity, life on earth has produced creatures with awareness, and at last, self-awareness. And through this possibility one creature brought forth knowledge. In the story of the universe it was a unique moment when life had the capacity to know itself.

On this small, insignificant planet that from space appeared no more than a blue orb bedecked with patches of white, self-consciousness had become part of the cosmic story.

From the beginning knowledge reflected not only on this life, but on the very nature of its origin. Brought forth by chemical interactions whose electric discharges shimmer across the surface of the brain, knowledge replicates the gossamer membrane of life that envelops the solid surface of this earth. The human brain seems poised as a vital point of equilibrium between the infinitesimal elements of the subatomic world and the infinitely large structures of interstellar space. In the spectrum of density that stretches from atomic structures to galactic masses, human beings stand at exactly the midpoint, ideally placed to observe the entire story.

And what a story! This life on earth arose from cosmic fragments gathered over the incomprehensibly vast period of three billion years and molded into unique microbial forms. The earth became a laboratory and workshop for life. After the nucleic structures that underpin all earth's life forms were gradually put in place, the self-organizing capacity of matter drew energy from the environment to create delicately balanced states of equilibrium and thus enabled the aggregation of ever more complex molecules. The biochemical processes of replication created a fractal beauty that would henceforth be the signature of all life within the earth's newly created biosphere.

A living tissue began to clothe this earth—the web of life. The development of such vital processes as replication, metabolism and photosynthesis enabled life to absorb energy and increase in complexity. All these functions began at the microbial level, which still accounts for 98 percent of the life forms on earth; yet so indiscernibly did these changes occur that all the great kingdoms of life lay so hidden from view that at one point this early period was called the 'azoic era'—the epoch without life.

How mistaken that was! Life had quite imperceptibly prepared all its tools for a magnificent burgeoning forth, an epiphany of its hitherto secret mysteries. Then, five hundred million years ago, the multicellular forms of life began to appear, and almost in the twinkling of an eye the thirty-five great phyla of the animal kingdom emerged. Indeed, the eye itself appeared and, for the first time, thousands of species began to look upon one another and the earth that was their common home. Life on earth crossed a vital threshold: the phanerozoic (visible) era had dawned.

Part 3—A Ravaged Earth

The biosphere now began to express itself in ever more numerous and diverse forms, exploding across the earth like a great pyrotechnic display. Every possible niche was soon colonized by some life form, and all creatures developed in size and survivability until they achieved their full potential. With their structural range poised between the microcosm of the molecules and the macrocosm of the stars, they became the mesocosm—the realm of the multicellular creatures.

But just as the story seemed to reach a dizzying apogee of biodiversity, the creatures with knowledge came forth, a development that would prove particularly fateful—if not fatal—for life on earth. At first, they were so awestruck by the incomprehensible majesty of the "blooming, buzzing confusion" they were part of that these humans—for this became their name, formed as they were from the earth, *humus*—not only venerated but worshiped nature and defined themselves in terms of animals that seemed to them models of superiority. They even built temples in which to worship them.

Then things changed. These clever humans, began to manipulate life to serve their own ends, reordering the established pattern of things to accord with their desires and their dreams. It seems typical of them that their oldest and greatest structures were erected for no practical reason, but in order that their builders could enjoy eternal life among the stars. Nature was not enough; they always wanted more—something greater than nature, a supernature. This infatuation would in large measure drive their future behavior, for with their minds on the heavens, the earth under their feet was no more than something to be trampled on whilst striving to fulfill their dreams.

It proved the beginning of the end. Many creatures learned to fear them, and those that didn't were the first to be exterminated. Ever more numerous, inventive, and powerful, humans became the lords of this earth. They adopted the view that all life was available to do with as they liked. But then, near what they called the end of the twentieth century, a time was reached when another decisive threshold in the history of the biosphere was crossed. Now humans were both consuming more than the earth could produce and in doing so destroying the planet's sources of life.

Just as crossing previous thresholds had defined distinct stages in the planet's life story, this new era needed a new name. Some called it the 'anthropocene,' the era of man, others the 'eremozoic,,' the era of solitude, since increasingly all other species were threatened with extinction. It is indeed frightening to consider the threatened extinction of 12 percent of the world's birds, 21 percent of its mammals, 30 percent of its amphibians, 31 percent of its reptiles, 37 percent of its fishes, and 70 percent of its plant species. But as sobering as the scale even more so was the speed at which this happened, for in no more than a few decades much of what had been perfected over millions of years of evolution was wiped out.

The rapidity of this ecocide was unprecedented in the earth's long history, and for the first time a single species had become a destructive geological force. Its claim of unique intelligence had led to the unique folly of threatening its own means of survival as well as that of many others. The tragic prospect was a scene of widespread desolation sometimes called the Great Thinning.

And just then the vice-president of the then most environmentally destructive nation on earth startled humanity by announcing the 'inconvenient truth' that civilization was destroying the planet. By destroying one hundred species a day, humans were destroying this earth—the forests were being felled, the earth torn open, the skies emptied of birds, the seas stripped of fish. Buzzing bees and songbirds would no longer be heard in the land. And all that solitude would be the lesser part of the catastrophe, for fuel driven technologies were poisoning the very air people breathed, temperatures were soaring, and the seas became acidified. *Homo sapiens*, the purportedly wise species, was not only condemning whole animal species to extinction, but destroying their entire habitat as well as the basis of its own survival. Life on earth was fast becoming unsustainable.

Nothing like this had happened to life on earth since the Permian crisis two hundred fifty million years earlier, when heating of the land and acidification of the seas produced by geological upheavals led to the disappearance of 95 percent of life forms on earth. Fortunately, earth showed its amazing powers of recovery by regaining the dynamic equilibrium at the very core of all life processes, but it took some twenty million years before the damage was repaired and new ecosystems created. The crisis in the eremozoic era was made more grievous by the incomparable richness and diversity that the flora and fauna had by then achieved.

As with all plagues, the *pestilentia hominorum*—the human pestilence—reached a crescendo of destructiveness and in the end ebbed away. It took less than a century. By the middle of the twenty-first century millions of people had been displaced from their homes by desertification, rising sea levels and a lack of fresh water as ever more desperate measure were proposed, such as dragging ice bergs from Antarctica to Arabia! Energy failures made life unsustainable in the vast urban sprawls where most of the population lived. Food shortages led to riots, and critical scarcities of most common resources led to widespread instability and to warfare fanned by extreme ideologies and irrational beliefs.

It was an apocalyptic age the like of which had never been seen in human history. To be sure, the collapse of the Roman Empire following the eruption of a supervolcanic in southern Asia that disrupted the global climate, and the disappearance of several early civilizations in Central and South America following environmental depredation and climate change, had provided foretastes. And a more recent warning had been the Great European War of the seventeenth century, which combined with climatic deterioration caused the loss of over one-third of the population and the near collapse of civil society. Now this was happening not just on a local but global scale. Small groups of humans clung on to life in miserable circumstances, reverting to the savagery that even in good times had never been entirely absent from civilized societies.

Much of humankind's vast store of knowledge disappeared, of course, but perhaps even more disastrous was the loss of essential survival skills. Urban populations had little or no knowledge of the land and the environmental skills needed to sustain life. Obsessed by technology, they had become estranged from the life of the earth on which they lived—the very derangement among the source of their problems. The final blow was the eruption of the supervolcano beneath Old Faithful in Yellowstone Park, for with this cataclysm that mighty natural force more than lived up to its name, and humans joined the 99 percent of species that nature had brought forth and then replaced by other life forms.

But as always, life on earth continued. Left to itself, nature corrected the planetary perturbation, and the cleansing effect of extinction allowed the ever-creative power of life on earth to bring forth new forms that were marvelously adapted to new circumstances. So a new age dawned. It could be called the ecozoic, when life regained the equilibrium of its natural rhythms; but perhaps more appropriate would be the name Cryptozoic 2, the age that as in the beginnings of life remained hidden and was destined to be forever unrecorded—unless many eons in the future it might be observed from one of the distant galaxies of the universe.

The relics of ages became fossils, reminders of earlier eras in the timeline of life. They included not only the remains of creatures but also those of anthropoid technical artifices, monumental machines, and inscribed remains of plans for a brave new world. The latter included bizarre religious texts that revealed an ultimate hubris—the conviction that this earthly life was not enough and the hopeful expectation of a blessed immortality. Such were the tombstones of these conquistadors of conspicuous consumption, who by wanting everything lost everything. Their fitting but unchiseled epitaph: Greed.

This chronicle can claim no further knowledge of this or subsequent epochs, but only that these events of the Anthropocene era took place when life on earth had run barely half its course. Now, freed from the threat of its insatiable offspring and having absorbed its stresses, the capacity of the earth to restore and create new life continued.

In the cycles of this life on earth it seemed that apocalyptic extinctions were simply preparations a for new beginnings. In the previous six great extinctions spikes of diversity were followed by troughs of decimation to be succeeded by a further flourishing of life that showed a restored but different pattern of diversity. Though recovery could take five to eight million years, this would be a mere blip in the life of earth, for unlike humans the planet always had plenty of time and was always able to respond with new and ever more diverse forms of life.

At last, of course, an even greater threat arose, for the energy that had from the beginning sparked and sustained life came not only from earth's biochemical processes, but from far beyond. The sun, for so long a largely benign neighbor, became ever more difficult to live with. As is the way with stars, it gradually expanded into a red giant and consumed the earth, and thus life on earth ended, an event of such insignificance in the vast emporium of the universe that it went unnoticed and unrecorded.

But it was not entirely without appreciation, for as this narrative testifies, the emergence and evolution of a biosphere was a wonderful and unparalleled achievement; a unique expression of the inherent life-giving potential of the universe. To have been a part of it was exhilarating. To be sure, the drama was replete with ironies. Perhaps the greatest of these is that the miracle of life led to the emergence of consciousness; yet just when that breakthrough made humankind aware of its place in the cosmic web of life, this creature that so prided itself on its wisdom fell victim to its animal nature. Driven by the instincts of reproduction and predation, and empowered by technological competence, humankind became so blinded by its preoccupation with the past and dreams for the future that it lost touch with the present and mistook its fantasies for reality.

The reality is that this life on earth was never more than a miniscule part of the life of the universe that enveloped it. This remains. Life has no purpose or destiny, only its ever creative self-expression. It simply is; it forever remains a presence that is its own epiphany. Its rhythms are eternal: ebb and flow, light and dark, systole and diastole, waxing and waning—all simple and unique, but above all beautiful. No genus or species is more than a part of this kaleidoscope. Like the prismatic raindrops that break open the rainbow in the summer storm or flecks of frost that cast diaphanous sparkles on the earth, and tiny flowers clothed in golden petals, beauty was its hallmark.

Consider the lilies of the field, marvel at the birds in the air and thrill to their song, observe the setting sun girdled with a glowing cauldron of clouds. All are minutiae of an awe-inspiring whole, reminders of a magic the mind can scarcely comprehend. Ponder this life while you can and glory in its fullness; value it above all, for there is no other.

Bibliography

Ali, Ayan Hirsi. *Heretic: Why Islam Needs a Reformation Now.* London: Harper, 2015.

Ali, Tariq. *The Clash of Fundamentalisms: Crusades, Jihads and Modernity.* London: Verso, 2002.

Al-Khalili, Jim. *Pathfinders: The Golden Age of Arabic Science.* London: Lane, 2010.

Allen, Charles. *Ashoka: The Search for India's Lost Emperor.* London: Abacus, 2013.

———. *The Buddha and the Sahibs: The Men Who Discovered India's Lost Religion.* London: Murray, 2002.

———. *God's Terrorists: The Wahhabi Cult and the Hidden Roots of Modern Jihad.* London: Abacus, 2006.

Appleyard, Bryan. *Understanding the Present: Science and the Soul of Modern Man.* London: Picador, 1992.

Armstrong, Karen. *Holy War: The Crusades and Their Impact on Today's World.* London: Macmillan, 1988.

Bachofen, J. J. *Myth, Religion, and Mother Right.* Translated by Ralph Manheim. Bollingen Series 84. Princeton: Princeton University Press 1973.

Baigent, Michael, and Richard Leigh. *The Inquisition.* London: Viking, 1999.

Barnes, Russell, dir. *World War Two: 1941 and the Man of Steel,* Parts 1 and 2. Starring David Reynolds. Produced by the BBC. 1 DVD (recorded off air). London: BBC, 2011. Broadcast on BBC Four on June 13, 2011.

Barbour, Henry, et al. "Growth & Opportunity Project." *Wall Street Journal,* March 18, 2013. https://online.wsj.com/public/resources/documents/RNCreport03182013.pdf/.

Baron-Cohen, Simon. *The Science of Evil: On Empathy and the Origins of Cruelty.* New York: Basic Books, 2011.

Bauman, Zygmunt. *Modernity and Ambivalence.* Cambridge: Polity, 1991.

———. *Modernity and the Holocaust.* Cambridge: Polity, 1989.

Bawden, Tom. "Climate Change Key in Syrian Conflict—and It Will Trigger More War in Future." *Independent,* March 2, 2015. https://www.independent.co.uk/news/world/middle-east/climate-change-key-in-syrian-conflict-and-it-will-trigger-more-war-in-future-10081163.html/.

Bayly, C. A. *The Birth of the Modern World, 1780–1914: Global Connections and Comparisons.* Blackwell History of the World. Oxford: Blackwell, 2004.

Berlin, Isaiah. *The Crooked Timber of Humanity: Chapters in the History of Ideas.* London: Murray 1990.

———. *Vico and Herder: Two Studies in the History of Ideas.* London: Hogarth, 1980.

Berry, Thomas. *Selected Writings on the Earth Community*. Selected and with an introduction by Mary Evelyn Tucker and John Grim. Modern Spiritual Masters Series. Maryknoll, NY: Orbis, 2014.

Blair, Tony. Speech delivered in Sedgefield on March 5, 2004. *Guardian*, March 5, 2004. https://www.theguardian.com/politics/2004/mar/05/iraq.iraq/.

Bonnett, Alastair. *The Idea of the West: Culture, Politics and History*. Basingstoke: Palgrave Macmillan, 2004.

Boulter, Michael. *Extinction: Evolution and the End of Man*. London: Fourth Estate, 2010.

Braudel, Fernand. *A History of Civilizations*. Translated by Richard Mayne. London: Penguin, 1993.

Brown, Peter. *Authority and the Sacred: Aspects of the Christianization of the Roman World*. Canto. Cambridge: Cambridge University Press, 1995.

———. *The Body and Society: Men, Women, and Sexual Renunciation in early Christianity*. Twentieth anniversary ed., with a new introduction. Columbia Classics in Religion. New York: Columbia University Press, 2008.

———. *Through the Eye of a Needle: Wealth, the Fall of Rome, and the Making of Christianity in the West, 350–550 AD*. Princeton: Princeton University Press, 2012.

Byrne. Lavinia. *Woman at the Altar: The Ordination of Women in the Roman Catholic Church*. New York: Continuum, 1999.

Cannadine, David. *Ornamentalism: How the British Saw Their Empire*. Oxford: Oxford University Press, 2001.

Carassava, Anthee. "200,000 Protest in Athens as Alexis Tsipras Government Teeters over Macedonia." *Sunday Times*, January 20 2019. https://www.thetimes.co.uk/article/200-000-protest-in-athens-as-alexis-tsipras-government-teeters-over-macedonia-lmnwcvncc/.

Carroll, James. "The Bush Crusade." History. *Nation*, September 2, 2004. https://www.thenation.com/article/bush-crusade/.

Childe, V. Gordon. *Man Makes Himself*. The Library of Science and Culture. Library of Science and Culture. London: Watts, 1936.

Christiansen, Eric. *The Northern Crusades*. New ed. London: Penguin, 1997.

Clark, Elmer T. *The Small Sects in America*. Nashville: Cokesbury, 1937.

Clark, J. C. D. *Our Shadowed Present: Modernism, Postmodernism and History*. London: Atlantic, 2003.

Cohn, Norman. *Cosmos, Chaos and the World to Come: The Ancient Roots of Apocalyptic Faith*. New Haven: Yale University Press, 1993.

———. *Europe's Inner Demons: The Demonization of Christians in Medieval Christendom*. London: Pimlico, 1993.

———. *The Pursuit of the Millennium: Revolutionary Millenarians and Mystical Anarchists of the Middle Ages*. London: Pimlico, 1993.

Conrad, Joseph. *Heart of Darkness*. Penguin Classics. London: Penguin, 2007.

———. *Heart of Darkness*. Giunti Classics. Florence: Giunti, 2001.

Cooper, Jago, presenter. *The Lost Kingdoms of Central America*. Produced and directed by Craig Collinson et al. 1 DVD. Australia: Distributed by Madman Entertainment 2015

Cowell, Alan. "Oskar Gröning, the 'Bookkeeper of Auschwitz,' Is Dead at 96." *New York Times*, March 12, 2018. https://www.nytimes.com/2018/03/12/obituaries/oskar-groning-the-bookkeeper-of-auschwitz-is-dead-at-96.html/.

Crossan, John Dominic. *How to Read the Bible and Still Be a Christian: Struggling with Divine Violence from Genesis through Revelation.* New York: HarperOne, 2015.

———. *Jesus and the Violence of Scripture: How to Read the Bible and Still Be a Christian.* London: SPCK, 2015.

———. *The Power of Parable: How Fiction by Jesus Became Fiction about Jesus.* New York: HarperOne, 2012.

Cupitt, Don. "All You Really Need Is Love." Originally published in the *Guardian* as a Face to Faith column, December 1994. On *Sea of Faith* (website): http://www.sof.org.nz/aynil.htm/.

———. *Ethics in the Last Days of Humanity.* Salem OR: Polebridge, 2015.

———. *Jesus and Philosophy.* London: SCM, 2009.

———. *The Meaning of the West: An Apologia for Secular Christianity.* London: SCM, 2008.

Dabiq. "The Extinction of the Grayzone." 7 (2015) 54–66. https://clarionproject.org/docs/islamic-state-dabiq-magazine-issue-7-from-hypocrisy-to-apostasy.pdf/.

D'Altroy, Terence N. *The Incas.* The Peoples of America. Malden, MA: Wiley-Blackwell, 2015.

Daily Mail. "Report: Radical Islamic Sect 'Has Half of Britain's Mosques in Its Grip.'" *Daily Mail*, September 7, 2007. http://www.dailymail.co.uk/news/article-480470/Radical-Islamic-sect-half-Britains-mosques-grip.html/.

Dampier, William Cecil. *A Shorter History of Science.* Cambridge: Cambridge University Press, 1944.

Darwin, Charles. "Life: An Autobiographical Fragment." Written in August 1838. In *Autobiographies*, 49–55. Edited by Michael Neve and Sharon Messenger. With an introduction by Michael Neve. Penguin Classics. London: Penguin, 2002.

Davidson, Thomas, ed. *Chambers's Twentieth Century Dictionary of the English Language.* London: Chambers, 1907.

Davies, Gareth. "The Shocking Aftermath of ISIS' Trail of Destruction: Iraqi Troops Discover the Iconic Tomb of the Prophet of Jonah Smashed to Smithereens as They Retake Parts of Mosul. *Daily Mail*, January 28, 2017. https://www.dailymail.co.uk/news/article-4166894/ISIS-destruction-popular-Mosque-prophet-Jonah.html/.

Davies, Nigel. *The Ancient Kingdoms of Mexico.* London: Penguin, 1982.

Diamond, Jared. *Collapse: How Societies Choose to Fail or Succeed.* Allen Lane Science. London: Lane, 2005.

Dickinson, Matt. "John Barnes Reminds Us We Have So Far Still to Travel on Racism." Football. *Times*, February 7, 2019. https://www.thetimes.co.uk/article/john-barnes-challenging-views-jolt-us-out-of-our-smug-complacency-about-racism-05phc6gbj/.

Dodd, C. H. *The Parables of the Kingdom.* London: Fontana, 1961.

Donald, Merlin. *Origins of the Modern Mind: Three Stages in the Evolution of Culture and Cognition.* Cambridge: Harvard University Press, 1991.

Douglas, Mary. *Implicit Meanings: Essays in Anthropology.* London: Routledge & Kegan Paul, 1975. Reprint. London: Routledge, 1978.

Edelman, Gerald M. *Bright Air, Brilliant Fire: On the Matter of the Mind.* London: Lane, 1992.

Egremont, Max. *Forgotten Land: Journeys among the Ghosts of East Prussia.* London: Picador, 2011.

Ellacuría, Ignacio, ed. "Fifth Centenary of Latin America: Discovery or Cover-Up?" Special issue, *Latin American Theological Review* 21 (1990).

Ferguson, Niall. *Civilization: The West and the Rest*. London: Lane, 2011.

Feuerbach, Ludwig. *The Essence of Christianity*. Translated from the 2nd German ed. by George Eliot. Cambridge Library Collection—Philosophy. Cambridge: Cambridge University Press, 2011.

Finkelstein, Israel, and Amihai Mazar. *The Quest for the Historical Israel: Debating Archaeology and the History of Early Israel*. Edited by Brian B. Schmidt. Archaeology and Biblical Studies 17. Atlanta: Society of Biblical Literature, 2007.

Finkelstein, Israel, and Neal Asher Silberman. *The Bible Unearthed: Archaeology's New Vision of Ancient Israel and the Origin of Its Sacred Texts*. New York: Free Press, 2001.

———. *David and Solomon: In Search of the Bible's Sacred Kings and the Roots of the Western Tradition*. New York: Free Press, 2006.

Fisher, H. A. L. *A History of Europe*. London: Arnold, 1936.

Flannery, Tim. *Here on Earth: A Twin Biography of the Planet and the Human Race*. London: Penguin, 2012.

Fotheringham, Alasdair. "Judge in the Dock to Defend Himself over Franco Investigation." *Independent*, February 1, 2012. https://www.independent.co.uk/news/world/europe/judge-in-the-dock-to-defend-himself-over-franco-investigation-6297649.html/.

Foucault, Michel. *The History of Sexuality*. Vol. 2. Translated by Robert Hurley. Peregrine Books. Hammondsworth, UK: Penguin, 1984.

Francis I, Pope. *On Care for Our Common Home: The Encyclical Letter "Laudato Sí."* Introduction by Msgr. Kevin W. Irwin. Mahwah, NJ: Paulist, 2015.

Frankl, Viktor E. *Man's Search for Meaning*. London: Hodder & Stoughton, 1946.

Fraser, James George. *The Golden Bough: A Study in Magic and Religion; A New Abridgement from the Second and Third Editions*. Edited with an introduction and notes by Robert Fraser. Oxford World's Classics. Oxford: Oxford University Press, 2009.

Freeman, Charles. *The Greek Achievement: The Foundation of the Western World*. London: Lane, 1999.

Fromm, Erich. *The Anatomy of Human Destructiveness*. Pimlico 262. London: Pimlico, 1997.

Fuentes, Carlos. *The Buried Mirror: Reflections on Spain and the New World*. London: Deutsch, 1992.

Fukuyama, Francis. *The End of History and the Last Man*. New York: Free Press, 1992.

———. *The End of History and the Last Man*. With a new afterword. New York: Free Press, 2006.

Geddes, Patrick. *Cities in Evolution*. London: Williams & Norgate, 1949.

Geering, Lloyd. *Christianity without God*. Salem OR: Polebridge, 2002.

———. *Christian Faith at the Crossroads: A Map of Modern Religious History*. Salem OR: Polebridge, 2001.

George, Alison. "Hidden Symbols." *New Scientist* 232/3099 (November 12, 2016) 36–39. https://www.newscientist.com/article/mg23230990-700-in-search-of-the-very-first-coded-symbols/.

Gilson, Etienne. *The Unity of Philosophical Experience*. The Scribner Library Books 113. New York: Scribner, 1937.

Gosden, Emily. "David Cameron 'Wrong and Counter-Productive', Says Muslim Council of Britain." *Telegraph*, June 19, 2015. https://www.telegraph.co.uk/news/uknews/terrorism-in-the-uk/11687455/david-cameron-wrong-isil-muslim-council.html/.

Gosse, Philip Henry. *Omphalos: An Attempt to Untie the Geological Knot*. London: Van Voorst, 1857.

Gould, Stephen Jay. "Adam's Navel." In *The Flamingo's Smile: Reflections on Natural History*, 99–103. New York: Norton, 1985.

Green, Edward. *Prophet John Wroe: Virgins, Scandals and Visions*. London: History Press, 2005.

Green, Toby. *Inquisition: The Reign of Fear*. London: Pan, 2008.

Greenfield, Trevor. *An Introduction to Radical Theology: The Death and Resurrection of God*. Winchester: O Books, 2006.

Gryn, Naomi, dir. *Chasing Shadows*. 1 DVD. Written by Hugo Gryn. Produced by See More Productions et al. Waltham, MA: National Center for Jewish Film, 2007. Originally released 1991.

Hall, Edith. *Introducing the Ancient Greeks*. London: Bodley Head, 2015.

Hannam, James. *God's Philosophers: How the Medieval World Laid the Foundations for Modern Science*. London: Icon 2009.

Harris, Sam. *The End of Faith: Religion, Terror and the Future of Reason*. New York: Norton, 2004.

Hasan, Usama. "Fatwa on Fasting in Ramadan during the UK Summer." *Unity* (blog), June 30, 2014. Updated June 18, 2015. https://unity1.wordpress.com/2014/06/30/fatwa-on-fasting-in-ramadan-during-the-uk-summer/.

Heer, Friedrich. *God's First Love: Christians and Jews over Two Thousand Years*. Translated from the German by Geoffrey Skelton. London: Phoenix, 1999.

———. *The Holy Roman Empire*. Translated by Janet Sondheimer. London: Weidenfeld & Nicolson, 1968.

Hill, Christopher. "God and the English Revolution." In *Disciplines of Faith: Studies in Religion, Politics, and Patriarchy*, edited by Jim Obelkevich et al., 393–409. History Workshop Series. London: Routledge & Kegan Paul, 1987.

Hobsbawm, E. J. *How to Change the World: Tales of Marx and Marxism*. London: Abacus, 2011.

Holthaus, Eric. "Hot Zone: Is Climate Change Destabilizing Iraq?" Future Tense. *Slate*, June 27, 2014. https://slate.com/technology/2014/06/isis-water-scarcity-is-climate-change-destabilizing-iraq.html/.

Huntington, Samuel P. *The Clash of Civilizations and the Remaking of World Order*. New York: Simon & Schuster, 1996.

Isaacs, Alan, ed. *The Macmillan Encyclopedia*. London: Macmillan, 1983.

James, Victoria (words), and Sébastien Thibault (illustrations). "The World Is Run by . . . the CIA.*" *Cambridge Alumni Magazine* (*CAM*) 80 (Lent 2017) 22–27. https://www.alumni.cam.ac.uk/sites/www.alumni.cam.ac.uk/files/documents/cam_80_0.pdf/.

John Paul II, Pope. *Memory and Identity: Personal Reflections*. London: Phoenix, 2005.

Jones, Jonathan. "Destruction of Timbuktu Manuscripts an Offence against the Whole of Africa." Opinion: Mali. *Guardian*, January 28, 2013. https://www.theguardian.com/world/2013/jan/28/destruction-timbuktu-manuscripts-offence-africa/.

Kamester Margaret, and Jo Vellacott, eds. *Militarism versus Feminism: Writings on Women and War*, by Catherine Marshall, C. K. Ogden, and Mary Sargant Florence. London: Virago, 1987.

Kazi, Tehmina. "Ramadan Fasting: Modern Opposition to Age-Old Rules." Indy/Life. *Independent*, June 16, 2015. https://www.independent.co.uk/life-style/food-and-drink/features/ramadan-fasting-modern-opposition-to-age-old-rules-10324718.html/.

Kelly, Colin P., et al. "Climate Change in the Fertile Crescent and Implications of the Recent Syrian Drought." *Proceedings of the National Academy of Sciences* 112 (March 17, 2015) 3241–46. https://www.pnas.org/content/112/11/3241/.

Klein, Naomi. *This Changes Everything: Capitalism vs. the Climate*. New York: Simon & Schuster, 2014.

Knapp, Robert. *The Dawn of Christianity: People and Gods in a Time of Magic and Miracles*. London: Profile, 2017.

Knox, Ronald. *Enthusiasm: A Chapter in the History of Religion*. Oxford: Clarendon, 1950.

Koonz, Claudia. *Mothers in the Fatherland: Women, the Family, and Nazi Politics*. London: Methuen, 1986.

Kriwaczek, Paul. *In Search of Zarathustra: The First Prophet and the Ideas That Changed the World*. London: Weidenfeld & Nicolson, 2002.

Lacey, Robert, and Danny Danziger. *The Year 1000: What Life Was Like at the Turn of the First Millennium; an Englishman's World*. London: Abacus, 2003.

Law, Stephen. *Philosophy*. Eyewitness Companions. London: Dorling Kindersley, 2007.

Leakey, Richard. *The Sixth Extinction: Biodiversity and Its Survival*. London: Weidenfeld & Nicolson, 1995.

Le Goff, Jacques. *The Birth of Europe*. The Making of Euorpe. Translated by Janet Lloyd. Malden, MA: Blackwell, 2005.

Leick. Gwendolyn. *Mesopotamia: The Invention of the City*. London: Penguin 2001.

Levack, Brian P. *The Witch-Hunt in Early Modern Europe*. 2nd ed. London: Longman, 1995.

———. *The Witch-Hunt in Early Modern Europe*. London: Longman, 1987.

Levi, Primo. *If This Is a Man*. Translated by Stuart Woolf. London: Abacus, 2007.

Lewis, Bernard *What Went Wrong? The Clash between Islam and Modernity in the Middle East*. London: Weidenfeld & Nicolson, 2002.

Lewis-Williams, J. David. *The Mind in the Cave: Consciousness and the Origin of Art*. London: Thames & Hudson, 2002.

Lewis-Williams, J. David, and David G. Pearce. *Inside the Neolithic Mind: Consciousness, Cosmos, and the Realm of the Gods*. London: Thames & Hudson, 2005.

Longley, Clifford. *Chosen People: The Big Idea That Shaped England and America*. London: Hodder & Stoughton, 2003.

Lovelock, James E. *The Ages of Gaia: A Biography of Our Living Earth*. Commonwealth Fund Book Program. Oxford: Oxford University Press, 1988.

———. *The Revenge of Gaia*. London: Lane. 2006.

Lumpkin, Joseph. *The Sacred Feminine: Searching for the Hidden Face of God*. Blounstville, AL: Fifth Estate, 2011.

MacCulloch, Diarmaid. *All Things Made New: Writings on the Reformation*. London: Lane, 2016.

———. "Evil Just Is." Review of *The Italian Inquisition*, by Christopher Black. *London Review of Books* 32/9 (13 May 2010) 23–24. https://www.lrb.co.uk/v32/n09/diarmaid-macculloch/evil-just-is/.

———. *A History of Christianity: The First Three Thousand Years*. London: Lane, 2009.

Martindale, Colin. *Cognition and Consciousness*. Dorsey Series in Psychology. Homewood, IL: Dorsey, 1981.

Martino, Renato Raffaele. "Statement by His Excellency Archbishop Renato Martino, Apostolic Nuncio, Permanent Observer of the Holy See to the United Nations and Head of the Delegation of the Holy See to the International Conference on Population and Development, 7 September 1994. https://www.un.org/popin/icpd/conference/gov/940908193315.html/.

Mazower, Mark. *Dark Continent: Europe's Twentieth Century*. London: Penguin, 1999.

Masood, Ehsan. *Science & Islam: A History*. London: Icon, 2009.

McKibben, Bill. *Eaarth: Making Life on a Tough New Planet*. New York: St. Martin, 2010

McKie, Robin. *Ape Man: The Story of Human Evolution*. London: BBC Worldwide Ltd. 2000.

Mellaart, James. *Catal Huyuk: A Neolithic Town in Anatolia*. New Aspects of Antiquity. London: Thames & Hudson 1967.

Merridale, Catherine. *Night of Stone: Death and Memory in Russia*. London: Granta, 2001.

Metz, Johann Baptitste, ed. "Through the Eyes of a European Theologian." *Concilium* 232 (1990).

Mill, John Stuart. "Coleridge." In *Essays on Bentham and Coleridge, 1838*. Edited by Jonathan Bennett. 2017. http://www.earlymoderntexts.com/assets/pdfs/mill1838.pdf/.

Milosz, Czesław. *The Captive Mind*. Penguin Classics. New York: Penguin, 2001.

———. *Native Realm: A Search for Self-Definition*. London: Penguin, 2017.

Mithen, Steven J. *The Prehistory of the Mind: A Search for the Origins of Art, Religion and Science*. London: Thames & Hudson, 1996.

Moody, Oliver. "AfD 'Pushes Racial Supremacy of Germans.'" *Times*, January 30 2019. https://www.thetimes.co.uk/article/afd-pushes-racial-supremacy-of-germans-kxnonbwo3/.

Moore, R. I. *The Formation of a Persecuting Society: Authority and Deviance in Western Europe, 950–1250*. 2nd ed. Oxford: Blackwell, 2007.

———. *The War on Heresy: Faith and Power in Medieval Europe*. London: Profile, 2012.

Mumford, Lewis. *The City in History*. Hammondsworth, UK: Penguin, 1966.

———. *The Myth of the Machine: Techniques in Human development*. London: Secker & Warburg, 1967.

Norfolk, Mark. "Muslim Leaders Opened Their Arms to Orator Who Spat Hate." *Times*, April 5, 2016. https://www.thetimes.co.uk/article/muslim-leaders-opened-their-arms-to-orator-who-spat-hate-b73q7fzdl/.

Novak, Michael. "Remembering the Secular Age." *First Things* 174 (June/July 2007) 35–40. https://www.firstthings.com/article/2007/06/003-remembering-the-secular-age/.

O'Brien, Conor Cruise. "Jean Jacques Rousseau." *Independent Magazine*, December 12, 1992, 62.

Oz, Amos. *In the Land of Israel*. San Diego: Harcourt Brace Jovanovich, 1983.

Pääbo, Svante. *Neanderthal Man: In Search of List Genomes*. New York: Basic Books, 2014.

Pappas, Stephanie, "The Social Mind: Brain Region Bigger in Popular People." *LiveScience* January 31, 2012. https://www.livescience.com/18230-brain-area-friends.html/.

Penn, Thomas. *Winter King: The Dawn of Tudor England*. London: Penguin, 2012.

Piggott, Stuart. *Ancient Britons and the Antiquarian Imagination: Ideas from the Renaissance to the Regency*. London: Thames & Hudson, 1989.

Power, Carla. Saudi Arabia Bulldozes over Its Heritage." *Time*, November 14, 2014.

Preston, Paul. *The Spanish Holocaust: Inquisition and Extermination in Twentieth Century Spain.* London: Harper, 2012.

Quammen, David. *The Tangled Tree: A Radical New History of Life.* New York: Simon & Schuster, 2018.

Renfrew, Colin, and Iain Morley, eds. *Becoming Human: Innovation in Prehistoric Material and Spiritual Culture.* Cambridge: Cambridge University Press, 2009.

Roberts, Alice. *The Incredible Human Journey: The Story of How we Colonised the Planet.* London: Bloomsbury, 2010.

Robertson, John. *Iraq: A History.* London: Oneworld, 2015.

Robinson, John A. T. *Honest to God.* London: SCM, 1963.

Rogers, Jane. *Mr Wroe's Virgins.* London: Faber & Faber, 1991.

Ronson, Jon. *The Psychopath Test.* London: Picador, 2011.

Rounding, V. *The Burning Time: The Story of the Smithfield Martyrs.* London: Macmillan, 2017.

Roy, Oliver. *Jihad and Death: The Global Appeal of Islamic State.* Translated by Cynthia Schoch. Comparative Politics and International Studies Series. London: Hurst, 2017.

Rubenstein, Richard L. *After Auschwitz: History, Theology and Contemporary Judaism.* 2nd ed. Johns Hopkins Jewish Studies. Baltimore: Johns Hopkins University Press, 1992.

Russell, Bertrand. *History of Western Philosophy.* London: Routledge, 1996.

Ruthven, Malise. *Islam in the World.* Oxford: Oxford University Press, 2006.

Sands, Shlomo. *The Invention of the Jewish People.* London: Verso, 2009.

Saunders, Doug. "Britain Has an Ethnic Problem: The English." Opinion. *Toronto Globe and Mail*, December 7, 2013. Updated February 20, 2018. https://www.theglobeandmail.com/opinion/britain-has-an-ethnic-problem-the-english/article15792740/

Scholem, Gershom. *Sabbatai Sevi: The Mystical Messiah.* The Littman Library of Jewish Civilisation. London: Routledge & Kegan Paul, 1973.

Schwagerl, Christian. *The Anthropocene: The Human Era and How It Shapes Our Planet.* Santa Fe: Synergetic, 2014.

Scurr, Ruth. *Fatal Purity: Robespierre and the French Revolution.* London: Vintage, 2007.

Sengupta, Kim. "Iran President Hassan Rouhani's First European Visit Shows His Country Is Coming in from the Cold." *Independent*, November 10, 2015. https://www.independent.co.uk/news/world/middle-east/iran-president-hassan-rouhanis-first-european-visit-shows-his-country-is-coming-in-from-the-cold-a6729421.html/.

Service, Elman R. *The Hunters.* Foundations of Modern Anthropology Series. Englewood Cliffs, NJ: Prentice-Hall, 1966.

Shalamov, Varlam. *Kolyma Tales.* Translated from the Russian by John Glad. New York: Norton, 1980.

Sheldrake, Philip, SJ. *Spirituality and History: Questions of Interpretation and Method.* London: SPCK, 1995.

Sheldrake, Rupert. *The Science of Delusion: Freeing the Spirit of Enquiry.* 1st paperback ed. London: Coronet, 2013.

Shlain, Leonard. *The Alphabet versus the Goddess: The Conflict between Word and Image.* New York: Penguin/Compass, 1999.

Siedentop, Larry. *Inventing the Individual: The Origins of Western Liberalism* London: Allan Lane, 2014.

Siegel, Ronald K. *Fire in the Brain: Clinical Tales of Hallucinations.* New York: Dutton, 1992.

Singer, Peter. *Hegel: A Very Short Introduction*. Very Short Introductions 49. Oxford: Oxford University Press, 2001.

Shoemaker, Stephen J. *Ancient Traditions of the Virgin Mary's Dormition and Assumption*. Oxford Early Christian Studies. Oxford: Oxford University Press, 2006.

Sim, Kevin, dir. *Islam: The Untold Story*. Written by and starring Tom Holland. 1 DVD. London: Channel 4, 2012. Broadcast on Channel 4 on June 24, 2016.

Sobrino, Jon. *The Principle of Mercy: Taking the Crucified People from the Cross*. Maryknoll, NY: Orbis, 1994.

Solomon, Andrew. "One Mother Lost Both Her Children in Boston." Voices. Comment *Independent*, April 26, 2013. https://www.independent.co.uk/voices/comment/one-mother-lost-both-her-children-in-boston-8589704.html/.

Spencer, Nick. *The Evolution of the West: How Christianity Shaped Our Values*. London: SPCK, 2016.

Suskind, Ron. "Faith, Certainty, and the Presidency of George W. Bush." *New York Times Magazine*, October 17, 2005. https://www.nytimes.com/2004/10/17/magazine/faith-certainty-and-the-presidency-of-george-w-bush.html/.

Swanson, Ana. "How Did China Use More Cement between 2011 and 2013 than the US Used in the Entire 20th Century?" *Independent*, March 25, 2015. https://www.independent.co.uk/news/world/asia/how-did-china-use-more-cement-between-2011-and-2013-than-the-us-used-in-the-entire-20th-century-10134079.html/.

Syed, Matthew. *Black Box Thinking: The Surprising Truth about Success*. London: Murray, 2015.

———. "Blame Doctors' Egos for These Disastrous Errors." Comment. *Times*, April 4, 2016. https://www.thetimes.co.uk/article/blame-doctors-egos-for-these-disastrous-errors-26qhct868/.

Taylor, Barbara. *Eve and the New Jerusalem: Socialism and Feminism in the Nineteenth Century*. Virago History. London: Virago, 1983.

Taylor, Jerome. "Atheist Defends Critical Focus on Islam." *Independent*, April 14, 2013. https://www.independent.co.uk/news/world/americas/atheist-defends-critical-focus-on-islam-8572632.html/.

Thomas, Keith. *Man and the Natural World: Changing Attitudes in England 1500–1800*. London: Penguin, 1984.

Thomas, Richard. "Britain's Complete U-Turn on Bulgaria," letter/editorial originally published in the *Independent* in 2014. https://johnblakey.wordpress.com/author/johnblakey/page/44/.

Thompson, E. P. *The Making of the English Working Class*. Hammondsworth, UK: Penguin, 1968.

Thomson, Hugh. *Cochineal Red: Travels through Ancient Peru*. London: Weidenfeld & Nicolson, 2006.

Thurley, Simon. *The Men from the Ministry: How Britain Saved Its Heritage*. New Haven: Yale University Press, 2013.

Toynbee, Arnold. "The Genesis of Pollution." *Horizon* 15/3 (1973) 4–9.

Ullmann, Walter. *The Carolingian Renaissance and the Idea of Kingship*. The Birbeck Lectures 1968–1969. Routledge Revivals. London: Routledge, 2010.

United States Department of Defense. "National Security Implications of Climate-Related Risks and a Changing Climate." Washington DC: Department of Defense, 2015. https://archive.defense.gov/pubs/150724-congressional-report-on-national-implications-of-climate-change.pdf/.

United States National Holocaust Memorial Museum. "Martin Niemöller: 'First They Came for the Socialists.'" In *Holocaust Encyclopedia* (website). https://encyclopedia. ushmm.org/content/en/article/martin-niemoeller-first-they-came-for-the-socialists

Usborne, David. "Life and Death of Stalin's 'Little Sparrow' Who Flew Far Away." *Independent*, November 30, 2011. https://www.independent.co.uk/news/world/ americas/life-and-death-of-stalins-little-sparrow-who-flew-far-away-6269765. html/.

Von Petzinger, Genevieve. *The First Signs: Unlocking the Mysteries of the World's Oldest Symbols*. New York: Atria, 2016.

Waal, F. B. M. de. *The Ape and the Sushi Master: Cultural Reflections by a Primatologist*. London: Lane, 2001.

Ward-Proud, Liam. "Charismatic Chief Executives Could Be Bad for Firms." *City A.M.* (website), October 29, 2014. https://www.cityam.com/charismatic-chief-executives-could-be-bad-firms/.

Weber, Thomas. *Hitler's First War: Adolf Hitler, the Men of the List Regiment, and the First World War*. Oxford: Oxford University Press, 2010.

Weinberg, Steven. *To Explain the World: The Discovery of Modern Science*. London: Lane, 2015.

Whitehead, Alfred North. *Science and the Modern World*. Lowell Lectures 1925. London: Free Association Press, 1985.

Whitworth, Damian. "The Man Who Knows the Isis Mindset." *Times*, January 16 2017. https://www.thetimes.co.uk/article/the-man-who-knows-the-isis-mindset-5ls7nvwtc.

Wikipedia. "Aboriginal Tasmanians." https://en.wikipedia.org/wiki/Aboriginal_Tasmanians.

———. s.v. "Anders Behring Breivik," https://en.wikipedia.org/wiki/Anders_Behring_Breivik.

Williams, Raymond. *Keywords: A Vocabulary of Culture and Society*. London: Fontana, 1988.

Wilson, E. O. *The Creation: An Appeal to Save Life on Earth*. New York: Norton, 2006.

Wistrich, Robert S. *Anti-Semitism: The Longest Hatred*. London: Methuen, 1991.

Wood, Graeme. *The Way of the Strangers: Encounters with the Islamic State*. London: Lane, 2017.

World Economic Forum Annual Meeting 2019 (website). "A Conversation with Sir David Attnborough and HRH The Duke of Cambridge" (video). January 22, 2019. https:// www.weforum.org/events/world-economic-forum-annual-meeting/sessions/an-insight-an-idea-with-david-attenborough?tab=Highlights/.

Wright, Ronald. *A Short History of Progress*. Massey Lectures Series. Edinburgh: Canongate, 2004.

Zamoyski, Adam. *Holy Madness: Romantics, Patriots and Revolutionaries 1776–1871*. London: Weidenfeld & Nicolson 1999.

Index

Lightning Source UK Ltd.
Milton Keynes UK
UKHW041323140819
347884UK00001B/78/P